Terminales

NOUVEAU PROGRAMME

Sous la direction de François GUAR
et Marie FORT-COUDERC

par

Mathieu BESMIER
Professeur agrégé

Marie FORT-COUDERC
Professeur certifié

Gaël MANESCAU
Professeur certifié

Sylvie PERSEC
Professeur agrégé

Serge TRIPODI
Professeur agrégé

Patricia VRINAT-HINDLE
Professeur agrégé

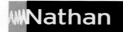

Cover photos

From top to bottom and from left to right: A teen chorus does The Telephone Hour during rehearsal for *Bye Bye Birdie*, a musical production by City Players, at Ruth Eckerd Hall, July 20, 2010 – Clearwater, FL, USA; SunHopes: it is an innovative concept for harvesting solar energy in a cost-efficient, environmentally friendly way using helium balloons. GEOTECTURA, an architectural studio founded by architect Dr. Joseph (Yossi) Cory, and Dr. Pini Gurfil of the Technion, Israel Institute of Technology, collaborated on the development of the technique; Ice palace for Bonhomme, the Carnival's guest of honour, Québec, Canada. Every year since 1954 the Québec City Winter Carnival in Québec City has featured ice palaces; Bombay: Selling balloons and wheel-burrow at Chopati beach, 2004; Ethnies: Eskimos Inuits, Umingmaktok.

Édition : Josiane Attucci-Jan

Iconographie : Sophie Suberbère

Conception de la couverture : Denis Hoch

Conception de la maquette : Frédéric Jély

Cartographie, graphiques et illustrations : AFDEC (p. 31, 110 et 156) ; Laurent Blondel (p. 24, 74) ; Philippe Tastet (p. 43, 66)

Le papier de cet ouvrage est composé de fibres naturelles, renouvelables, recyclables et fabriquées à partir de bois provenant de forêts gérées de manière responsable et durable.

Bienvenue dans *New Bridges Terminales* et dans la deuxième année du cycle terminal du lycée !

Cette année, il s'agit pour vous de continuer à développer votre autonomie dans la pratique de l'anglais, de confirmer votre progression vers le niveau avancé B2 attendu en fin de classe de terminale et, bien sûr, d'obtenir votre baccalauréat !

Objectif bac

Commençons par là ; *New Bridges Terminales* vous propose de vous préparer efficacement aux épreuves du baccalauréat. Vous trouverez donc dans ce manuel :

• À la fin de chaque unité, des entraînements aux épreuves orales (compréhension pour les séries ES, S et ST, expression pour toutes les séries) et aux épreuves écrites (compréhension et expression) (voir la présentation des épreuves, p. 12-13).

• Des pages « Spécial bac » vous fournissant :

– des conseils pratiques pour chacune des épreuves ;

– des fiches *Use your grammar* pour utiliser au mieux les structures grammaticales au cours des épreuves d'expression orale et écrite.

• Un index des documents du manuel classés par notion culturelle pour vous aider à préparer l'épreuve d'expression orale.

Cependant, votre réussite au bac sera d'autant plus assurée qu'elle n'est pas votre unique ambition. *New Bridges Terminales* vous propose de continuer à explorer les cultures du monde anglophone et à approfondir votre maîtrise linguistique par le biais d'une démarche visant à vous rendre acteur de votre apprentissage.

Pour cela, votre manuel vous propose :

• **Un enrichissement culturel**

Le programme culturel du cycle terminal « **Gestes fondateurs et mondes en mouvement** » est structuré autour de quatre notions : **Mythes et héros**, **Espaces et échanges**, **Lieux et formes du pouvoir** et **L'idée de progrès**. Chaque unité s'articule autour de deux notions de ce programme et s'appuie sur des supports de toute nature (textes, images, documents audio, extraits de film) qui vous permettront de mieux connaître les sociétés anglo-saxonnes.

Les pages *Spotlight* éclairent la thématique de l'unité à travers le prisme d'un des domaines du programme suivants : Arts, Croyances et représentations, Histoire et géopolitique, Langue et langages, Littérature, Sciences et techniques, Sociologie et économie.

• **Une tâche finale à accomplir à l'issue de chaque unité**

La tâche finale est annoncée en début d'unité : il s'agit d'une mise en situation de communication autour d'un scénario dont vous serez – seul, à deux ou en groupe – l'acteur ou les acteurs. Deux activités langagières seront mises en jeu pour la réalisation de cette tâche. Tout au long de l'unité, des entraînements à partir de supports variés, ainsi que des micro-tâches vous guideront vers cette tâche.

• **Un entraînement systématique dans chaque activité langagière**

Les pages *Focus on* de chaque unité vous permettront de vous entraîner dans une activité langagière dominante, liée à la réalisation de la tâche finale. Vous trouverez également, au cours de chaque unité, un entraînement dans les autres activités langagières.

Chaque unité vous permettra ainsi d'améliorer vos compétences dans les activités de réception (compréhension de l'oral et compréhension de l'écrit), de production (expression orale en continu et expression écrite) ainsi que dans les activités d'interaction orale.

L'objectif est de vous aider à atteindre le niveau B2 (utilisateur indépendant) du Cadre européen commun de référence pour les langues (CECRL).

Enfin, rappelez-vous que ce livre a été élaboré pour vous. Apprenez à bien le connaître, les deux pages qui suivent vous aideront à l'utiliser au mieux. N'oubliez pas de consulter régulièrement les dernières pages du manuel : les *Culture keys*, la Méthodologie et le Précis grammatical. Ce sont des pages de référence qui vous seront utiles tout au long de l'année.

Nous souhaitons vivement que, grâce à *New Bridges Terminales*, vous soyez à même de tirer le meilleur parti de vos cours, d'accomplir de réels progrès en anglais, d'enrichir votre connaissance du monde anglo-saxon et bien entendu de réussir au baccalauréat.

All the best!

Les auteurs

OUVERTURE

Découverte de la thématique de l'unité
Présentation de la tâche finale

Expression orale

- ***Keywords*** : lexique essentiel de la thématique
- ***Spécial bac*** : documents liés aux notions culturelles du programme

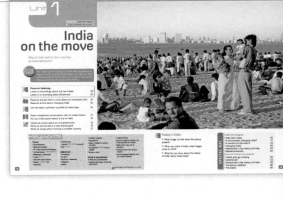

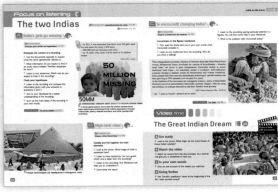

FOCUS ON

Activité langagière dominante de l'unité

- Trois exercices d'entraînement
- Renvois aux pages de Méthodologie traitant de la compétence travaillée
- ***Video time*** : étude d'un document vidéo ou ***Webquest*** : réalisation de tâches à partir d'une recherche sur Internet

LISTENERS' CORNER

Entraînement à la compréhension de l'oral

WRITERS' CORNER

Entraînement à l'expression écrite

SPEAKERS' CORNER

Entraînement à l'expression orale en continu et à l'interaction orale

- Activités guidées pour renforcer chacune des compétences.

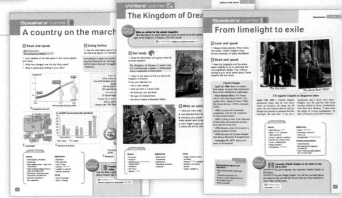

TEXT 1 / TEXT 2

Entraînement guidé à la compréhension d'un ou deux texte(s) de fiction ou de presse

- ***Warming up*** : préparation à la lecture
- ***Understanding the text*** : compréhension écrite et reformulation
- ***Writing time*** (Text 2) : expression écrite à partir du texte
- ***Going further*** : approfondissement
- ***Language training*** : Savoir prononcer, Pratiquer la grammaire, en lien avec le texte

Logos utilisés dans le manuel

 Compréhension de l'oral   **Compréhension de l'écrit**   **Expression orale en continu**   **Interaction orale**   **Expression écrite**

 CD de l'élève   **CD pour la classe**   **DVD** DVD avec les vidéos   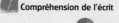 **Activités en lien avec les technologies de l'information et de la communication pour l'éducation**

Rubriques récurrentes

toolbox Lexique pour parler du document

function box Structures de communication

your task Activité en lien avec le document

LANGUAGE WORKSHOP
Renforcement de points clés

Grammaire – Grammaire de l'oral – Lexique

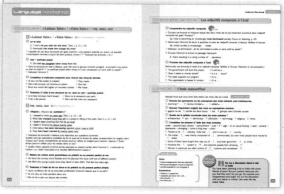

SPOTLIGHT
Enrichissement culturel autour d'un domaine du programme

■ Activités à partir de documents divers

FINAL TASK
Une tâche finale organisée autour de deux activités langagières

■ **Je me situe par rapport au CECRL** : des critères pour s'évaluer par rapport aux niveaux du Cadre européen

BAC ORAL – BAC ÉCRIT
Entraînement aux épreuves du baccalauréat

Compréhension de l'oral, expression orale, compréhension de l'écrit, expression écrite

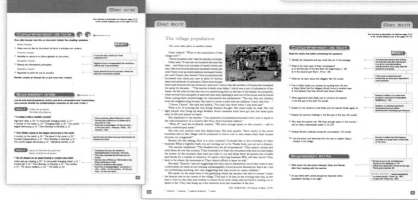

Fin du manuel

■ **Reading** : Entraînement à la lecture autonome
■ **Culture keys** : Certains aspects de la culture anglophone
■ **Méthodologie** : Renforcement des méthodes dans les cinq activités langagières

■ **Bac** : Conseils pratiques – Aide à l'expression (*Use your grammar*)
■ Précis grammatical
■ Verbes irréguliers
■ **Bac** : Index par notion culturelle

Breaking the ice 1

L'idée de progrès
Lieux et formes du pouvoir

2

L'idée de progrès
Espaces et échanges

Fiction & science

3

Lieux et formes du pouvoir
Espaces et échanges

Powers and counter-powers

4

L'idée de progrès
Espaces et échanges

5

Lieux et formes du pouvoir
Mythes et héros

This is Britain

Focus on writing ✍
Snapshots of Britain
Write about life in Britain today.   74

Webquest
London's changing skyline   75

Text 1 📖
Consumerist zombies (Jonathan COE)   76
▶ YOUR TASK ◀ Write an article about today's
young generation.   77

Listeners' corner 📞
Students protest   78
▶ YOUR TASK ◀ Have a discussion about the cost
of going to university.   78

Speakers' corner 👤👥
A sporting nation   79
▶ YOUR TASK ◀ Discuss organizing a trip
to a sporting event.   79

Text 2 📖
Black Britons (*The Guardian*)   80
▶ YOUR TASK ◀ Prepare a recording for an
e-twinning project.   81

Language workshop
Grammaire : Les propositions en *-ING* – Prétérit
et *present perfect*   82
Lexique : Le Royaume-Uni   83
▶ YOUR TASK ◀ Have a discussion with your
parents.   83

Spotlight The arts
Kings and queens on screen   84

Video time
Elizabeth: the Golden Age (S. KAPUR)   85

▶ Final task ◀ 👤✍
– Present the content of the article you will write
about your traineeship in Britain.
– Write the article.   86

(Bac oral) The UK monarchy debate   87

(Bac écrit) Challenges (Vikram SETH)   88

Staging ambition

Focus on discussing 👤
Improv games
Act out games about ambition.   92

Video time
Pygmalion (John GLENISTER)   93

Text 1 📖
Educating Rita (Willy RUSSELL)   94
▶ YOUR TASK ◀ Write an essay about Rita's
reactions to *Macbeth*.   95

Listeners' corner 📞
First day on the job   96
▶ YOUR TASK ◀ Act out a conversation between
an employee and his boss.   96

Writers' corner ✍
Reaching for the stars   97
▶ YOUR TASK ◀ Write a script about a young
man's ambitions.   97

Text 2 📖
Friends, Romans, countrymen…
(William SHAKESPEARE)   98
▶ YOUR TASK ◀ Recite a famous monologue.   99

Language workshop
Grammaire : Traduction de « devoir » – Pronoms
relatifs   100
Lexique : Théâtre et ambition   101
▶ YOUR TASK ◀ Express your disagreement about
your parents' expectations.   101

Spotlight Literature
Shakespeare and ambition   102

Webquest
Shakespeare forever   103

▶ Final task ◀ 👤
– Discuss which scene you should stage to perform
a scene on the topic "Ambition and drama".
– Rehearse the scene you choose.   104

(Bac oral) J.K. Rowling's speech
to Harvard students   105

(Bac écrit) The Crock (T. RATTIGAN)   106

6

7

sommaire

À l'issue du cycle terminal des séries générales et technologiques, le niveau de compétence attendu pour la langue vivante 1 est **B2**, pour la langue vivante 2, **B1**.

	Compréhension de l'oral	Compréhension de l'écrit	Expression orale en continu	Interaction orale	Expression écrite
B1	**Comprendre les points essentiels d'une intervention énoncée dans un langage clair et standard.** • comprendre ce qui est dit pour réaliser une tâche en situation réelle ou simulée ; • comprendre une information factuelle sur des sujets de la vie quotidienne ou étudiés ; • suivre une conversation en situation réelle ou simulée ; • comprendre les points principaux d'une intervention sur des sujets familiers ou étudiés, y compris des récits courts ; • suivre le plan général d'un exposé court sur un sujet connu ; • comprendre les points principaux de bulletins d'information et de documents enregistrés simples portant sur des sujets connus.	**Comprendre des textes essentiellement rédigés dans une langue courante.** • comprendre des instructions et consignes détaillées ; • comprendre suffisamment pour entretenir une correspondance suivie ; • localiser des informations recherchées ou pertinentes pour s'informer et réaliser une tâche ; • comprendre un enchaînement de faits ; • reconnaître les grandes lignes d'un schéma argumentatif.	**S'exprimer de manière simple sur des sujets variés.** • prendre la parole devant un auditoire, mettre en voix un texte ; • restituer une information avec ses propres mots, éventuellement à partir de notes ; • relater des expériences vécues, en rendre compte (événements, dialogues, texte écrit ou oral) ; • décrire ; • expliquer ; • exprimer des sentiments, une opinion personnelle ; • argumenter pour convaincre.	**Faire face à des situations variées avec une relative aisance à condition que la langue soit standard et clairement articulée.** • engager la conversation et maintenir le contact pour échanger des informations, réagir à des sentiments, exprimer clairement un point de vue ; • prendre part à une discussion pour expliquer, commenter, comparer et opposer ; • interviewer et être interviewé, conduire un entretien préparé et prendre quelques initiatives ; • faire aboutir une requête.	**Rédiger un texte articulé et cohérent, sur des sujets concrets ou abstraits, relatif aux domaines qui lui sont familiers.** • restituer une information avec ses propres mots, paraphraser simplement de courts passages écrits ; • prendre des notes sous forme d'une liste de points ; • rédiger un courrier personnel (incluant des avis sur des sujets abstraits ou culturels) ; • rendre compte d'expériences, de faits et d'événements ; • écrire un court récit, une description, un poème, de brefs essais simples ; • rédiger des messages courts de type informatif ou injonctif.
B2	**Comprendre l'essentiel d'une intervention longue, d'une argumentation complexe énoncée dans un langage standard.** • suivre une grande partie de ce qui est dit dans une longue conversation ; • comprendre la plupart des émissions, reportages et films en langue standard, reconnaître le point de vue et l'attitude du locuteur ; • comprendre l'essentiel d'une conférence, d'un discours ou d'un exposé complexes à condition que le sujet soit assez familier.	**Lire avec un grand degré d'autonomie et utiliser les références convenables de manière sélective.** • identifier rapidement le contenu et la pertinence d'une information, d'un article ou d'un reportage dans une gamme étendue de sujets ; • comprendre un texte littéraire contemporain en prose ; • comprendre des articles et des rapports sur des problèmes contemporains et dans lesquels les auteurs adoptent une position ou un point de vue particuliers.	**S'exprimer de manière organisée sur une gamme étendue de sujets relatifs à ses domaines d'intérêt.** • développer un exposé de manière claire et méthodique en soulignant les éléments significatifs ; • faire une description claire et détaillée sur un sujet connu ou étudié ; • exprimer avec finesse et précision des sentiments, une opinion personnelle ; • développer une argumentation claire, nuancée et enchaîner les arguments avec logique.	**Participer à des conversations avec spontanéité et aisance, avec des locuteurs natifs.** • échanger des informations précises, expliciter, demander des éclaircissements ; • prendre part à une conversation sur des sujets connus ou étudiés : exposer son propre point de vue, évaluer les points de vue d'autrui, émettre des hypothèses ; • interviewer et être interviewé, conduire un entretien avec efficacité et aisance de manière de plus en plus autonome ; • corriger lapsus et erreurs après en avoir pris conscience.	**Écrire des textes clairs et détaillés sur une gamme étendue de sujets relatifs à son domaine d'intérêt.** • résumer un large éventail de textes ; • résumer l'intrigue et la suite des événements d'un film ou d'une pièce ; • écrire des lettres exprimant différents degrés d'émotion, souligner ce qui est important ; • écrire des descriptions élaborées d'événements et d'expériences dans un texte articulé ; • écrire un essai ou un rapport qui développe une argumentation de façon méthodique.

D'après le *Bulletin officiel* n° 43, 24 novembre 2011

Séries ES, S, ST

Partie orale de l'épreuve

1. La compréhension de l'oral (LV1 et LV2)

Durée : 10 minutes (le temps d'écoute n'est pas inclus dans cette durée)

Cette évaluation a lieu dans le cadre habituel de formation de l'élève. Elle est annoncée aux élèves. Les enseignants l'organisent au cours du deuxième trimestre de l'année de terminale sur des supports, audio ou vidéo, sélectionnés en fonction des apprentissages effectués en classe.

Supports : Un ou des documents audio ou vidéo liés aux notions du programme, non étudiés précédemment en classe et d'une durée maximale d'une minute trente. Il peut s'agir d'extraits d'émissions de radio, de documentaires, de films, de journaux télévisés.

Modalités : Le titre donné à l'enregistrement est communiqué aux candidats. Le candidat a droit à trois écoutes, séparées chacune d'une minute. Il peut prendre des notes pendant chaque écoute et dispose ensuite de dix minutes pour rendre compte par écrit en français de ce qu'il a compris, sans exigence d'exhaustivité.

2. L'expression orale (LV1 et LV2)

Durée : 10 minutes

Temps de préparation : 10 minutes

Modalités : Les enseignants organisent cette évaluation au cours du dernier trimestre de terminale. Elle est annoncée aux candidats. Le candidat tire au sort une des notions du programme étudiées dans l'année. Après dix minutes de préparation, il dispose d'abord de cinq minutes pour présenter cette notion. Cette prise de parole en continu servira d'amorce à une conversation conduite par le professeur, qui prendra appui sur l'exposé du candidat. Cette phase d'interaction aura une durée maximale de cinq minutes.

Partie écrite de l'épreuve

Durée : Séries ES et S LV1 : 3 heures LV2 : 2 heures
Série ST   LV1   et / ou LV2 : 2 heures

L'épreuve écrite comprend deux sous-parties : la première porte sur la compréhension de l'écrit et la deuxième sur l'expression écrite. Chaque sous-partie est notée sur 10 points, au demi-point près.

1. L'épreuve de compréhension écrite

Elle prend appui sur un, deux ou trois documents. Ces documents peuvent relever de différents genres (extraits d'œuvres littéraires ou d'articles de presse) et être informatifs, descriptifs, narratifs ou argumentatifs. Certains documents peuvent comporter des éléments iconographiques. Ils renvoient aux notions du programme sans exiger de connaissances trop spécifiques.

En LV1 et LV2, les candidats seront évalués selon leur aptitude à :

– identifier le sujet ou la thématique générale des différents documents ;

– repérer dans un ou plusieurs documents les informations importantes relatives à un thème ou une problématique donnés ;

– comprendre les événements ou informations essentiels présents dans les documents ;

– comprendre les liens logiques, chronologiques ou thématiques entre les informations ou événements relatés ou évoqués dans les documents ;

– comprendre les motivations et réactions des personnages, du narrateur ou de l'auteur quand elles sont clairement exprimées ;

– comprendre les conclusions d'une argumentation.

En LV1, on tiendra aussi compte de l'aptitude des candidats à :

– comprendre les détails significatifs d'un document informatif ou factuel ;

– percevoir les points de vue, les opinions, les contrastes dans les documents et / ou dans leur mise en relation.

2. L'épreuve d'expression écrite

En LV1 et LV2, les candidats devront rédiger un ou plusieurs textes construits, prenant appui sur des événements, des faits ou des prises de position qu'il aura identifiés dans les documents servant de support à l'épreuve de la compréhension.

De plus, il est demandé aux candidats de LV1 de construire une argumentation personnelle à partir des mêmes documents ou d'un nouveau document « tremplin » en relation thématique avec les documents de la compréhension écrite.

Cette épreuve vise à évaluer l'aptitude du candidat à rédiger un ou des textes cohérents et clairement articulés dans une langue correcte et directement compréhensible (niveau B1 du CECRL).

Pour les LV1, est évaluée aussi l'aptitude à exprimer une opinion de façon nuancée et argumentée, en présentant les avantages ou les inconvénients d'une proposition, les points forts et les limites d'une prise de position dans une langue correcte aussi précise que possible (niveau B2 du CECRL).

Série L

Partie orale de l'épreuve

1. L'épreuve d'expression orale

Durée : 20 minutes

Temps de préparation : 10 minutes

Modalités (LV1 et LV2) : Le candidat présente à l'examinateur la liste des notions du programme qu'il a étudiées dans l'année et les documents qui les ont illustrées. L'examinateur choisira l'une de ces notions. Après dix minutes de préparation, le candidat dispose d'abord de dix minutes maximum pour présenter cette notion.

Cette prise de parole en continu servira d'amorce à une conversation conduite par l'examinateur, qui prendra appui sur l'exposé du candidat. Cette phase d'interaction aura une durée maximale de dix minutes.

Partie écrite de l'épreuve

Durée : LV1 et LV2 : 3 heures

L'épreuve écrite comprend deux sous-parties : la première porte sur la compréhension de l'écrit et la deuxième sur l'expression écrite. Chaque sous-partie est notée sur 10 points, au demi-point près.

2. L'épreuve de compréhension écrite

Elle prend appui sur un, deux ou trois documents. Ces documents peuvent relever de différents genres (extraits d'œuvres littéraires ou d'articles de presse) et être informatifs, descriptifs, narratifs ou argumentatifs. Certains documents peuvent comporter des éléments iconographiques. Ils renvoient aux notions du programme sans exiger de connaissances trop spécifiques. En LV1 et en LV2, les candidats seront évalués selon leur aptitude à :

– identifier le sujet ou la thématique générale des différents documents ;

– repérer dans un ou plusieurs documents les informations importantes relatives à un thème ou une problématique donnés ;

– comprendre les événements ou informations essentiels présents dans les documents ;

– comprendre les liens logiques, chronologiques ou thématiques entre les informations ou événements relatés ou évoqués dans les documents ;

– comprendre les motivations et réactions des personnages, du narrateur ou de l'auteur quand elles sont clairement exprimées ;

 – comprendre les conclusions d'une argumentation.

En LV1, on tiendra aussi compte de l'aptitude des candidats à :

– comprendre les détails significatifs d'un document informatif ou factuel ;

– percevoir les points de vue, les opinions, les contrastes dans les documents et / ou dans leur mise en relation.

3. L'épreuve d'expression écrite

En LV1 et LV2, les candidats devront rédiger un ou plusieurs textes construits, prenant appui sur des événements, des faits ou des prises de position qu'il aura identifiés dans les documents servant de support à l'épreuve de la compréhension.

De plus il est demandé aux candidats de LV1 de construire une argumentation personnelle à partir des mêmes documents ou d'un nouveau document « tremplin » en relation thématique avec les documents de la compréhension écrite.

Cette épreuve vise à évaluer l'aptitude du candidat à rédiger un ou des textes cohérents et clairement articulés dans une langue correcte et directement compréhensible (niveau B1 du CECRL).

Pour les LV1, est évaluée aussi l'aptitude à exprimer une opinion de façon nuancée et argumentée, en présentant les avantages ou les inconvénients d'une proposition, les points forts et les limites d'une prise de position dans une langue correcte aussi précise que possible (niveau B2 du CECRL).

Épreuve orale pour la langue choisie comme enseignement de spécialité (langue vivante approfondie)

Durée : 30 minutes

Temps de préparation : 10 minutes

Le candidat a choisi deux des notions étudiées dans l'année et a constitué pour chacune d'elles un dossier comportant deux documents étudiés en classe et un document de son choix (présenté en deux exemplaires et qui n'est pas pris dans un manuel scolaire) qui illustre ou complète cette notion. L'examinateur choisit l'une des notions. Après dix minutes de préparation, le candidat dispose de dix minutes pour présenter son dossier et justifier ses choix. Cette prise de parole en continu sert d'amorce à une conversation conduite par l'examinateur, qui prend appui sur l'exposé du candidat. Cette phase d'interaction n'excède pas vingt minutes.

The music scene

A Speaking

1 Protest songs of the 1960s-1970s

a. Name each singer, then match him with the extract from a song opposite.

b. What did these singers protest against?

c. Explain why the protest song movement was so important in the 60s-70s.

Come you masters of war
You that build the big guns
You that build the death planes
You that build all the bombs
You that hide behind walls
You that hide behind desks
I just want you to know
I can see through your masks.

Preacher man, don't tell me,
Heaven is under the earth.
I know you don't know
What life is really worth.
It's not all that glitters is gold;
'Alf the story has never been told:
So now you see the light, eh!
Stand up for your rights. Come on!
Get up, stand up: stand up for your rights!

Two, one, two, three, four
Everybody's talking about
Bagism, Shagism, Dragism, Madism, Ragism, Tagism
This-ism, that-ism, is-m, is-m, is-m.
All we are saying is give peace a chance
All we are saying is give peace a chance.

2 Singers emblematic of the 1980s-1990s

a. First, name each singer, then match him / her with one of the sentences below.

b. In your opinion, which of these singers is the most emblematic of the 1980s-1990s? Explain why and give as many details as you can about him / her.

c. Can you think of any other singer who could figure on the list of the top-five singers of that period? Justify your choice.

1 This singer was born in the USA and nicknamed "the Boss".

2 This singer was thrilled to learn that one of her / his albums was the best-selling album of all time.

3 This singer is known for continuously reinventing his / her image and music.

4 This singer is famous not only for his / her songs but also for his / her involvement in humanitarian causes, particularly in Africa.

 Listening

❶ The topic

a. Describe the photo taken in New York in 2011. In what circumstances do you think it was taken?

b. You are going to listen to the interview of Dorian Lynskey, the author of *33 Revolutions per Minute, a History of Protest Songs*, published in March 2011. What questions would you have asked him if you had interviewed him?

❷ Listen ⓌORKBOOK → p. 3

Listen to the interview. You will find some help in your *Workbook*.

❸ In your own words

How does Dorian Lynskey explain the rise and fall in popularity of protest songs? What examples does he give?

 Discussing

Pair work

If you had to pick three songs emblematic of the last decade, which ones would you choose? Discuss your choice with a classmate and try to agree on three songs.

 **Reading**

A Tucker fan

Tucker Crowe is an American singer-song writer. Duncan has taken his girlfriend, Annie, on a trip through the USA, visiting the
5 *various places where Tucker Crowe had lived.*

Nick HORNBY

was born in 1957 in England. His first novel, *Fever Pitch* (about his being a devoted Arsenal fan), made him a literary star in the UK. It was adapted for the screen as well as several of his best-selling novels: *High Fidelity, About a Boy, An Education.*

"I promise that after this holiday I won't be so Tuckercentric," he said.

"That's OK, I don't mind."

"I've wanted to do this for a long time."

10 "I know."

"I'll have got him out of my system."

"I hope not."

"Really?"

"What would there be left of you, if you did?"

15 She hadn't meant it cruelly. She'd been with Duncan for nearly fifteen years, and Tucker Crowe had always been part of the package, like a disability. To begin with, the condition hadn't prevented him from living a normal life: yes, he'd written a book, as yet unpublished, about Tucker, lectured on him, contributed to a radio documentary for the BBC and organized conventions, but somehow
20 these activities had always seemed to Annie like isolated episodes, sporadic attacks.

And then the Internet came along and changed everything.

When, a little later than everyone else, Duncan discovered how it all worked, he set up a website called "Can Anybody Hear Me?", the title of a track from an obscure EP[1] recorded after the wounding[2] failure of Crowe's first album. Until
25 then, the nearest fellow fan had lived in Manchester, sixty or seventy miles away, and Duncan met up with him once or twice a year; now the nearest fans lived in Duncan's laptop, and there were hundreds of them, from all around the world, and Duncan spoke to them all the time. There seemed to be a surprising amount to talk about. The website had a "Latest News" section, which never failed to
30 amuse Annie, Tucker no longer being a man who did an awful lot. ("As far as we know," Duncan always said.) There was always something that passed for news among the faithful, though – a Crowe night on an Internet radio station, a new article, a new album from a former band-member, an interview with an engineer. The bulk[3] of the content, though, consisted of essays analysing lyrics, or
35 discussing influences, or conjecturing, apparently inexhaustibly, about the silence. It wasn't as if Duncan didn't have other interests. But these were all flirtations, by comparison. Tucker Crowe was his life-partner. If Crowe were to die – to die in real life, as it were, rather than creatively – Duncan would lead the mourning.

Nick HORNBY, *Juliet, Naked* (2009)

1. Extended Play: musical recording between the single and the full album or LP

2. *blessant*

3. *essentiel*

➊ Reading comprehension ⓌORKBOOK → p. 4

urn to your *Workbook* for help in understanding the text.

➋ Key questions

. What shows that Duncan's interest for Tucker has grown bsessional? What parallel does he make when he says *"I'll have ot him out of my system"* (l. 11)?

. What is paradoxical about Tucker's fans' interest in their idol since he birth of Internet?

. Analyse Annie's attitude toward Duncan's addiction to Tucker Crowe.

. Do you agree with Annie when she refers to Duncan's addiction terms of disability?

toolbox

Nouns
- pilgrimage: *pèlerinage*
- addict /'ædɪkt/
- expert
- icon /'aɪkɒn/

Adjectives
- obsessed /əb'sest/
- obsessive /əb'sesɪv/
- addicted /ə'dɪktɪd/
- ironical /aɪ'rɒnɪkəl/
- unhealthy: *malsain*

Verbs & expressions
- dedicate one's life to
- keep V-ING: *ne pas arrêter de*
- look up to = admire
- idolize
- be on drugs
- make fun of: *se moquer de*

Fans during a vigil on the 10th anniversary of Kurt Cobain's death in Seattle

▤ Writing ✎

Music pilgrimages
- A Seattle tour takes Nirvana's fans to the house where Kurt Cobain lived and died.
- Graceland, home of rock 'n' roll star Elvis Presley is a magnet to thousands each year.
- The tomb of Jim Morrison, The Doors' lead singer, in the Père Lachaise Cemetery in Paris, is one of the city's top attractions.

Would you be ready to undertake a music pilgrimage? Why or why not? (200 words)

LES ÉVALUATIONS DIAGNOSTIQUES
Vous venez de vous entraîner dans les cinq activités langagières. Votre professeur va maintenant vous fournir des fiches vous permettant de vous évaluer et de déterminer à quel niveau du CECRL vous vous situez dans ces cinq activités.

Unit 1

L'idée de progrès

Lieux et formes du pouvoir

India on the move

Why is India said to be a country of contradictions?

final task It's "India week" in your school. After listening to reports and reading about India, you give an oral presentation of one aspect of modern-day India that you find particularly interesting.

Keywords

Nouns
- subcontinent
- high technology
- IT / information technology
- entrepreneur /ˌɒntrəprəˈnɜː/
- billionaire: *milliardaire*
- caste /kɑːst/
- second-class citizen
- dowry /ˈdaʊrɪ/: *dot*
- contrast
- democracy
- custom /ˈkʌstəm/: *coutume*
- sari /ˈsɑːrɪ/

Adjectives
- emerging
- hi-tech
- thriving = booming
- religious
- Hindu
- (un)fair: *(in)juste*
- oppressive
- open-minded ≠ narrow-minded
- (un)skilled /skɪld/ ≠ *(non) qualifié*
- urban ≠ rural

Verbs & expressions
- climb the social ladder
- make ends meet: *joindre les deux bouts*
- make a living
- go from rags to riches = go from poverty to wealth
- fight one's way out of poverty
- come a long way: *faire du chemin*
- be on an equal footing: *être sur un pied d'égalité*

LANGUAGE WORKSHOP → p. 29

 ## Today's India

1. What image of India does this picture present?

2. When you think of India, what images come to mind?

3. What do you know about the history of India? about India today?

The two Indias

Ⓜ ÉTHODOLOGIE **COMPRÉHENSION DE L'ORAL** → p. 16

Ⓦ ORKBOOK → p. 5–

Ⓐ India's girls go missing 8-9

Ⓜ ÉTHODOLOGIE
Anticiper puis vérifier ses hypothèses → p. 161

Anticipate the content of a recording.

1. Use the documents opposite to explain what the word "gendercide" alludes to.

2. What information do you expect to find in an audio report entitled "Families desperate for sons"?

3. Listen to two sentences. Which one do you expect to hear in the recording?

Check your hypotheses.

4. Listen to the recording and compare the information given with your answers to questions 2 and 3.

5. Turn to your *Workbook* for a better understanding of the recording.

6. Sum up the main ideas of the recording in your own words.

culture key   The dowry tradition → p. 151

– In 2011 it was estimated that there were 940 girls age‹ six and under for every 1,000 boys.
– 600,000 girls go missing every year.
– In 18 years' time, India will be short of 10 million brides.

India's 2011 censu

50 MILLION MISSING

50MM

AN INTERNATIONAL CAMPAIGN ABOUT INDIA'S 50 MILLION MISSIN

In three generations, more than 50 million women have been selectively eliminated from India's population through infanticide, dowry-related murders, and other gendercide practices.

Infosys Technologies Ltd. headquarters in Bangalore, India

Ⓑ High-tech cities  10-12

Ⓜ ÉTHODOLOGIE
Classer, relier, hiérarchiser → p. 162

Classify and link together the main elements.

1. Look at the photo. What image of India presented here?

2. Listen to three sentences. Can you gues‹ which one is taken from the recording?

3. Listen to the recording. Your *Workbook* ‹ help you to understand it.

4. Summarize the report.

C Is microcredit changing India?

13-15

ⓂÉTHODOLOGIE
Repérer et mémoriser les nombres → p. 162

Concentrate on the figures mentioned.

1. First, read the article and say in your own words what microcredit consists in.

2. Listen to two sentences from the recording. Who do you think is talking?

3. Listen to the recording paying particular attention to figures. You will find some help in your *Workbook*.

4. What is the problem with microcredit today?

When Bangladeshi economist, founder of Grameen Bank and Nobel Peace Prize winner, Muhammad Yunus, developed the concept of microfinance – whereby small loans[1] are given to poor entrepreneurs financially unable to secure traditional bank loans – he essentially started a revolution. Self-sufficiency suddenly became a realistic notion for businessmen and women worldwide. India jumped full-force onto the microfinance bandwagon[2] and the industry has been growing at 70% annually over the past five years.

At the forefront of the movement are courageous women – many of them Dalits (formerly known as untouchables) from India's poorest villages – who are using microfinance to extricate themselves and their families from poverty.

SEE Change Magazine (Dec. 7th 2010)

1. *prêt*   2. *sauter sur l'occasion / prendre le train en marche*

culture key   The Dalits → p. 151

Video time

The Great Indian Dream 🎬 ⓓⓥⓓ

Visions of India, a BBC documentary (2010)

A Get ready

1. Look at the photo. What might be the Great Dream of these Indian women?

B Watch the video

2. Watch an extract from the documentary. Your teacher will give you a worksheet to help you.

C In your own words

3. Give an oral account of the extract you watched.

D Going further

4. Has Gandhi's prediction, heard at the beginning of the film, been proved correct?

Text 1

Another girl

culture key The dowry tradition → p. 151

Shilpi SOMAYA GOWDA

was born (1970) and raised in Toronto, Canada. Her parents migrated there from Mumbai. She holds an MBA from Stanford University. In 1991, she spent a summer as a volunteer in an Indian orphanage, which seeded the idea for her first novel, *Secret Daughter*. It was translated into 19 languages.

A Warming up

Use the *Culture key* and the picture of the girls in an Indian orphanage to guess what the text is about.

Kavita has decided to give birth to her child in an abandoned hut, not far from her home.

No one heard my prayers. Kavita closes her eyes and her body shudders with silent tears. She leans forward, seizes the midwife's[1] hand, and whispers,

5 "*Daiji*[2], don't tell anyone. Go quickly, fetch Rupa[3], and bring her here. No one, you hear?"

"Yes, my child. Blessings to you and your baby. You rest now, please. I will bring some food." The midwife steps outside into the night.

As the early light of dawn seeps into the hut, Kavita awakens and feels the

10 throbbing[4] ache in her pelvis. She shifts her body, and her gaze falls upon the newborn sleeping peacefully beside her.

It is not long before the door creaks open and bright sunlight spills in. Jasu enters, his eyes gleaming. "Where is he?" He beckons playfully with his hands. "Where is my little prince? Come, come… let me see him!" He walks toward

15 her, arms outstretched.

Kavita stiffens. She clutches the baby to her chest and tries to sit up. "She is here. Your little princess is right here." She sees blackness cloud his eyes. Her arms tremble as she wraps them tightly around the baby, shielding her small body.

20 "Another girl? What is the matter with you? Let me see!" he shouts.

"No. I will not. You are not taking her." She hears the shrillness of her voice, feels the tension flood into her limbs[5]. "This is my baby, *our* baby, and I will not let you take her." She sees bewilderment[6] in his eyes as they search her face for some understanding. She has never spoken to anyone, let alone[7] her husband,

25 with such defiance.

He takes a few steps toward her, then his face softens and he falls to his knees next to her. "Look, Kavita, you know we can't keep this baby. We need a boy to help us in the fields. As it is, we can hardly afford one child, how can we have two? My cousin's daughter is twenty-three and still not married, because
30 he can't come up with the dowry. We are not a rich family, Kavita. You know we can't do this."

Her eyes fill again with tears, and she shakes her head until they spill out. Her breath becomes ragged[8]. She squeezes her eyes closed for several breaths. When she opens them again, she looks squarely at her husband. "I won't let
35 you take her this time. I won't. If you try, if you even *try*, you will have to kill me first."

"Kavita, come, you're not thinking straight. We can't do this."

He throws his hands in the air. "She will become a burden to us, a drain[9] on our family. Is that what you want?" He stands, towering over her again.
40 Her mouth is dry. She stumbles over the words she has not quite allowed to form except in the distant corners of her mind. "Give me one night. Just one night with my child. You can come fetch her tomorrow."

Jasu remains silent, looking down at his feet.

"*Please.*"

Shilpi SOMAYA GOWDA, *Secret Daughter* (2010)

1. *sage-femme* 2. *sage-femme (en hindi)* 3. *Kavita's sister* 4. *lancinant*
5. *membres* 6. *perplexité* 7. *encore moins* 8. /ˈrægɪd/ *irrégulière* 9. *(ici) gouffre*

B Understanding the text ⓌORKBOOK → p. 7-8

1. Turn to your *Workbook* for help in understanding the text.

2. Use your *Workbook* to explain what happened after the baby's birth.

C Going further

3. What does Kavita mean when she says *"No one heard my prayers"* (l. 1)?

4. Why does Kavita tell the midwife not to tell anyone?

5. Explain Jasu's change of attitude.

6. Analyse Kavita's reactions and feelings.

7. Guess why Kavita says *"Give me one night"* (l. 41).

D Language training

8. Savoir prononcer 4-5 17-18

Les consonnes muettes

9. Pratiquer la grammaire

« Laisser faire » / « Faire faire » ●LANGUAGE WORKSHOP → p. 28

TELL et le style indirect ⓌORKBOOK → p. 11

toolbox

Nouns
- despair
- infanticide /ɪnˈfæntɪsaɪd/

Adjectives
- motherly: *maternel*
- unwanted
- dreadful /ˈdredfʊl/ = awful
- broken-hearted = devastated
- helpless: *impuissant, désespéré*

Verbs & expressions
- give birth to: *donner naissance à / accoucher de*
- grant a wish / prayer: *exaucer un vœu / une prière*
- break the news: *annoncer la nouvelle*
- expect
- reject
- snatch / grab sth from sb: *arracher*
- fear / tremble for
- abandon = give up
- compel = oblige
- vanish = disappear
- beg: *(ici) implorer*
- get rid of: *se débarrasser de*

 Your task

✎ **Continue the story**
Imagine how Jasu reacts to Kavita's demand and what happens afterwards.

Ⓜ ÉTHODOLOGIE
Continuer un récit → p. 171

23

A country on the march

A Read and speak

(M)ÉTHODOLOGIE
Dire des données chiffrées → p. 164

1. Look carefully at the data given in the various graphs and charts.

2. What has changed over the last thirty years?

3. What is particularly striking in your view?

B Going further

4. Use the information given in this page to comment on the following figures on well-being in India.

> According to a study on overall well-being, 17% people describe themselves as "thriving", a majority of Indians (64%) believe they are "struggling", while 19% think they are "suffering".
>
> *The Times of India* (April 20)

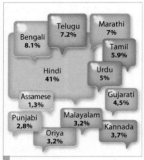

Population

2 — 1.7bn
1.5 — 1.2bn
1 —
0.5 — 319m
0 — estimate
1941 — 2011 — 2050
Will overtake China by 2030

▌ **Population growth**

India's population
17.5% of the world's population
Two-child families encouraged by family planning programmes
940 females for 1,000 males
Life expectancy: 66.8 (UK: 79.4)

Number of billionaires
55 (fourth-highest in the world)

People living below 80p (0.93€) a day
42% in 2005 (60% in 1981)
Literacy rate: 74% (Male: 83% – Female: 65%)

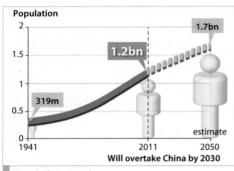

Bengali 8.1%
Telugu 7.2%
Marathi 7%
Tamil 5.9%
Hindi 41%
Urdu 5%
Assamese 1,3%
Gujarati 4,5%
Punjabi 2,8%
Malayalam 3,2%
Oriya 3,2%
Kannada 3,7%

▌ **Languages**

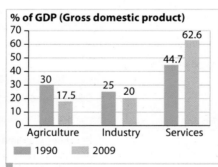

% of GDP (Gross domestic product)

70 —
60 — 62.6
50 — 44.7
40 —
30 — 30
25
20 — 17.5 — 20
10 —
0 — Agriculture — Industry — Services

▬ 1990 ▬ 2009

▌ **Sectors of activity**

Hinduism **80.5%**

Islam **13.4%**

Jainism **0.4%**

Buddhism **0.8%**

Christianity **2.3%**

Sikhism **1.9%**

▌ **Religions**

toolbox

Nouns
- discrepancy: *décalage*
- social gap
- (the) needy (noun + adj.): *(les) nécessiteux*
- (the) underprivileged (noun + adj.): *(les) défavorisés*
- the haves ≠ the have-nots *(les nantis ≠ les démunis)*
- growth: *croisssance*
- sex-selection

Adjectives
- populous
- fast-growing
- vast = huge
- diverse /darˈvɜːs/
- wealthy = well-off
- poverty-stricken

Verbs
- thrive = prosper
- shift = change

Your task

Present a profile of India today

Use the data to give an oral account about modern day India to the class.

(M)ÉTHODOLOGIE
Rendre compte d'un document → p. 163

Writers' corner

The Kingdom of Dreams

Your task

Write an article for the school magazine
After listening to an audio report, you write an article about the opening night of the Kingdom of Dreams. (250-300 words)

Ⓜ ÉTHODOLOGIE **Rédiger un article de presse** → p. 172

A Get ready

1. Read the information and guess what the pictures represent.

> The Kingdom of Dreams is India's first live entertainment complex: a Bollywood theme park comparable to Disneyland.

2. Listen to the report to find out about the Kingdom of Dreams.
Focus your attention on:
– why it was created;
– what you find in Culture Gully;
– the food you can eat there;
– the type of entertainment;
– the show hosted at Nautanki Mahal.

B Write an article

3. Here are a few hints:

a. Use elements from the audio report, but make your own sentences.

b. Introduce your article so as to make people want to read it.

c. Don't forget to give your article a catchy title and to conclude.

function box

Expressing surprise
- I can't / couldn't believe it / my eyes!
- You can't imagine what I saw!
- How surprised I was!
- It was truly amazing!
- How fantastic it was!
- How astonishing to see such...!
- I was amazed by / stunned by / astounded by...

Expressing enthusiasm
- It must be great / terrific...
- How fantastic!
- I'd just love to...
- I was so impressed by...
- I can't wait to see that!

toolbox

Nouns
- live show
- musical
- performance /pəˈfɔːməns/: représentation
- rehearsal
- set: décor
- palace /ˈpælɪs/

Adjectives
- fake: factice
- impressive
- glamorous
- sparkling: étincelant
- colourful

Verbs
- stage: mettre en scène
- recreate
- feature /ˈfiːtʃə/: représenter
- perform: se produire
- attract
- enjoy = delight in

Changing India

Anand GIRIDHARADAS

is the author of *India Calling: An Intimate Portrait of a Nation's Remaking* (2011). He writes for *The New York Times* and the *International Herald Tribune*. A native of Cleveland, Ohio, and a graduate of the University of Michigan, he worked in Mumbai as a management consultant until 2005, when he began reporting from that city.

A Warming up

Use the picture and the title to anticipate the content of the article.

The first thing I ever learned about India was that my parents had chosen to leave it.

My cousins in India would sometimes
5 ask if I was Indian or American.

"American," I would say, because it was the truth, and because I felt that to say otherwise would be to accept a lower berth in the world.

10 I moved to India six years ago in an effort to understand it on my own terms, to render mine what had until then only belonged to my parents.

India was changing when I arrived
15 and has changed dramatically, viscerally, improbably in these 2,000 days: farms giving way to factories; ultra-cheap cars being built; companies buying out rivals abroad. But the greatest change I have
20 witnessed is elsewhere. It is in the mind: Indians now know that they don't have to leave, as my parents left, to have their personal revolutions.

It took me time to see. At first, my
25 old lenses[1] were still in place – India the frustrating, difficult country – and so I saw only the things I had ever seen.

But as I traveled the land, the data did not fit the framework. The children of the
30 lower castes were hoisting themselves up one diploma and training program at a time. The women were becoming breadwinners through microcredit and decentralized manufacturing. The young people were finding in their cellphones
35 a first zone of individual identity. The couples were ending marriages no matter what "society" thinks, then finding love again. The vegetarians were embracing meat and meat-eaters were turning
40 vegetarian, defining themselves by taste and faith, not caste.

Indians from languorous villages to pulsating cities were making difficult
45 new choices to die other than where they

were born, to pursue vocations not their father's, to live lives imagined within their own skulls. And it was addictive, this improbable rush of hope.

50   The shift is only just beginning. Most Indians still live impossibly grim[2] lives. Trickle down[3], here more than most places, is slow. But it is a shift in psychologies, and you rarely meet an 55 Indian untouched by it.

Grabbing hold of their destinies, these Indians became the unlikely cousins of my own immigrant parents in America: restless, ambitious, with dreams vivid 60 only to themselves. But my parents had sought[4] to beat the odds in a bad system.

What has changed since they left is a systemic lifting of the odds for those who stay. It is a milestone in any nation's 65 life when leaving becomes a choice, not a necessity.

[Indians] no longer angrily berate[5] America, because they are too busy building their own country. Indian 70 accents are now cooler than British ones. No one asks if I feel Indian or American. How delicious to see that unconcern[6]. How fortunate to live in a land you needn't leave to become your fullest 75 possible self.

Anand GIRIDHARADAS,
"Farewell to an Indian I Hardly Knew",
in *The New York Times* (July 4th 2009)

1. *lentilles*   2. *tristes*   3. *retombées économiques dont bénéficient les moins favorisés*   4. seek – sought – sought: *chercher*   5. *fustiger*
6. *insouciance*

B Understanding the text ⓦORKBOOK → p. 9-10

1. Turn to your *Workbook* which will help you to understand the text.

2. Explain in what way(s) India is changing.

C Going further

3. What did the writer go to India for?

4. Explain the sentence: "*At first, my old lenses were still in place*" (l. 24).

5. In the journalist's opinion, what is the greatest change in India?

6. What reservations does the journalist express about India's evolution?

7. In your opinion, what changes are the most striking?

D Writing time

8. **Essay** (150-200 words) Ⓜ ÉTHODOLOGIE
Rédiger un essai → p. 172

Would you be ready to leave your country "*to become your fullest possible self*"?

a. Précisez ce que l'expression "*your fullest possible self*" signifie pour vous.

b. Analysez les avantages et les inconvénients que vous auriez à émigrer.

c. Étoffez votre argumentation à l'aide d'exemples.

d. Utilisez la *Toolbox* et les *Expressions utiles pour communiquer*, p. 173-174.

E Language training

9. Savoir prononcer 🎧 6-7 💿 20-21 ⓦORKBOOK → p. 10

La prononciation des lettres -*ou*

La place de l'accent de mot

10. Pratiquer la grammaire

For, since, ago 🔵LANGUAGE WORKSHOP → p. 28
Would – Comparatif ou superlatif ? ⓦORKBOOK → p. 11

toolbox

Nouns
- stereotype /'stɪərɪətaɪp/
- prejudice
- self-confidence
- optimism
- state of mind: *état d'esprit*
- roots: *racines*

Adjectives
- (un)biased /'baɪəst/: *(im)partial*
- confident: *confiant*

- tremendous /trə'mendəs/: *énorme*
- hopeful
- proud

Verbs & expressions
- check
- achieve: *réaliser*
- have blinkers: *avoir des œillères*
- turn into: *(se) transformer en*
- break with fate: *refuser son destin*
- become westernized

Your task

Have a telephone conversation with an Indian friend

Put yourself in the narrator's shoes. You have a telephone conversation with an Indian friend of yours who still lives in the USA. You try to persuade him / her to return to India.

Ⓜ ÉTHODOLOGIE
Conversation au téléphone → p. 165

Grammaire | **«Laisser faire»** / **«Faire faire»** – *FOR, SINCE, AGO*

A «Laisser faire» / «Faire faire» ⓟRÉCIS GRAMMATICAL → 36B, 36C

① *LET* et *MAKE*

1. *"I won't **let you take** her this time."* (Text 1, p. 23, l. 34)
2. *Eventually **she made him change** his mind.*

a. Laquelle de ces deux structures (en gras) exprime «une pression exercée sur autrui» et laquelle «l'autorisation donnée à autrui de faire quelque chose»? **b.** Traduisez les énoncés 1 et 2.

② *HAVE* + participe passé

3. *She **had her daughter taken away** from her.*

a. Dans la structure en *HAVE* ci-dessus, quel rôle joue le groupe nominal souligné : accomplit-il une action ou bien la subit-il? **b.** Le participe passé *taken away* a-t-il par conséquent un sens actif ou passif? **c.** Traduisez l'énoncé 3.

③ Complétez la traduction proposée pour chacun des énoncés donnés.

a. Ils leur ont fait quitter la maison. → *They made…*
b. Elle a fait envoyer cet homme en prison. → *She had…*
c. Nous leur avons fait signer un nouveau contrat. → *We made…*

④ Traduisez à l'aide d'une structure en *LET, MAKE* ou *HAVE* + participe passé.

a. Je la ferai renvoyer (*send away*).　　**c.** Nous ne la laisserons pas partir.
b. Il les a fait pleurer.　　**d.** Elle s'est fait voler son passeport.

B *FOR, SINCE, AGO* ⓟRÉCIS GRAMMATICAL → 7.

⑤ «Depuis», «il y a» ou «pendant»?

1. *I **moved** to India <u>six years ago</u>.* (Text 2, p. 26, l. 10)
2. *What **has changed** <u>since they left</u> is a systemic lifting of the odds.* (Text 2, p. 27, l. 62)
3. *I **hadn't seen** anything like that <u>for so long</u>!*
4. *I **lived** in America <u>for about twenty years</u>.*
5. *Child labour **has been decreasing** regularly <u>since I was a child</u>.*
6. *They **have been married** <u>for twenty years now</u>.*

a. Traduisez les énoncés ci-dessus puis répondez aux questions suivantes :
Quelles sont les traductions possibles de *for* et quel est le temps du verbe correspondant en anglais dans chaque cas? Quels compléments de temps peut-on utiliser en anglais pour traduire «depuis»? Quels temps peut-on utiliser pour les verbes dans ce cas?

b. Quelle notion apporte la forme *BE+ING* associée au *present perfect* dans l'énoncé 5 : «continuité de l'action» ou «bilan mesurable d'un résultat définitivement acquis»?

⑥ Mettez les verbes entre parenthèses au prétérit ou au *present perfect BE+ING*.

a. *He (tour) the country since October and he (discuss) this issue with lots of different people.*
b. *We (film) this young couple since they (land) in New Delhi. That (be) two days ago.*

⑦ Traduisez à l'aide de *for* ou *since* et du prétérit ou du *present perfect* simple.

a. Leurs conditions de vie se sont-elles améliorées (*improve*) depuis que tu es parti?
b. Ils ont vécu en Inde pendant deux ans.
c. Elle ne les a pas vus depuis des années.

Grammaire de l'oral | **Les adjectifs composés à l'oral**

8 Comprendre les adjectifs composés 22-24

a. Écoutez cet énoncé et indiquez lequel des deux mots est le plus fortement accentué dans l'adjectif composé (en gras). Pourquoi ?

> **1a.** *India is becoming an increasingly* **male-dominated** *society.* (Focus on listening, p. 20)

b. Reformulez l'énoncé de façon à expliciter le sens de l'adjectif composé ci-dessus. Vérifiez à l'écoute.

> **1b.** *Indian society is increasingly … males.*

c. Déduisez : la terminaison *-ed* de *dominated* a-t-elle un sens actif ou passif ?

d. Écoutez l'énoncé et écrivez le passage manquant.

> **2.** *That's resulting in a rising number of … abortions.*

9 Produire des adjectifs composés à l'oral 25

Reformulez ces énoncés à l'aide d'un adjectif composé. Vérifiez à l'écoute. (Attention à l'accentuation.)

1. *The government will fund the project.* → *It will be a …*
2. *Does it relate to money issues?* → *Is it a … issue?*
3. *The state supports our program.* → *It's a …*
4. *The organization is based in London.* → *It's a …*

Lexique | **L'Inde aujourd'hui**

Assurez-vous que vous avez bien retenu les mots clés de l'unité. → **Keywords p. 18**

10 Donnez les synonymes ou les antonymes des mots suivants, puis traduisez-les.
a. *booming* = … **b.** *narrow-minded* ≠ … **c.** *skilled* ≠ …

11 Donnez l'équivalent anglais des mots ou expressions suivants.
a. gagner sa vie **b.** joindre les deux bouts **c.** dot **d.** grimper dans l'échelle sociale

12 Quelle est la syllabe accentuée dans les mots suivants ?
a. *entrepreneur* **b.** *sari* **c.** *democracy* **d.** *billionaire* **e.** *technology* **f.** *religious* **g.** *Hindu*

13 Complétez les phrases à l'aide des mots suivants.
unfair – second-class citizens – subcontinent – rural – IT – rags – on an equal footing – caste – poverty – oppressive – emerging – come a long way – urban

a. *Thanks to its …1… industry, India has …2… and is now an …3… country.*
b. *The Indian …4… was mainly composed of …5… communities, but now most people have moved to …6… areas.*
c. *Some of them have fought their way out of …7… and even gone from …8… to riches.*
d. *However the …9… system is …10… and prevents people from all being …11….*
e. *Women in particular are often victims of …12… customs and considered …13….*

Your task

 Act out a discussion about a trip to India

You have been planning a trip to India with some friends of yours. But your parents have just told you that they won't let you go. You express your disagreement and anger. Act out the discussion with your father or mother. Use verbs like **let**, **make**, **have**.

Milestones in the history of India

From British dominion to the largest democracy in the world.

A Hinduism, the oldest religion in the world

Read the text and explain why Hinduism is often considered more a way of life than a religion.

Men praying along the banks of the Ganges River

HINDUISM HAS ELEMENTS which stretch back many thousands of years. Unlike most other religions, Hinduism has no single founder. Throughout its extensive history, there have been many key figures teaching different philosophies and writing numerous holy[1] books. For these reasons, writers often refer to Hinduism as "a way of life" or "a family of religions" rather than a single religion.

Hindus believe in a single collective soul named Brahman, divided into different lesser gods such as Brahma (the Creator), Vishnu (the Preserver), and Shiva (the Destroyer).

Life is seen as cyclical, and Hinduism teaches both reincarnation and karma. Hindus believe that the soul is eternal: when the body dies, the soul lives on and is given a new body. Karma – the culmination of all the actions of a person in his life – affects the form his next life will take. Hindus believe that both animals and humans have souls; thus most Hindus abstain from meat (vegetarianism depends on caste), and beef is forbidden to all.

Millions of pilgrims[2] from all over India gather in many holy places such as Benares on the Ganges[3] every year.

1. *sacrés* 2. *pèlerins* 3. /ˈgændʒiːz/

B The jewel in the crown

FROM THE 16TH CENTURY, European powers established trading posts in India. British Rule began in 1600 with the arrival of the British East India Company trading mainly in cotton, silk, indigo dye[1], tea and spices. The Company established its own army composed of British troops as well as native soldiers called sepoys[2].

The Indian Mutiny erupted in May 1857, when sepoys mutinied against their British commanders because they had supplied them rifle cartridges[3] greased with pig and cow fat,

Queen Victoria (1819-1901)

which was unacceptable for both Hindu and Muslim soldiers. Uprisings[4] spread throughout British India. The conflicts were brutal and bloody.

For most of the 19th century India was considered the jewel in the crown of the British Empire. Queen Victoria was made Empress of India in 1877.

1. *teinture* 2. /ˈsiːpɔɪ/ 3. *cartouches* 4. *insurrection*

1 Read the text once.
2 Give an oral account of the text.
The following guidelines will help you. Make your own sentences and link them.
a. When and why did the British establish a trading company in India?
b. What caused the Indian Mutiny?
c. What happened in 1877?

C Towards independence

Read the text and find out why the end of British Empire resulted in the creation of separate states.

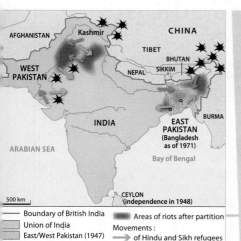

The partition of British India (1947)

500 km

Boundary of British India
Union of India
East/West Pakistan (1947)
★ Border conflicts

Areas of riots after partition
Movements:
→ of Hindu and Sikh refugees
→ of Muslim refugees

ALTHOUGH MOST OF INDIA RALLIED to the British flag, many Indians started fighting for independence. In 1922, Mahatma Gandhi started an anti-British campaign of non-violent civil disobedience to obtain independence. Along with the desire for independence, tension between Hindus and Muslims developed over the years. The Muslims were a minority and worried about a possible exclusively Hindu government. So the Muslim League demanded the division of India into two separate states: Muslim and Hindu. When the British left in 1947, India became independent, the separate states of Pakistan and Bangladesh were created and violence erupted. Muslim and Hindu minorities in the areas fled in opposite directions. In a few weeks, half a million people died in the course of one the greatest migrations of human beings in the history of the world.

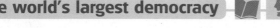
culture key Mahatma Gandhi → p. 151

D The world's largest democracy

1 Do you know why India is said to be the largest democracy in the world?

2 Read the text to check your answer to question 1.

INDIA'S GOVERNMENT IS MODELED on the British parliamentary system. The Parliament, located in India's capital, New Delhi, is made up of two houses. India's President is elected for five years by members of both houses and the Prime Minister is chosen by the President.

1947-1964: Jawaharlal Nehru, India's first Prime Minister, defends a policy of nonalignment.

1964-1977: Nehru's daughter Indira Gandhi: first female Prime Minister.

1980-1984: Indira Gandhi's second term – assassinated by her Sikh bodyguards.

2001: Rise in tension with Pakistan over Kashmir.

2007: Pratibha Patil becomes the first female President of India.

In just over 50 years, India has become an independent democracy. Overpopulation, poverty, and internal conflicts threaten Indian stability from time to time. However India has survived the past half-century without a government collapse or military takeover.

Pratibha Devisingh Patil

Webquest From Bombay to Mumbai TICE

1 Browse the web to find out about Mumbai. The following guidelines will help you.

a. When and why did Bombay become Mumbai?

b. Give information about its geographical location, climate, population.

c. What are the places of interest?

d. Why is it such an important city?

e. Find out about the Dharavi slum.

2 Give an oral presentation of the city (3 to 4 minutes) with the information you collected.

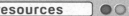

◄ ► Web resources ○ ○ ○
• www.mumbainet.com/
• ngm.nationalgeographic.com/
• www.lonelyplanet.com/

Why is India said to be a country of contradictions?

It's "India week" in your school. After listening to reports and reading about India, you give an oral presentation of one aspect of modern-day India that you find particularly interesting.

¹ Listen to a radio report 8-9 26-27

Ⓜ ÉTHODOLOGIE **COMPRÉHENSION DE L'ORAL** → p. 161

Ⓐ Get ready

Do you think that this illustration could be used as a poster to advertise "India week" in your school?
Explain why or why not.

Ⓑ Now listen

■ The worksheet your teacher will give you will help you to understand a report entitled *Two stories*.

■ Explain what the stories of Suhas Gopinath and Bisu Das illustrate.

★ ★ ★
Je me situe par rapport au CECRL **B2**

LORSQUE J'ÉCOUTE CE REPORTAGE :
Je peux comprendre un reportage audio en langue standard, reconnaître le point de vue et l'attitude du locuteur.

Hindu God Ganesh going hi-tech

² Present an aspect of modern-day India

Ⓜ ÉTHODOLOGIE **EXPRESSION ORALE EN CONTINU** → p. 163

■ Use the document you have just listened to as an introduction to your presentation.

■ Choose one aspect of modern India that you would like to present to the class. The various documents you have worked on in this unit should help you to make your choice. Browse the Internet or use other information sources to find out more about the topic.

■ Make complete sentences and link them. Your presentation should last 3 to 4 minutes.

★ ★ ★
Je me situe par rapport au CECRL **B2**

LORSQUE JE PARLE DE CE SUJET DE SOCIÉTÉ :
Je peux développer un exposé de manière claire et méthodique en soulignant les éléments significatifs.

function box

Expressing surprise
● It was just unbelievable!
● Just imagine!
● Fancy that!
● It was incredible!
● What a sight! / What strange things!...
● What I find the most incredible / unpleasant / shocking is that...

Giving one's opinion
● To my mind / In my opinion...
● It seems to me that...
● I feel / believe that...
● I can't help thinking that...
● My feeling is that...
● As a matter of fact, I am convinced that...
● For my part, I consider that...

Vous trouverez la présentation de l'épreuve pages 12-13
et des conseils pratiques pour le bac pages 175-179.

Compréhension de l'oral

 10 28 WORKBOOK → p. 12

Vous allez écouter trois fois un document intitulé *Two duelling narratives*.

Avant l'écoute

1. Aidez-vous du titre du document de façon à anticiper son contenu.

Première écoute

2. Identifiez la nature et le thème général du document. ←

Deuxième écoute

3. Relevez les informations principales. ←

Troisième écoute

4. Rapportez le point de vue du locuteur. ←

Rendez compte en français de ce que vous avez compris.

| TIPS |

En quoi les deux récits sur l'Inde s'opposent-ils ?

Repérez à quoi correspondent les nombreux chiffres que vous entendez.

Soyez attentif au ton du locuteur. Notez les adjectifs et adverbes utilisés.

Expression orale

WORKBOOK → p. 13

Lors de votre prise de parole en continu, puis de la conversation avec l'examinateur, vous pourrez aborder les problématiques suivantes en lien avec l'unité 1.

Notion 1 **L'idée de progrès**
The idea of progress

■ **Is today's India a modern country?**

High-tech cities, p. 20 • Is microcredit changing India?, p. 21 •
A country on the march, p. 24 • Changing India, p. 26 • The world's
largest democracy, p. 31 • From Bombay to Mumbai, p. 31 ←

- Citez quelques villes indiennes hi-tech.
- Donnez des chiffres sur la baisse de la pauvreté en Inde.
- Exprimez le **contraste** : *On the one hand... on the other hand... Whereas / While... Yet / However / Still...*

■ **From British colony to the largest democracy in the world**

A country on the march, p. 24 • The jewel in the crown, p. 30 •
Towards independence, p. 31 • From Bombay to Mumbai, p. 31 •
The world's largest democracy, p. 31 • Mahatma Gandhi, p. 151 ←

Mentionnez les dates les plus importantes de l'histoire de l'Inde.

Notion 2 **Lieux et formes du pouvoir**
Seats and forms of power

■ **Are all citizens on an equal footing in modern-day India?**

India's girls go missing, p. 20 • Is microcredit changing India?, p. 21 •
Another girl, p. 22 • From Bombay to Mumbai, p. 31 • Two stories,
p. 32 • The dowry tradition, p. 151 • The Dalits, p. 151 ←

- Comparez les taux de natalité et d'alphabétisation hommes / femmes.
- Citez des exemples de femmes qui ont réussi.
- Donnez des chiffres sur l'élimination des filles pratiquée en Inde.
- Parlez du système des castes.
- Exprimez la **comparaison** : *Compared to / with... Unlike... On the contrary... On the one hand... on the other hand...*

The village population

The scene takes place in southern India.

Daisy [asked] "What is the population of this village now?"

"Seven hundred-odd," said the teacher promptly.

5 Daisy said, "It was just six hundred last year this time… and there is an increase of nearly twenty per cent. Has your food production increased twenty per cent? Have your accommodations increased twenty per cent? I know they haven't. Your production has 10 increased only three per cent in spite of various improved methods of cultivation. Have more houses been built between the last monsoon[1] and now? I know that the number of houses has remained the same for decades…" The teacher looked crest-fallen[2]; which was a sort of admission of her thesis. He felt relieved that she was not questioning him on the size of his family; but presently, 15 when several boys and girls of assorted sizes kept dashing in and out of his house and he found Daisy eyeing them questioningly, he volunteered the explanation: "You see, they are children from the neighbouring houses, they have to come to play with my children. I have only four…"

"I know, I know," she said and added, "You had only three when I was here last!"

What a lot of policing she was doing! Raman thought. She must really be mad! She will 20 fight people who bring up large families. Some madness must have got into her head quite early in life and stayed on there.

She explained to the teacher, "Our quantum of population-increase every year is equal to the total population of a country like Peru, that's fourteen million."

"What if!" said the foolhardy teacher. "We have enough space in this country – still so 25 many undeveloped areas."

She was very patient with this dialectician. She said quietly, "How many of the seven hundred-odd in this village will be prepared to move over to new areas when their homes become too congested?"

Raman felt like asking, How is it your concern? If people like to live crowded, it's their 30 business. What a frightful bully you are turning out to be. Thank God, you are not a dictator.

The teacher explained, "The families here are all stonemasons[3]. They quarry stones and send them all over the country. Their business is to blast the mountain-side and cut and shape the stones. At the moment, they have an order to cut and dress three thousand tons of slabs and blocks for a temple in America. It's quite a thriving business. Why will they move? They 35 have to be where the mountain is. They cannot afford to leave its side."

She said, "Exactly. I am not suggesting that they uproot themselves, but if they want to stay comfortable, let them avoid creating unmanageable crowd around themselves, that's all. I am not prohibiting anything, but only suggesting that they avoid too many children."

She spoke on the same lines to the gathering which the teacher was able to muster[4] under 40 the banyan tree in the centre of the village. This had to be late on the evening next day, as she had to wait for the men and women to return from work, wash, and eat before coming out to listen to her. They had hung up a few lanterns from the branches of the tree.

R.K. NARAYAN, *The Painter of Signs* (1976)

1. *mousson* 2. *penaud* 3. *tailleurs de pierres* 4. *réunir*

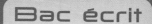
Vous trouverez la présentation de l'épreuve pages 12-13
et des conseils pratiques pour le bac pages 175-179.

Compréhension de l'écrit

Read the whole text before answering the questions.

1. Identify the characters and say what they do in this passage.

2. What is the main topic of their conversation?
   a. In the first part of the text (from the beginning to l. 18).
   b. In the second part (from l. 19 to l. 30).

3. What do we learn about the villagers' life? (40 words)

4. True or false? Justify your answer by quoting from the text.
   a. Daisy thinks that the villagers should move to another area.
   b. She believes that they should have fewer children.

5. What arguments does Daisy use to convince the teacher
in the first part of the text? (50 words)

6. Explain in one sentence what Daisy and the teacher finally agree on.

7. Analyse the teacher's feelings in the first part of the text. (60 words)

8. Why does the teacher say *"We have enough space in this country –
still so many undeveloped areas"* (l. 24-25)?

9. Analyse Raman's attitude during the conversation. (40 words)

10. Use the photo and elements from the text to explain Daisy's
mission in the village.

Expression écrite

1. Write down the discussion between Daisy and Raman
after their meeting with the teacher.

2. Do you think birth control should be imposed when
population density is too high?

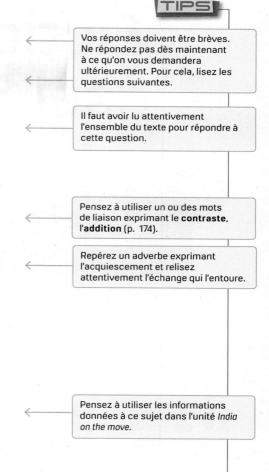

TIPS

Vos réponses doivent être brèves.
Ne répondez pas dès maintenant
à ce qu'on vous demandera
ultérieurement. Pour cela, lisez les
questions suivantes.

Il faut avoir lu attentivement
l'ensemble du texte pour répondre à
cette question.

Pensez à utiliser un ou des mots
de liaison exprimant le **contraste**,
l'**addition** (p. 174).

Repérez un adverbe exprimant
l'acquiescement et relisez
attentivement l'échange qui l'entoure.

Pensez à utiliser les informations
données à ce sujet dans l'unité *India
on the move.*

• Pensez à suivre les conseils pour
l'écriture d'un dialogue, p. 172.
• Utilisez les réponses courtes et les *tags* :
Précis grammatical, 30.

Use your grammar
• Opposer «idées générales» et «situation
particulière» : **fiche 1** (p. 180)
• Exprimer un jugement : **fiche 4** (p. 182)

Unit 2

L'idée de progrès
Espaces et échanges

Fiction & science

Does fiction draw inspiration from science or is it the other way round?

final task
You take part in a competition on the Greatest Scientific Breakthroughs. You enter it by sending an audio recording about a fascinating scientific innovation and / or a written presentation of a techno-scientific invention imagined by a sci-fi writer or film-maker.

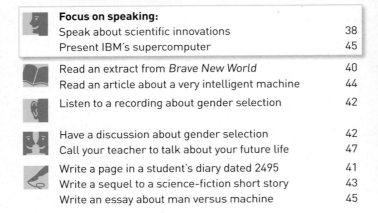

Keywords

Nouns
- **pro**gress (*indén.*) / an advance
- **break**through: *découverte capitale*
- fantasy ≠ reality
- plot: *intrigue*
- utopia /juːˈtəʊpɪə/ ≠ dystopia /dɪsˈtəʊpɪə/
- robotics /rəʊˈbɒtɪks/
- genetics
- electronics
- AI /eɪˈaɪ/ = artificial intelligence
- android
- IVF /ˌaɪviːˈef/ = in-vitro fertilization
- prosthesis /prɒsˈθiːsɪs/
- hybrid /ˈhaɪbrɪd/ (noun + adj.)
- DNA /ˌdiːenˈeɪ/: *ADN*

Adjectives
- state-of-the-art: *dernier cri / de pointe*
- **ground**breaking: *révolutionnaire*
- promising
- enhanced /ɪnˈhɑːnst/: *augmenté*
- risk-free = reliable
- hazardous /ˈhæzədəs/ = risky
- out of control
- ethical /ˈeθɪkəl/
- human-like
- genetically engineered: *manipulé génétiquement*

Verbs & expressions
- unfold: *se dérouler*
- carry out an experiment
- make things easier
- enable sb to
- play with fire
- raise an issue /ˈɪʃuː/

LANGUAGE WORKSHOP → p. 47

Do you want to dance?

1. This is a still from *Short Circuit*, a film directed by John Badham in 1986. Describe the situation.

2. What is funny about the woman's attitude?

3. Do you think you can expect to see such a scene in the near future?

Science or fiction?

ⓂÉTHODOLOGIE **EXPRESSION ORALE EN CONTINU** → p. 16

A I, Robot

ⓂÉTHODOLOGIE
Expliquer → p. 163

Describe and explain.

1. Observe the two robots.
One is a fictional robot featured in Alex Proyas's film, *I, Robot*, released in 2004.
The other is HRP-4C. It was designed and created by a team of scientists in 2009. Describe the two robots and say which is which.

2. The film is based on Isaac Asimov's short story collection of the same name. The robots are designed to obey the Three Laws of Robotics devised by Asimov. Read the *Culture Key* about these laws. In your opinion, why did he imagine the Three Laws?

3. Roboticists say we will soon be taking their creations into our homes and workplaces.

a. In what ways could robots improve our quality of life?

b. Do you see any drawbacks to their increasing role in our daily life? Explain why or why not.

culture key Three Laws of Robotics → p. 152

culture key Robot: HRP-4C → p. 152

B I, Cyborg

ⓂÉTHODOLOGIE
Rendre compte d'un article → p. 163

Give an oral account of the article.

1. Do you know what a cyborg /ˈsaɪbɔːg/ is? In your opinion, what does the picture illustrate?

2. Read the article below and explain what the picture actually illustrates.

3. Give an oral account of what you have read, explaining what Kevin

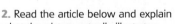

Warwick's research consists in and why he calls himself a cyborg.

4. Can you imagine how Warwick's experiment might be used?

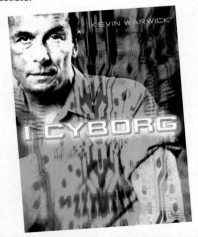

My body, my laboratory

AT THE RADCLIFFE HOSPITAL in Oxford, England, in March 2002, doctors wheeled Kevin Warwick, a professor of cybernetics at the University of Reading, into an operating theater for what has to be one of the world's only cases of elective neurosurgery on a healthy patient. Warwick belongs to a rare breed of scientists who experiment on themselves. He had volunteered to go under the knife so surgeons could hammer[1] a silicon chip with 100 spiked[2] electrodes directly into his nervous system via the median nerve fibers in his forearm. The goal was to fire electrical impulses into his brain to see whether a human could learn to sense, interpret and reply to computer-generated stimuli. The chip in Warwick's arm did what it was intended to do, picking up neural action potentials – the signals sent from the cortex when a person thinks of moving a limb but does not actually do it. That allowed Warwick to use thoughts to control an electric wheelchair and, through an Internet connection, an artificial hand back in his lab in Reading.

Time (February 28th 2011)

1. *enfoncer* 2. *à pointe*

The bionic age

MÉTHODOLOGIE
Rendre compte d'un reportage audio → p. 163

Give an oral account of the recording.

1. Read the following definition of "bionic". Then explain why the man on the magazine cover is a bionic man.

"Having anatomical structures or physiological processes that are replaced or enhanced by electronic or mechanical components."

2. Listen to MIT Professor Hugh Herr.

3. Explain what happened to Hugh Herr when he was a young man and how he became involved in biomechatronics.

toolbox

Nouns
- pioneer /ˌpaɪə'nɪə/
- limb /lɪm/: *membre*
- household chores /tʃɔːz/ (Am.) = housework (Br.)
- task
- capability /ˌkeɪpə'bɪlɪtɪ/
- the elderly: *les personnes âgées*
- the handicapped

Adjectives
- humanoid = human-like
- automated

- daily
- sophisticated
- disabled = crippled

Verbs & expressions
- perform: *exécuter*
- interact
- take care of
- behave: *se comporter*
- entertain
- upgrade = improve

KEVIN SMITH

THE BIONIC MAN

KEVIN SMITH
PHIL HESTER
JONATHAN LAU
IVAN NUNES
SIMON BOWLAND
DYNAMITE

Video time

The intelligence revolution 📺 DVD

Visions of the Future, a BBC documentary (2009)

A Get ready

1. In the extract from the documentary film that you are about to see, leading theoretical physicist Dr Michio Kaku predicts that by 2020 intelligence will be everywhere, practically in every object.

In the photo, you can see Dr Kaku standing in front of a car.
What do you think an intelligent car can do?

B Watch the video

2. Watch the extract from the documentary film. Your teacher will give you a worksheet to help you.

C In your own words

3. Use the worksheet to summarize what you saw.

D Going further

4. Do you look forward to living with such intelligent machines?

"O brave new world!"

culture key Brave New World society → p. 152

Aldous HUXLEY

(1894-1963), the grandson of a famous biologist, was born in Surrey, England. At 16, he became totally blind for 18 months. He recovered his eyesight sufficiently to continue his studies but not to pursue his chosen career as a scientist. He turned to writing and wrote a dozen books before achieving worldwide fame with *Brave New World*.

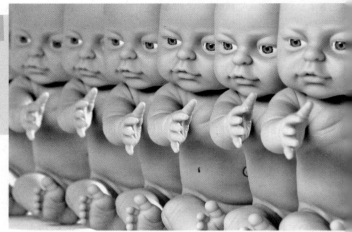

A Warming up

What could explain the fact that the babies in the picture are identical?

"I shall begin at the beginning," said the D.H.C.[1] and the more zealous students recorded his intention in their notebooks: *Begin at the beginning*. "These," he waved his hand, "are the incubators." And opening an insulated[2] door he showed them racks[3] upon racks of numbered test-tubes.

5 "Bokanovsky's Process," repeated the Director, and the students underlined the words in their little notebooks.

One egg, one embryo, one adult-normality. But a bokanovskified egg will bud[4], will proliferate, will divide. From eight to ninety-six buds, and every bud will grow into a perfectly formed embryo, and every embryo into a full-
10 sized adult. Making ninety-six human beings grow where only one grew before. Progress.

"Essentially," the D.H.C. concluded, "bokanovskification consists of a series of arrests of development. We check the normal growth and, paradoxically enough, the egg responds by budding."
15 *Responds by budding*. The pencils were busy.

He pointed. On a very slowly moving band a rack-full of test-tubes was emerging. Machinery faintly purred[5]. It took eight minutes for the tubes to go through, he told them. Eight minutes of hard X-rays being about as much as an egg can stand. A few died; of the rest, the least susceptible divided into two;
20 most put out four buds; some eight. Two, four, eight, the buds in their turn budded; and having budded – bud out of bud out of bud – were thereafter left to develop in peace. By which time the original egg was in a fair way to becoming anything from eight to ninety-six embryos – a prodigious improvement, you will agree, on nature. Identical twins – but not in piddling twos and threes[6] as
25 in the old viviparous days, when an egg would sometimes accidentally divide; actually by dozens, by scores at a time.

"Scores," the Director repeated and flung out his arms[7], as though he were distributing largesse. "Scóres."

But one of the students was fool enough to ask where the advantage lay.

30 "My good boy!" The Director wheeled sharply round on him. "Can't you see? Can't you see?" He raised a hand; his expression was solemn. "Bokanovsky's Process is one of the major instruments of social stability!"

Major instruments of social stability.

Standard men and women; in uniform batches[8]. The whole of a small factory 35 staffed with the products of a single bokanovskified egg.

"Ninety-six identical twins working ninety-six identical machines!" The voice was almost tremulous with enthusiasm. "You really know where you are. For the first time in history." He quoted the planetary motto. "Community, Identity, Stability." Grand words. "If we could bokanovskify indefinitely the 40 whole problem would be solved."

Solved by standard Gammas, unvarying Deltas, uniform Epsilons. Millions of identical twins. The principle of mass production at last applied to biology.

Aldous HUXLEY, *Brave New World* (1932)

1. Director of Hatcheries (*couveuses*) and Conditioning   **2.** *isolante*   **3.** *casiers*
4. *bourgeonner*   **5.** *ronronner*   **6.** *pas en nombre ridiculement petit*   **7.** *fling – flung – flung*: (*ici*) *lever les bras*   **8.** *groupes*

B Understanding the text WORKBOOK → p. 14-15

. Turn to your *Workbook* which will help you to understand the text.

. Explain why the D.H.C. gives the students a tour of the hatchery.

C Going further

. Describe the D.H.C.'s attitude toward the students.

. What about the students' attitudes?

. After reading the *Culture key* on Huxley's *Brave New World* society, explain what the goal of the Bokanovsky's Process is.

6. What kind of society did Aldous Huxley devise? In your view, what was his aim in imagining such a society?

7. What scientific discoveries anticipated in the novel have become possible in today's society?

D Language training

8. Savoir prononcer 11-12   31-32

Les groupes de sens – La prononciation de la lettre -*i*-

9. Pratiquer la grammaire

L'hypothèse LANGUAGE WORKSHOP → p. 46

most / the most – Adjectifs composés WORKBOOK → p. 19

toolbox

Nouns
- clone (noun + verb) /kləʊn/
- therapeutic /ˌθerəˈpjuːtɪk/ / reproductive cloning
- upper classes ≠ lower classes
- ruling class: *classe dirigeante*
- elite /ɪˈliːt/ (noun + adj.)
- proletarian (noun + adj.)
- satire /ˈsætaɪə/

Adjectives
- custom-made: *fait sur mesure*
- haughty /ˈhɔːtɪ/: *hautain*
- disciplined

- submissive
- obedient
- predestined /priːˈdestɪnd/
- standardized /ˈstændədaɪzd/
- totalitarian

Verbs & expressions
- manipulate
- talk sb down: *réduire au silence*
- enforce: *mettre en application*
- be conditioned into V-ING
- dare: *oser*
- warn (against)

Your task

Write a page in a student's diary dated 2495

The student who asked about the advantage of the Bokanovsky's Process writes a diary. Imagine and write down the entry he wrote on that day.

MÉTHODOLOGIE
Écrire une page de journal intime → p. 171

From *Gattaca* to Los Angeles

A The topic

1. Read this extract from the script of Andrew Niccol's film *Gattaca* (1997). Then look at the *Newsweek* cover and say what Andrew Niccol had anticipated.

> **GENETICIST:** Your extracted eggs... Maria, have been fertilized with... Antonio's sperm and we have performed an analysis of the resulting pre-embryos[1]. After screening[2] we're left with two healthy boys and two healthy girls. Naturally, no critical pre-dispositions to any of the major inheritable diseases. All that remains is to select the most compatible candidate.
>
> First, we may as well decide on gender. Have you given it any thought?
>
> **MARIA** (*referring to the toddler on her knee*): We would like Vincent to have a brother... you know, to play with.
> *The Geneticist nods.*
>
> 1. /'embrɪəʊ/ 2. checking

BEYOND IOWA: THE RUTHLESS GAME OF 'OPPO'

Newsweek

Girl or Boy?
Now You Can Choose.
But Should You?
The New Science of Sex Selection.

B Open your ears 33

2: Before listening to the report, you will hear three sentences. Which one could be said by the journalist, a doctor, a customer of the clinic?

C Listen 34-35 ⓦORKBOOK → p. 16

3. Listen to a CBS News report. You will find some help in your *Workbook*.

D In your own words

4. Explain what the Los Angeles Fertility Institutes propose.

5. Is the procedure different from the one explained by the geneticist in *Gattaca*?

6. Do all doctors agree with this type of gene manipulation?

function box

Giving one's opinion
- To my mind / In my opinion...
- As for me...
- I'm convinced that...
- I can't help thinking that...
- It seems to me that...

Expressing disagreement
- How can you say that...?
- This is nonsense / ridiculous / silly!
- Don't be silly!
- I don't see things that way.
- That's not how I see it.

toolbox

Nouns
- gender / sex selection
- designer baby: *bébé sur mesure*
- feature /ˈfiːtʃə/: *caractéristique*
- dysfunction
- disease /dɪˈziːz/: *maladie*
- ethical issue /ˈɪʃuː/
- chance: *hasard*

Adjectives
- wealthy = well-off

Verbs
- manipulate
- eliminate
- avoid: *éviter*
- prohibit = ban

 Your task

 Have a discussion about gender selection

You disagree on the question of whether or not people should choose their baby's sex.

Ⓜ ÉTHODOLOGIE
Discussion contradictoire → p. 166

Writers' corner

The materializer

Your task

Write a sequel to a science-fiction short story

Unfortunately, the second part of this short story has been lost… You decide to write the sequel. (150-200 words)

Ⓜ ÉTHODOLOGIE
Continuer un récit → p. 171

A Get ready

1. Read the beginning of this short story. Make sure that you understand it perfectly:

a. Deduce what a "materializer" is.

b. Why did Ned Quinn have "a lot to learn"?

2. Think of what Ned Quinn could wish for next.

3. Imagine the possible consequences of the new materialization(s).

B Write the sequel to this story

4. Study the text carefully so as to imitate its characteristics. Ask yourself:

– what tenses are used;

– whether the sentences are long or short;

– whether there are any repetitions;

– whether the narrative includes direct speech, free indirect speech.

5. Give an unexpected twist to the story in accordance with the title of the novel.

THE MATERIALIZER WAS COMPLETED. Ned Quinn stood back, wiped his hands, and admired the huge bank of dials, lights and switches. Several years and many fortunes had gone into his project. Finally it was ready.

Ned placed the metal skullcap on his head and plugged the wires into the control panel. He turned the switch to ON and spoke: "Pound note".

There was a whirring sound[1]. In the Receiver a piece of paper appeared. Ned inspected it. Real.

"Martini," he said.

A whirring sound. A puddle[2] formed in the Receiver. Ned cursed silently. He had a lot to learn.

"A bottle of beer," he said.

The whirring sound was followed by the appearance of the familiar brown bottle. Ned tasted the contents and grinned.

Chuckling[3], he experimented further.

Ned enlarged the Receiver and prepared for his greatest experiment. He switched on the Materializer, took a deep breath and said…

R.T. KUROSAKA, *A Lot to Learn* (1978)

1. *ronronnement* 2. *flaque* 3. *glousser*

Man vs machine

culture key   IBM's supercomputer → p. 152

THE HUFFINGTON POST

or *Huff Post* is an American news website – with several international editions – founded by Arianna Huffington in 2005. Its slogan is "The Internet Newspaper: News, Blogs, Video, Community". Its community is active indeed with one million comments posted each month.
Website: huffingtonpost.co.uk/

A Warming up

Describe the situation in the photo.
What do you think Watson is?

Machines first out-calculated us in simple math. Then they replaced us on the assembly lines, explored places we couldn't get to,
5 even beat our champions at chess. Now a computer called Watson has bested our best at "Jeopardy[1]!"

A gigantic computer created by IBM specifically to excel at answers-and-
10 questions left two champs of the TV game show in its silicon dust after a three-day tournament, a feat that experts call a technological breakthrough.

Watson's victory leads to the question:
15 What can we measly[2] humans do that amazing machines cannot do or will never do?

The answer, like all of "Jeopardy!", comes in the form of a question: Who –
20 not what – dreamed up Watson? While computers can calculate and construct, they cannot decide to create. So far, only humans can.

"The way to think about this is: Can
25 Watson decide to create Watson?" said Pradeep Khosla, dean of engineering at Carnegie Mellon University in Pittsburgh. "We are far from there. Our ability to create is what allows us to
30 discover and create new knowledge and technology."

Experts in the field say it is more than the spark of creation that separates man from his mechanical spawn[3]. It is the
35 pride creators can take, the empathy we can all have with the winners and losers, and that magical mix of adrenaline, fear and ability that kicks in when our backs are against the wall and we are in
40 survival mode.

What humans have that Watson, IBM's earlier chess champion Deep Blue, and all their electronic predecessors and software successors do not have and will
45 not get is the sort of thing that makes song, romance, smiles, sadness and all that jazz[4]. It's something the experts in computers, robotics and artificial intelligence know very well because
50 they can't figure out how it works in people, much less duplicate it. It's that indescribable essence of humanity.

Nevertheless, Watson, which took 25 IBM scientists four years to create,

55 is more than just a trivia[5] whiz[6], some experts say.

Richard Doherty, a computer industry expert and research director at the Envisioneering Group in Seaford, N.Y., 60 said he has been studying artificial intelligence for decades. He thinks IBM's advances with Watson are changing the way people think about artificial intelligence.

65 "This is the most significant breakthrough of this century," he said. "I know the phones are ringing off the hook[7] with interest in Watson systems. 70 For this century, it's the most significant advance in computing."

And yet Watson's creators say this breakthrough gives them an extra appreciation for the magnificent machines we call people.

75 "I see human intelligence consuming machine intelligence, not the other way around," said David Ferrucci, IBM's lead researcher on Watson.

The Huffington Post (February 17th 2011)

1. /ˈdʒepədɪ/ péril 2. misérables 3. progéniture 4. (ici) et tout ce qui s'ensuit
5. jeu portant sur des questions de culture générale 6. champion
7. (expr.) ne pas arrêter de sonner

B Understanding the text ⓦORKBOOK → p. 17-18

1. Read the text with the help of your *Workbook*.

2. Explain what type of machine Watson is and the reactions to this new technological advance.

C Going further

3. Read the *Culture key* and imagine the TV viewers' reactions when watching the game show.

4. Explain why the experts consider Watson *"the most significant breakthrough of this century"* (l. 65).

5. What is the fear lying behind this advance?

6. What is man's superiority over machines according to the experts mentioned in the article?

D Writing time

ⓂÉTHODOLOGIE
Rédiger un essai → p. 172

7. **Essay** (200-250 words)

Science-fiction movies have long predicted that an epic battle would take place between man and machine. Do you think that some day, in the near (or distant) future, men will have to wage war on machines?

a. Trouvez des exemples dans les œuvres de science-fiction où l'homme est aux prises avec la machine.

b. Appuyez-vous sur l'article étudié pour parler des avancées spectaculaires dans le domaine de l'intelligence artificielle.

c. N'hésitez pas à entrer, à votre tour, dans l'univers de la science-fiction pour répondre à la question posée.

d. Utilisez les mots de liaison permettant d'exprimer but, cause et conséquence (p. 174).

E Language training

8. **Savoir prononcer** 13-14   36-37   ⓦORKBOOK → p. 18

La prononciation de la lettre *-a-*

9. **Pratiquer la grammaire**

Le possible   ⬤LANGUAGE WORKSHOP → p. 46
Present perfect *BE+ING* et présent *BE+ING* ⓦORKBOOK → p. 19

toolbox

Nouns
- quiz show / game
- competitor
- riddle: *énigme*
- skill = *ability*

Adjectives
- tricky = *difficult*
- enigmatic
- subtle /ˈsʌtl/
- learned /ˈlɜːnɪd/: *érudit*
- tough /tʌf/: *coriace*

- astounded: *abasourdi*
- sophisticated

Verbs & expressions
- rival /ˈraɪvəl/
- outdo: *l'emporter sur*
- surpass /sɜːˈpɑːs/
- outwit: *se montrer plus malin que*
- pit one's wits against: *se mesurer avec*
- baffle: *déconcerter*
- hail = *salute*

Give an oral presentation of IBM's supercomputer

You are impressed by Watson's capacities and decide to present IBM's supercomputer on the school web radio.

ⓂÉTHODOLOGIE
Rendre compte d'un article → p. 163

Grammaire | L'hypothèse – Le possible

A L'hypothèse ⓅRÉCIS GRAMMATICAL → 39

1 **Les subordonnées en *if***

1. *"If we could bokanovskify indefinitely the whole problem **would** be solved."* (Text 1, p. 41, l. 39)
2. *"If we let them grow, they **will** develop into full-sized adults."*
3. *"If we had let them go on with it, we **would have** made a terrible mistake."*
4. *"If we used this new technique, we **would** produce dozens of identical beings."*

a. Relevez pour chaque énoncé le temps de la subordonnée en ***if*** et la forme correspondante dans la principale (*will, would* ou *would have*). Indiquez dans chaque cas si la subordonnée en *if* exprime : **1.** une hypothèse que l'on envisage pour l'avenir ; **2.** une hypothèse envisageable mais incertaine ou **3.** une hypothèse qui ne s'est pas réalisée.

b. Laquelle de ces deux formes ***would*** ou ***would have*** implique que l'action ne s'est pas produite ?

c. Traduisez les énoncés **1**, **2**, **3** et **4**.

2 **Traduisez les énoncés.**

a. Que se produirait-il s'ils arrivaient (*manage*) à créer des centaines d'êtres humains identiques ?
b. Que feront-ils s'ils échouent ?
c. Auriez-vous travaillé avec eux si vous en aviez eu la possibilité ?
d. S'ils nous en parlaient, nous leur dirions combien c'est dangereux.

B Le possible ⓅRÉCIS GRAMMATICAL → 14, 15

3 ***Could* / *could have* et l'expression de la capacité**

1. *"Then they (…) explored places we **couldn't** get to."* (Text 2, p. 44, l. 2)
2. *You know that they **could** beat us if they wanted to.*
3. *We **could** have stopped him but we thought it was better not to.*

a. Indiquez pour chacun des modaux en gras s'il renvoie à une capacité ou une incapacité passée ou irréelle (imaginée).

b. Laquelle de ces deux formes ***could*** ou ***could have*** implique que l'action était possible mais ne s'est **pas** produite ?

c. Traduisez les énoncés à l'aide de «pouvoir» et nommez les temps que vous utilisez en français.

4 ***May* / *may have* et l'expression de la probabilité**

1. *This new machine **may turn out** to be one of the most significant advances in computing.*
2. *Some of these scientists **may be trying** to create a new machine. Who knows?*
3. *They **may have decided** to stop their research, which would be a disaster.*

a. Indiquez pour chacune des formes en gras si elle désigne la probabilité d'un fait présent, passé ou à venir.

b. Traduisez les énoncés **1**, **2** et **3** à l'aide de «Il est possible que… ».

5 **Traduisez à l'aide de l'une des deux formes proposées.**

● ***could* ou *could have*** :
a. Je pourrais leur envoyer un mail, mais c'est un peu risqué.
b. Ils auraient pu nous aider, non ?
c. Je leur ai écrit, mais ils n'ont pas pu me répondre.

● ***may* ou *may have*** :
d. Il est possible qu'ils soient en train d'essayer de nous appeler.
e. Il est possible qu'ils aient déjà résolu le problème.
f. Il est possible que nous trouvions une solution dans les jours à venir (*in the next few days*).

| **Interpréter les formes en *BEING* à l'oral**

6 **Connaître les formes verbales en *being* et *been*** 38

a. Lisez ces quatre énoncés. Identifiez les formes verbales (présent BE+ING, *present perfect* simple ou *present perfect* BE+ING) en indiquant s'il s'agit de la voix active ou passive.

   1. *"It **is being used** for something very different."* (Listeners' corner, p. 42)

   2. *For years, it **has been used** for something different.*

   3. *He **has been using** this technology for years.*

   4. *He **is using** new technology.*

b. Écoutez ces mêmes énoncés et indiquez quelles sont les syllabes accentuées. Pourquoi certaines des formes verbales utilisées semblent-elles assez difficiles à distinguer à l'oral ?

7 **Interpréter le sens des formes verbales à l'oral** 39-40

a. Écoutez les passages suivants et, en vous appuyant sur le contexte, indiquez si la forme verbale entendue est la forme **1** ou la forme **2**.

a.1. *we've seen*	**a.2.** *we're seeing*	**c.1.** *being treated*	**c.2.** *been treating*
b.1. *we've seen*	**b.2.** *we're seeing*	**d.1.** *been treated*	**d.2.** *being treated*

b. Écrivez les énoncés que vous entendez en donnant la forme pleine des auxiliaires.

| **Science et fiction**

Assurez-vous que vous avez bien retenu les mots clés de l'unité. → **Keywords p. 36**

8 **À quoi correspondent les acronymes suivants ?** **a.** IVF = … **b.** DNA = … **c.** AI = …

9 **Sur quelle syllabe se trouve l'accent des mots terminés en *-ics* ?**
première syllabe – dernière syllabe – avant-dernière syllabe

10 **Donnez les synonymes ou les antonymes des mots suivants.**
a. *reality* ≠ … **b.** *utopia* ≠ … **c.** *risky* = … **d.** *reliable* = …

11 **Traduisez :** **a.** un progrès **b.** dernier cri

12 **Complétez les phrases à l'aide des mots suivants en faisant les changements nécessaires.**
enable – enhanced – plot – ethical – unfold – prosthesis – groundbreaking – carry out – issue – human-like – easier – out of control

a. *The …¹… of this science-fiction film …²… in 2076.*

b. *Scientists have …³… a …⁴… experiment which will …⁵… man to travel through time.*

c. *Robots make things …⁶… but some fear they might get …⁷… .*

d. *The fact that they are increasingly …⁸… may raise …⁹… …¹⁰… .*

e. *His capacities have been …¹¹… thanks to his new …¹²… .*

---

toolbox

Nouns
- application: *candidature*
- test scores: *résultats d'examen*
- admissions standards: *niveau de recrutement*

Adjectives
- upset: *bouleversé*
- devastated: *anéanti*

Verbs
- graduate (from a university): *obtenir un diplôme*
- appeal (against a decision): *faire appel*

Your task

Call your teacher to talk about your future life
You applied for admission to a famous university but you were rejected. You phone one of your teachers and you tell him / her how you feel about it. You both try to figure out what your options are now. Imagine the conversation. Use *if*-clauses, **would / would have, could / could have.**

From fantasy to reality

When science fiction becomes science facts...

A Fiction

Read the following timeline. Choose one of these science-fiction novels or films. Browse the web to know more about it and present it to the class. Say whether it predicted a techno-science discovery.

1818 *Frankenstein* by Mary Shelley → **man creates artificial life**

1895 *The Time Machine* by Herbert George Wells → **one of the first time travel stories**

1927 *Metropolis*, a movie directed by Fritz Lang → **androids**

1932 *Brave New World* by Aldous Huxley → **cloning** (Text 1, p. 40)

1942 *Runaround* and *The Robots* by Isaac Asimov (Focus, p. 38) → **the Three Laws of Robotics**

Metropolis, Fritz Lang, 1927

1946 *A Logic Named Joe* written by Murray Leinster → **first appearance of a personal computer**

1949 *Nineteen Eighty-Four* written by George Orwell → **surveillance networks**

1950 *Destination Moon* by Irving Pichel → **a lunar mission**

1950 *The Martian Chronicles* by Ray Bradbury → **earthlings invade Mars**

1951 *The Foundation* series written by Isaac Asimov → **a futuristic galactic empire**

1958 *The Fly*, a movie directed by Kurt Neumann and remade by David Cronenberg in 1986 → **creation of a mutant by DNA fusion**

1966 *Star Trek*, the first episode of the great American TV series → **a space opera**

1968 *2001, A Space Odyssey* directed by Stanley Kubrick → **artificial intelligence**

1968 *Planet of the Apes*, a film by Franklin J. Schaffner based on Pierre Boulle's novel published in 1963 → **interstellar travel**

1977-2005 The six episodes of the *Star Wars* film series → **a space opera saga**

1982 *Tron* directed by Steven Lisberger → **dematerialization of a human being into a computer mainframe**

1984 *Terminator* directed by James Cameron → **archetypal cyborg-machine**

1985 *Back to the Future* directed by Robert Zemeckis → **time travel, hoverboard**

1987 *RoboCop* directed by Paul Verhoeven → **archetypal human cyborg**

1990 *Total Recall* directed by Paul Verhoeven, adapted from Philip K. Dick's *We Can Remember It for You Wholesale* (1966) → **Mars colonization and memory implant**

1997 *Gattaca*, a film directed by Andrew Niccol (Listeners, p. 42) → **genetic manipulation**

2000 *Mission to Mars* directed by Brian De Palma → **space mission to Mars**

2001 *A.I. Artificial Intelligence* directed by Steven Spielberg (Final task, p. 50) → **humanoid robots**

2002 *Minority Report* directed by Steven Spielberg, adapted from the 1956 novel by Philip K. Dick → **Mutant human beings**

2004 *I, Robot* a film by Alex Proyas based on Isaac Asimov's short story collection (Focus, p. 38) → **humanoid robots**

2009 *Avatar* directed by James Cameron → **avatars and genetically created hybrids**

2010 *Tron: Legacy* directed by Joseph Kosinski, a sequel to the 1982 film → **virtual reality**

2001: a space odyssey

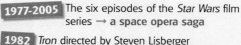
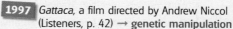
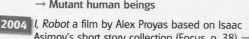

Techno-sciences

Read the timeline of the most significant techno-science breakthroughs since the beginning of the 20th century. Which of these advances were anticipated by a sci-fi writer or film director?

1905 Albert Einstein revolutionizes the concept of space-time with the special **theory of relativity** and, in 1916, the **theory of general relativity**.

1953 Discovery of the double helix **structure of DNA**.

1957 Launch of the **first satellite**, *Sputnik 1*.

1968 Olean, New York State: first city to install **video cameras** in an effort to **fight crime**.

1969 Neil Armstrong takes the **first step on the Moon**.

1971 First human artifact touches down on Mars, released by the **Mars 3** probe.

1972 **First genetic engineering**: American scientists introduce a foreign DNA fragment into a bacterium.

1979 First generation (1G) analogue **cell phone network**.

1981 **First portable microcomputer.** Computing becomes personal.

1989 Project begins to determine the sequence of the **human genome**.

1990 **Launch of the Web** for public navigation becomes possible on the Internet.

1993 First version of Honda **humanoid robot**, named P1.

1995 **GPS** satellite geolocation system invented by the U.S. Army becomes operational.

1997 **First robot** to travel over the **Martian surface**: Pathfinder mission's Sojourner rover.

1997 **First successful cloning** of a mammal, Dolly the sheep, by Scottish scientists.

1998 **Project Cyborg.** First stage: RFID (Radio Frequency IDentification) chip implanted in a man's arm. Second stage in 2002 (Focus, p. 38).

2000 Launch of the **International Space Station** (ISS).

2005 **First "bionic" arm transplant** (first person to control a prosthesis by thought) (Focus, p. 39).

2009 HRP-4C, a human-like robot (Focus, p. 38).

2009 The LA Fertility Institutes offers **gender selection** (Listeners, p. 42).

2009-2010 The **Voyager 1** probe, launched in 1977, is now beyond our solar system.

2010 **Robonaut 2** (alias R2), a humanoid robot that will assist astronauts in outer space.

2011 Watson, IBM's supercomputer: machine intelligence beats human intelligence (Text 2, p. 44).

2011 Magsurf: first super-conduction skateboard built by French researchers.

2011: Curiosity, the Mars Science Laboratory, launched on Nov. 25

Webquest **Men in space** TICE

1 Browse the web to find about the ISS, International Space Station.

2 Make an oral presentation to the class. You can use the following guidelines:

a. What is the mission of the ISS?

b. What countries share the project?

c. When was it launched and where is it now?

d. How long does an expedition last? How many expeditions and crew members have been launched to the station?

e. What about life on board?

 **Web resources** ○○○

• nasa.gov/mission_pages/station/main
• guardian.co.uk/science
• esa.int/esaHS/iss.html

final task

Does fiction draw inspiration from science or is it the other way round?

You take part in a competition on the Greatest Scientific Breakthroughs. You enter it by sending an audio recording about a fascinating scientific innovation and/or a written presentation of a techno-scientific invention imagined by a sci-fi writer or film-maker.

 1 ## Present a fascinating breakthrough

Ⓜ ÉTHODOLOGIE **EXPRESSION ORALE EN CONTINU** → p. 163

■ You can choose, among the breakthroughs presented in the unit, the one you consider the most fascinating. You can also present another invention which you find particularly striking.

■ Browse the web so as to be able to give details about the invention.

■ You must explain what the invention consists in. Don't forget to mention when it was invented, who invented it and what the applications are.

■ Your presentation should last 2 to 3 minutes. Make complete sentences and link them. When you think you're ready, record yourself.

★ ★ ★ ★
Je me situe
par rapport
au CECRL
B2

LORSQUE JE PARLE DE CETTE INVENTION :
Je peux faire une description détaillée et développer un exposé de manière claire et méthodique en soulignant les éléments significatifs.

 2 ## Write about an imaginary invention

Ⓜ ÉTHODOLOGIE **EXPRESSION ÉCRITE** → p. 170

Many sci-fi novels and films present imaginary inventions which have not yet been created (see Spotlight, p. 48).
For instance, Steven Spielberg's *A.I. Artificial Intelligence* (2001) features advanced humanoids capable of copying human thoughts and emotions.

■ Among these imaginary inventions, choose one which, in your opinion, could become reality in the near future.

■ Your text should include the following elements:
– a description of the device / invention / process;
– the reasons why you think it is likely to be invented;
– the impact this invention could have on people's daily life;
– your feeling(s) towards this future achievement: enthusiasm, indifference, fear…

A.I. Artificial Intelligence,
Steven Spielberg, 2001

★ ★ ★ ★
Je me situe
par rapport
au CECRL
B2

LORSQUE J'ÉCRIS CE TEXTE :
Je fais une description élaborée et je développe une argumentation dans un texte articulé.

Vous trouverez la présentation de l'épreuve pages 12-13 et des conseils pratiques pour le bac pages 175-179.

Compréhension de l'oral
  WORKBOOK → p. 20

Vous allez écouter trois fois un document intitulé
Creating intelligent machines.

Avant l'écoute

1. Aidez-vous du titre du document de façon à anticiper son contenu.

Première écoute

2. Identifiez le thème général du document. ←

> **TIPS**

> Quelles sont les insuffisances des robots d'aujourd'hui ?

Deuxième écoute

3. Relevez les informations principales. ←

> Vers quoi la recherche s'oriente-t-elle ?

Troisième écoute

4. Relevez des détails significatifs. ←

> Soyez attentif au deuxième domaine de la recherche qui permet cette avancée. Il est mentionné deux fois.

Rendez compte en français de ce que vous avez compris.

Expression orale
WORKBOOK → p. 21

Lors de votre prise de parole en continu, puis de la conversation avec l'examinateur, vous pourrez aborder les problématiques suivantes en lien avec l'unité 2.

Notion 1 L'idée de progrès
The idea of progress

■ **Man-machine and machine-man**

I, Robot, p. 38 • *I, Cyborg*, p. 38 • The bionic age, p. 39 • "O brave new world!", p. 40 • Man vs machine, p. 44 ←

> Parlez des deux grands axes de recherche liés à l'homme et la machine : l'homme aux capacités augmentées et la machine dont l'intelligence se rapproche de celle de l'homme.

■ **Should we fear progress?**

I, Robot, p. 38 • *I, Cyborg*, p. 38 • The bionic age, p. 39 • "O brave new world!", p. 40 • From *Gattaca* to Los Angeles, p. 42 • Man vs machine, p. 44 • Isaac Asimov's Three Laws of Robotics, p. 152 • Robot: HRP-4C, p. 152 • IBM's supercomputer, p. 152

> Vous pourrez vous appuyer sur ces documents pour évoquer la crainte que l'homme ne maîtrise plus les machines qu'il crée.
> • Exprimez le **contraste** : *On the one hand... on the other hand... Whereas / While... Yet / However / Still...*

Notion 2 Espaces et échanges
Places and exchanges

■ **New fields of scientific discovery**

I, Robot, p. 38 • *I, Cyborg*, p. 38 • The bionic age, p. 39 • The intelligence revolution, p. 39 • From *Gattaca* to Los Angeles, p. 42 • Man vs machine, p. 44 • From fantasy to reality, p. 48 • Men in space, p. 49 • Robot: HRP-4C, p. 152

> • Insistez sur le caractère international des recherches scientifiques.
> • Choisissez un domaine scientifique qui vous a particulièrement intéressé au cours de l'étude des documents de l'unité 2. Présentez-le et justifiez votre choix.
> • Reliez vos idées avec des mots de liaison : **cause** (*as... since...*), **conséquence** (*consequently... as a result...*).

TEXT 1 – Designer baby

The narrator, Campbell, is a lawyer. He has been asked for legal advice by thirteen-year-old Anna.

"They had me so that I could save Kate," the girl explains. "They went to special doctors and everything, and picked the embryo that would be a perfect genetic match."

There had been ethics courses in law school, but I usually skipped them. Still, anyone who tuned
5 in periodically to CNN would know about the controversies of stem cell[1] research. Spare parts[2] babies, designer infants, the science of tomorrow to save the children of today.

I tap my pen on the desk, and Judge – my dog – sidles closer. "What happens if you don't give your sister a kidney[3]?"

"She'll die."
10 "And you're okay with that?"
Anna's mouth sets in a thin line. "I'm here, aren't I?"

"Yes, you are. I'm just trying to figure out what made you want to put your foot down, after all this time."

She looks over at the bookshelf. "Because," she says simply, "it never stops."
15 Suddenly, something seems to jog her memory. She reaches into her pocket and puts a wad of crumpled bills and change onto my desk. "You don't have to worry about getting paid, either. That's $136.87. I know it's not enough, but I'll figure out a way to get more."

It's not that I'm a particularly charitable man, but rather that legally, this case is a lock: she doesn't want to give a kidney; no court in its right mind would force her to give up a kidney; I
20 don't have to do any legal research, the parents will cave in before we go to trial, and that will be that. Plus, the case will generate a ton of publicity for me, and will jack up my pro bono for the whole damn decade. "I'm going to file a petition for you in family court: legal emancipation for medical purposes," I say.

"Then what?"
25 "There will be a hearing, and the judge will appoint a guardian *ad litem*[4], which is –" "– a person trained to work with kids in the family court, who determines what's in the child's best interests," Anna recites. "Or in other words, just another grown-up deciding what happens to me."

Jodi PICOULT, *My Sister's Keeper* (2004)

TEXT 2 – Saviour sibling[5]

Charlie Whitaker, who suffered a debilitating and extremely rare genetic condition, has been given the all clear by doctors and can now live a normal, healthy life, his parents, Jayson and Michelle, disclosed yesterday.

Now aged 12, he was saved by stem cells transplanted from the umbilical cord of his brother
5 Jamie, who was born by IVF specifically to provide a tissue match.

In a case which prompted fierce debate, the Whitakers had to go to the United States for the procedure which was banned at the time in Britain.

Last night Mrs Whitaker, 38, said: "People would use the term 'designer' or 'harvest baby' to talk about Jamie, to make it sound like he was born for spare parts, but that is completely wrong.
10 I really like the term saviour sibling because that is what he is. Charlie is now completely healthy, I know his little brother saved him and he knows that too, which is wonderful."

The Telegraph (May 7th 2011)

1. *cellule souche*   2. *pièces détachées*   3. *rein*   4. *tuteur pour la procédure juridique*   5. *frère ou sœur*

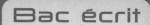

Vous trouverez la présentation de l'épreuve pages 12-13
et des conseils pratiques pour le bac pages 175-179.

Compréhension de l'écrit

Read the two texts before answering the questions.

TEXT 1

1. Explain in one sentence why and how Anna was conceived.

2. What can you deduce about Kate's health?

3. Explain what a spare parts baby (or designer baby) is.

4. Is Campbell an expert on stem cell research? (30 words)

5. What made Anna eventually ask for legal advice? Quote the text.

6. Among the following adjectives, choose those that best describe Campbell's character. Use the adjectives chosen to explain what sort of man he is.

charitable – cynical – opportunist – money-minded – impatient – unpleasant

7. Analyse Anna's character. (50 words)

TEXT 2

8. Explain why Jamie was conceived.

9. Explain why the Whitakers had to go to the USA. Quote the text.

10. Why does Mrs Whitaker prefer to call her son a *"saviour sibling"*?

TEXT 1 AND TEXT 2

11. Point out the similarities and differences between Anna's and Jamie Whitaker's stories.

Expression écrite

1. On her way home from her appointment with the lawyer, Anna meets a friend and tells her what happened.

2. The Whitakers' case *"prompted fierce debate"* (Text 2, l. 6). Give your own view on the topic.

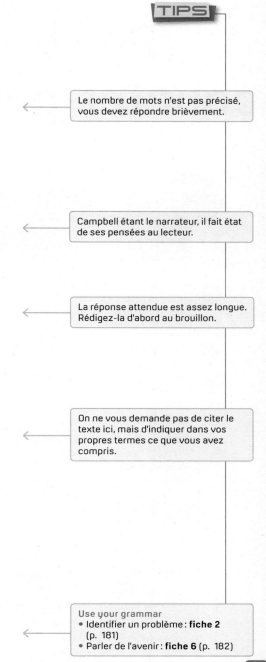

TIPS

Le nombre de mots n'est pas précisé, vous devez répondre brièvement.

Campbell étant le narrateur, il fait état de ses pensées au lecteur.

La réponse attendue est assez longue. Rédigez-la d'abord au brouillon.

On ne vous demande pas de citer le texte ici, mais d'indiquer dans vos propres termes ce que vous avez compris.

Use your grammar
• Identifier un problème : **fiche 2** (p. 181)
• Parler de l'avenir : **fiche 6** (p. 182)

Unit 3

Lieux et formes du pouvoir

Espaces et échanges

Powers and counter-powers

Are counter-powers growing in influence?

final task You have been invited to a TV debate on the rise of counter-powers in today's society. After listening to reports and reading about powers and counter-powers, you take part in the debate.

Keywords

Nouns
- influence (noun + verb)
- supremacy (over sb)
- greed: *avidité*
- empowerment: *responsabilisation*
- the indignant /ɪnˈdɪgnənt/ movement
- demonstrator = protester
- the Fourth Power = the power of the press
- watchdog: *comité de surveillance*
- activist: *militant*

Adjectives
- powerful = mighty
- influential /ɪnfluˈenfəl/
- corporate /ˈkɔːpərɪt/: *de l'entreprise*
- financial /faɪˈnænfəl/
- well-off = wealthy /ˈwelθɪ/

- worldwide = global
- determined = strong-willed
- debt-ridden /detˈrɪdn/: *criblé de dettes*

Verbs & expressions
- empower: *responsabiliser, donner du pouvoir*
- rule: *gouverner, dominer*
- dominate
- question: *remettre en cause*
- rise up = protest (against)
- resist (sth / sb) = stand up to

- stand up / fight for one's rights
- challenge (sb) = confront (sb)
- assert one's rights: *faire valoir ses droits*
- make oneself heard: *faire entendre sa voix*
- raise awareness: *faire prendre conscience, sensibiliser*
- take to the streets = demonstrate /ˈdemənstreɪt/
- repress = crack down on

LANGUAGE WORKSHOP → p. 65

Watchdogs of the sea

1. The photo shows Greenpeace activists trying to stop oil exploration off the Alaskan coast. Describe the scene.

2. In what fields do Greenpeace and other environmental organizations intervene?

3. Do you believe such actions are efficient?

The Fifth Power

Ⓜ ÉTHODOLOGIE **COMPRÉHENSION DE L'ORAL** → p. 161

Ⓦ ORKBOOK → p. 22-23

After studying the various documents on these pages, say what the Fifth Power is.

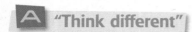 **"Think different"** 42-44

Ⓜ ÉTHODOLOGIE
Anticiper → p. 161

Anticipate the content of a recording.

1. Look at the cartoon. Why is Steve Jobs said to have been a visionary?

2. You are going to listen to a recording entitled "Think different". What does the title evoke for you? Deduce the topic of the recording.

3. Listen to three sentences. Which ones do you expect to hear in the recording?

4. Listen to the recording. Your *Workbook* will help you to understand it.

5. Summarize this report.

APPLE'S VISIONARY
Steve Jobs
1955~2011

 **The power of Google** 45-47

Ⓜ ÉTHODOLOGIE **Utiliser tous les indices** → p. 161

culture key Google → p. 153

Pay attention to the different voices and points of view.

1. Before listening to a recording entitled "The power of Google", look at the photo, read the *Culture key* about Google and the text below.

a. Describe the picture. What is this car used for? What does it show about Google?

b. Say what Google was accused of in the text.

2. You are going to listen to three sentences. Which two sentences mention other reasons why Google is criticized?

3. Listen to the recording. Your *Workbook* will help you to understand it. How many voices can you hear? What points of view are expressed?

4. Sum up the main ideas in your own words.

Google received its first fine[1] for improperly gathering and storing data for its Street View application on Monday when it was penalized by France's privacy watchdog. The €100,000 ($141,300) penalty – the largest ever by French body CNIL – sanctions Google for collecting personal data from Wi-Fi networks – including e-mails, web browsing histories and online banking details – from 2007 to 2010 through its roaming camera-mounted cars and bicycles.

The fine is the first against Google over the data-gathering, which more than 30 countries have complained about.

Associated Press (March 22nd 2011)

1. *amende*

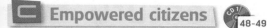 **Empowered citizens** 48-49

Ⓜ **ÉTHODOLOGIE**
Repérer l'idée principale → p. 161

Memorize the main idea while listening.

1. Look at the picture. What is the woman on the left doing?

2. Use the picture and the title of the recording ("Empowered citizens") to guess its topic.

3. One of the three sentences you are going to hear is taken from the recording. Can you guess which one?

4. Listen to the recording and try to memorize the main idea. Your *Workbook* will help you to understand it.

5. Give an oral account of what you have heard.

toolbox

Nouns
- **CEO** /ˌsiːiːˈəʊ/ = Chief Executive Officer: *P.-D.G.*
- **entrepreneur** /ˌɒntrəprəˈnɜː/
- **chairman** /ˈtʃeəmən/: *président*
- **visionary** /ˈvɪʒənərɪ/
- **billionaire** /ˌbɪljəˈnɛə/: *milliardaire*
- **pioneer** /paɪəˈnɪə/

- **monopoly** /məˈnɒpəlɪ/
- **amateur** /ˈæmətə/ **reporter / journalist**

Adjectives
- **iconic** /aɪˈkɒnɪk/
- **creative** /kriːˈeɪtɪv/
- **staggering**: *stupéfiant*
- **ubiquitous** /juːˈbɪkwɪtəs/: *omniprésent*

Verbs & expressions
- **found**: *fonder*
- **envision** /ɪnˈvɪʒən/: *imaginer*
- **do without**
- **infringe on sth**: *porter atteinte à*
- **invade sb's privacy**
- **act as**: *s'improviser comme*

Webquest ⟲▭ **What kind of Internet user are you?** TICE

1 Browse the website below to find out how the Internet has affected people's lives. Here are a few guidelines to help you.
www.bbc.co.uk/worldservice/specialreports/superpower_internet_changed_my_life.shtml

a. Choose one of the subjects proposed.
b. Click on the corresponding link, then watch the video.
c. Report back to the class on what you have just watched and learnt.

2 What do you use the Internet for? In your answer, use the information that you have collected from the website as well as what you have learnt from your classmates.

Welcome to the 21st century

Gavin ESLER

(born in 1953) is an award-winning television and radio broadcaster, novelist and journalist, who has interviewed world leaders and reported for news and documentary programmes across the world. He is also the author of five novels, and he wrote a book on American discontent, *The United States of Anger* (1998).

A Warming up

Describe the picture briefly. What can you deduce about the two men from their attitude?
Use the title and the picture to imagine the subject of the text.

I heard the news late because I had my mobile phone switched off all day, working, and because I had a row with my client. This never happens. I am too polite for that kind of thing, but he was an up-himself New York corporate lawyer from a private equity firm[1] that was trying to buy up half of
5 eastern Europe, and I was helping them. I'm not particularly proud of it, but there you are. Not many people in London speak fluent Czech, and they paid me five times my normal fee for a bit of translation and a bit of interpreting, and probably would have paid me twenty times if I'd had the nerve to ask. The New York lawyer and I finished going through the paperwork enabling
10 his company to buy a sizeable slice of the Czech economy which he told me he intended to "remodel". He signed the contract as I spoke to his opposite number in Prague confirming the deal. At the same time he talked to his office in Manhattan… I could hear him gloating[2].

I was at the other end of the room but could still hear him yakking[3]. He
15 told me to give him the thumbs up the moment I had confirmation the contract was signed in Prague. When I did so, he told New York, "It's done," and then put the phone down. He was beaming, as if he had just had sex. Maybe at that point he needed someone to boast to and I was the only one in the room. Whatever the reason he turned to me and said that in
20 that one instant, in that one stroke of a pen, his company had made more than seven hundred million dollars. He personally had pocketed around thirteen million, and was going to find a club and what he called some "broadminded women" to celebrate with. I ran off at the mouth.

"You're celebrating putting thousands of Czech workers out of a job?"

25 He looked as if I had just hit him, then he laughed and started putting his papers into his attaché case.

"Interpret this, Harry: Welcome to globalization. Welcome to the world where you make dust or you eat dust. Welcome to the twenty-first century."

Then he handed me my cheque with all the good grace of a client stuffing
30 money into the bra[4] of a lap dancer[5].

"Your interpreting fee. A thousand. Don't spend it all at once."

I wanted to hit him. He waved a finger at me.

"You wanna know why people like you don't like Americans, Harry? Because we're so goddamn successful in every field of human endeavour[6]."

35 That angered me even more. It had nothing to do with his nationality. It had everything to do with his behaviour.

"I do like Americans," I protested. "Most of them. But some of you don't travel so well. The ones who have no values except what you can pay for. People like you."

Gavin ESLER, *A Scandalous Man* (2005)

1. *société de capital / investissement* 2. *jubiler* 3. *jacasser*
4. *soutien-gorge* 5. *stripteaseuse* 6. /ɪnˈdevə/ *activité humaine*

B Understanding the text ⓌORKBOOK → p. 24-25

1. Your *Workbook* will help you to understand the text.

2. Give a summary of the situation.

C Going further

3. Draw the portrait of the New York corporate lawyer.

4. Analyse Harry's feelings in this passage. What does he think of the lawyer he works for?

5. Explain the sentence: *"Welcome to the world where you make dust or you eat dust"* (l. 27).

6. According to the lawyer, what are Americans criticized for? Does Harry agree with him?

7. Do you agree with the lawyer's vision of today's world?

D Language training

8. Savoir prononcer 16-17 51-52

Les formes faibles

9. Pratiquer la grammaire
Les temps du récit 🔘 LANGUAGE WORKSHOP → p. 64
Quantifieurs – Nombres ⓌORKBOOK → p. 28

function box

Expressing anger
- I've had enough of sb / sth / V-ING...
- I'm fed up with sb / sth / V-ING...
- It infuriates me (that + should)...
- Enough is enough...
- I can't stand him / V-ING...
- He drives me mad...
- I can't take it anymore...
- I'm sick and tired of sb / sth / V-ING...

toolbox

Nouns
- opportunist /ˌɒpəˈtjuːnɪst/
- stereotype /ˈstɪərɪətaɪp/

Adjectives
- frustrated /frʌsˈtreɪtɪd/: *contrarié*
- resentful /rɪˈzentfʊl/: *plein de ressentiment*
- ashamed
- cynical
- insensitive (to sb): *insensible*
- cold-hearted = heartless: *impitoyable*
- unmoved (by sth): *indifférent (à)*
- arrogant /ˈærəgənt/

Verbs & expressions
- bear / have a grudge /grʌdʒ/ against sb: *en vouloir à qqn*
- make a fortune /ˈfɔːtʃən/
- roll in money: *rouler sur l'or*
- money talks: *l'argent est roi*
- be appalled /əˈpɔːld/ (at sb): *être consterné*
- hold back one's anger /ˈæŋgə/: *rentrer sa colère*
- betray (*trahir*) ≠ stick to (one's principles)
- despise (sb for sth / V-ING): *mépriser*

Your task

 Write an e-mail about your meeting
Put yourself in the narrator's shoes. The next day, you write an e-mail to a friend about the meeting you had with the corporate lawyer.

Ⓜ ÉTHODOLOGIE
Écrire un courriel → p. 171

"We are the 99%"

A Look and listen CD 1/53

1. Read the information given in the box. Study the cartoon and explain the cartoonist's message.

2. You are going to listen to a recording about the "Occupy Wall Street Movement".

a. Use the cartoon to anticipate the content of the recording.

b. Listen to the audio report and then write down the main ideas.

> "We are the 99%" is a political slogan chanted by the protesters of the "Occupy Wall Street Movement", referring to the 99% of Americans who have almost nothing compared to the wealthiest 1% who have everything.

Chattanooga Times Free Press BENNETT

B Speak

3. With the help of the cartoon and the recording, prepare an oral presentation of the "Occupy Wall Street Movement".

4. Use your notes, but don't read them. You may also use what you have heard about this movement.

C Going further

5. What do you think about the "Occupy Wall Street Movement"? Do you feel personally concerned? Why (not)?

function box

Giving one's opinion
- It seems to me that...
- In my opinion...
- As I see it...
- I can't help thinking that...

Expressing protest
- I object to V-ING...
- I disapprove of V-ING...
- How can they...?
- How dare they...?
- What right have they to...?

toolbox

Nouns
- placard /'plækɑːd/: *pancarte*
- thief /θiːf/ = **r**obber
- culprit /'kʌlprɪt/: *coupable*
- social gap
- (the) needy (noun + adj.): *(les) nécessiteux*
- the haves ≠ the have-nots
- (the) underprivileged (noun + adj.): *(les) défavorisés*

Adjectives
- masked
- innocent /'ɪnəsnt/ ≠ guilty

- fair ≠ unfair
- poverty-stricken
- shocking = outrageous

Verbs & expressions
- thrive /θraɪv/ = prosper
- go looting: *se livrer au pillage*
- make a difference (in sth): *changer (qqch)*
- tackle (an issue): *s'attaquer à (un problème)*
- infuriate /ɪn'fjʊərɪeɪt/: *rendre furieux*

Your task

 Interview an "Occupy Wall Street Movement" protester

A journalist working for the *New York Times* reports live from Wall Street where a crowd of protesters are demonstrating.
Decide who you want to be and act out the interview.
Student A You are the reporter. Think of the questions you will ask the protester.
Student B You are the protester. Imagine the questions you will be asked and prepare your answers.

Ⓜ MÉTHODOLOGIE
Interview → p. 166

Writers' corner

Should WikiLeaks be banned?

culture key   WikiLeaks → p. 153

Your task

Write a letter to a newspaper about WikiLeaks

You write a letter to the "Readers' opinion" column in *The Sydney Morning Herald*, in which you express your own opinion on whether WikiLeaks should be banned or authorized.

MÉTHODOLOGIE Écrire une lettre → p. 171

A Get ready

1. Read the *Culture key* about WikiLeaks, p. 153.

2. Read the two statements about WikiLeaks in *The Sydney Morning Herald*.

B Write your letter

3. Here are a few hints:
a. Refer to the statements that you have read.
b. Explain whether you agree or disagree with the two points of view.
c. Write down your own arguments.

JENNIFER ROBINSON, *lawyer, London* – Without question, WikiLeaks has made a remarkable contribution to free speech, human rights and the operation of democracy, by offering better protection to journalistic sources and by holding governments to account by revealing abuse and empowering the public to make better-informed democratic choices.

As a human rights and media defence lawyer, to me it is an incontrovertible fact that WikiLeaks is a force for good, for revealing human rights abuse and protecting the human rights of journalists and their sources.

Pr MICHAEL FRASER, *director of the Communications Law Centre at UTS* – Publication is not its own justification. In our democracy we value and protect the fundamental right of freedom of expression and the public's right to know. But we limit even these rights where we need to balance them against other important rights that we also enjoy as citizens. The purpose of WikiLeaks' mass publication of hundreds of thousands of other classified diplomatic communications is a political attack on US communications and the outcome will be more government secrecy. That is not in the public interest.

The Sydney Morning Herald (June 11th 2011)

toolbox

Nouns
- censorship /'sensəʃɪp/: *censure*
- source /sɔːs/
- news leaks: *fuites journalistiques*
- national security
- state / official secret

Adjectives
- anonymous /ə'nɒnɪməs/
- ethical ≠ unethical
- classified
- sensitive: *sensible*
- legal ≠ illegal

Verbs & expressions
- censor /'sensə/: *censurer*
- disclose = unveil: *divulguer*
- conceal: *dissimuler*
- keep sth private /'praɪvɪt/
- release /rɪ'liːs/: *publier*
- blame sb for sth / V-ING
- tell the truth (about sth) ≠ lie
- put sb at risk / in danger
- break the law = be against the law
- keep sb informed

function box

Expressing agreement / disagreement
- I (dis)agree with... / about...
- That's (not) how I see it...
- I couldn't agree more...
- I don't see things that way...

Expressing one's opinion
- I can't help thinking that...
- I'm convinced that...
- I do believe that...
- It seems to me that...

Flash mobs 📖

CourierPostOnline.com

is a daily newspaper based in New Jersey. Established in 1875, it is the fourth largest paper in New Jersey. The newspaper's employees are paid by the number of papers delivered each day.
Website: www.courierpostonline.com

Cable News Network (CNN) is an American cable news channel which was founded in 1980 by Ted Turner, a media magnate. CNN, which was the first TV channel to offer 24/7 news coverage, is present in more than 212 countries and territories worldwide.
Website: www.cnn.com

A Warming up

Use the picture and the titles of the two articles to anticipate their content.

Culture performance

THEY SIDLED UP to a shoe kiosk at Macy's Grand Court last holiday season, holding empty shopping bags – and their breaths. Though nervous, Victoria Burhman
5 and her friends tried not to look suspicious.

"We faked as if we actually were shopping," recalls the 17-year-old Woodstown resident. "We would touch things to make it look like we were shopping."
10 But they had little intention of buying anything.

In fact, they and about 650 accomplices came to the Center City site to sell something instead – a spectacle that shocked and
15 stopped busy holiday shoppers at the foot of the Wanamaker Organ[1].

As shoppers on the three floors of the Grand Court united in a rendition of the "Hallelujah" chorus from Handel's "Messiah[2]," it became
20 clear this was a case of organized chime[3].

Before disappearing back into the crowd, the performers ended the five-minute performance to general applause and with a message: "You've just experienced a Random[4]
25 Act of Culture."

The Opera Company of Philadelphia was behind this particular Random Act, a nationwide initiative by the Knight Foundation aimed at taking classical arts out
30 of the theaters and into the community.

Defining these Random Acts as "a series of unexpected, spontaneous cultural performances in nontraditional settings," the Knight Foundation has helped make the zany[5]
35 and unusual common place.

The Courier Post Online (December 5th 2011)

1. the largest operational pipe organ in the world
2. /mɪˈsaɪə/ 3. *carillon* 4. *aléatoire* 5. *loufoque*

Flash looting

IN THE PAST, people seemed to require a massive "cue[1]" to form a mob. The New York blackouts of the summer of 1977 resulted in citywide looting, not just because alarm systems were down, but because a whole lot of hot, angry, frustrated people had an excuse to act en masse.

Media can certainly accelerate or even reproduce this process. Radio gave Hitler a way to unify angry crowds as never before, and it both inspired and facilitated the chasing down and murder of about 800,000 Tutsis by gangs with machetes in Rwanda.

Are social media such as Facebook and Twitter serving a similar function? This year, we've certainly become aware of how these technologies can coordinate the activities of protesters and rebels acting against repressive regimes. The Arab Spring was initiated on Facebook pages, orchestrated through Twitter accounts, and video recorded on cell phones. But as we're also beginning to witness, these same technologies are being used to orchestrate "flash" looting of stores and almost entirely destructive (or at least poorly justified) riots in England. A mob beating in Wisconsin was reportedly organized through social networks, as were attacks in Cleveland, Chicago, and Washington.

Is access to technology through which a network of friends can so easily be turned into a gang of thieves or assailants just too dangerous for people to handle? By putting what had formerly been the capability of broadcast networks in the hands of everyone owning smartphones, have we unwittingly[2] empowered the "mob" and given new life to the lowest form of crowd behavior?

CNN (August 17th 2011)

1. *signal* 2. *involontairement*

B Understanding the texts Ⓦ ORKBOOK → p. 26-27

. Turn to your *Workbook*. It will help you to understand the two articles.

. Sum up the main ideas in both articles.

C Going further

. Describe and explain the performers' attitude before their show in the article from *The Courier Post Online*.

. Why did their spectacle shock and stop *"busy holiday shoppers"* (l. 14)?

. What do you think of such a *"Random Act of Culture"* (l. 24)?

. Compare the influence of yesterday's and today's media as described in the CNN article.

. Why does the journalist wonder whether today's social media are *"too dangerous for people to handle"* (l. 28)?

. After studying the two articles, point out what is paradoxical in the use of social media today.

toolbox

Nouns
- (prearranged) signal
- gathering = rally
- word-of-mouth: *bouche à oreille*

Adjectives
- unexpected: *inattendu*
- spontaneous
- anonymous /ə'nɒnɪməs/
- pointless ≠ useful /'juːsfʊl/
- temporary /'tempərərɪ/ = short-lived
- harmless ≠ dangerous
- illegal = against the law

Verbs & expressions
- spread: *faire circuler*
- assemble /ə'sembl/ = gather
- converge (on)
- perform
- disperse
- be authorized
- participate in = take part in
- take sth / sb seriously /'sɪərɪəslɪ/
- be held responsible / accountable for sth / V-ING
- condemn /kən'dem/
- misbehave: *se conduire mal*

D Writing time

Ⓜ ÉTHODOLOGIE
Rédiger un essai → p. 172

9. Essay (150-200 words)

Do you think that today's social networks give people too much power?

a. Prenez appui sur les deux articles, mais développez également vos propres idées et construisez votre argumentation en donnant des exemples précis liés ou non à l'actualité.

b. Vous devez exprimer un point de vue. Prenez position en utilisant les expressions de l'opinion.

c. Pensez à utiliser les *Keywords* (p. 54), la *Toolbox* et les mots de liaison appropriés.

E Language training

10. Savoir prononcer 18-19 54-55 Ⓦ ORKBOOK → p. 27

La prononciation de la lettre -*u*-
La prononciation des lettres -*ea*-

11. Pratiquer la grammaire

Cause, condition, concession ● LANGUAGE WORKSHOP → p. 64
Adjectifs composés, date, durée, âge Ⓦ ORKBOOK → p. 28

Your task

 Act out a conversation with a friend about a flash mob

A flash mob has been organized. Decide the reason for the flash mob. You and your friend disagree about taking part. Act out the conversation.

Ⓜ ÉTHODOLOGIE
Conversation → p. 165

Grammaire | **Les temps du récit – Cause, condition, concession**

A Les temps du récit ℗RÉCIS GRAMMATICAL → 4, 8

1 **Valeurs des formes verbales passées**

 1. *I heard the news late…* (Text 1, p. 58, l. 1)
 2. *a (…) firm that was trying to buy up half of eastern Europe (…)* (Text 1, p. 58, l. 4)
 3. *He personally had pocketed around thirteen million (…)* (Text 1, p. 58, l. 21)
 4. *He looked as if I had just hit him, then he laughed and started (…)* (Text 1, p. 59, l. 25)

a. Relevez les verbes au prétérit simple, au prétérit BE+ING et au *pluperfect* et associez à chacune de ces formes verbales l'une des valeurs suivantes : sert à présenter des faits passés sous l'angle du déroulement, exprime l'antériorité dans le passé d'un fait ou exprime une succession de faits passés sans commentaire.
b. Laquelle de ces trois formes est essentielle pour faire progresser le récit ? Quelles autres formes verbales donnent des indications complémentaires (description, retour en arrière) ?
c. Parmi les verbes au prétérit simple ci-dessus, lesquels sont des verbes d'état et ne pourraient donc pas s'utiliser à la forme BE+ING ?

2 **Traduisez le passage suivant.**

a. Beaucoup de choses se produisirent ce jour-là. **b.** J'avais été récemment promu et nous fêtions cela (*celebrate*). **c.** Mon client essayait désespérément de me joindre sur mon téléphone portable lorsque j'eus la confirmation que je venais de gagner 2 millions de dollars. **d.** J'avais l'air à la fois heureux et stupéfait (*astonished*). **e.** Et j'affichais un large sourire (*smile broadly*).

B Cause, condition, concession ℗RÉCIS GRAMMATICAL → 39, 40, 41

3 *As, since, provided, unless, though*

 1. *Though [they were] nervous, Victoria Burhman and her friends tried not to look suspicious.* (Text 2, p. 62, l. 4)
 2. *The New York blackouts (…) resulted in citywide looting, (…) **because a whole lot of hot, angry, frustrated people had an excuse to act en masse.*** (Text 2, p. 63, l. 2)
 3. ***As shoppers on the three floors of the Grand Court united in a** (…) **chorus** (…), it became clear this was a case of organized chime.* (Text 2, p. 62, l. 17)
 4. ***As they did not intend to buy anything**, they didn't have any money.*
 5. ***Since there was nothing to do after the show**, they went straight back home.*
 6. *No such thing has ever happened **since smartphones appeared on the market**.*
 7. *"There is nothing dangerous about it, **unless the police find out**," they said.*
 8. *"We will all be safe **provided we take the proper precautions**."*

a. Associez à chacune des subordonnées en gras ci-dessus l'une des notions suivantes : cause, concession, condition, temps.
b. Lequel de ces subordonnants, AS, SINCE, PROVIDED, UNLESS, THOUGH, exprime une condition **négative** ?
c. Quelles sont les différentes valeurs de AS d'une part et de SINCE d'autre part ?
d. Traduisez les énoncés 1 à 6.

4 **Traduisez à l'aide de *as, since, provided, unless* ou *though*.**

a. Bien qu'ils aient eu peur, ils n'ont pas bougé.
b. Ils ne feront rien à moins que vous le leur demandiez.
c. Puisque ces technologies sont utilisées partout, nous devons nous adapter.
d. Comme ils avaient un réseau très efficace (*efficient*), ils ont organisé une manifestation (*protest march*).
e. C'est autorisé à condition que vous respectiez les règles.

Grammaire de l'oral | *Do / did* dans les énoncés affirmatifs

5 Repérez l'accentuation

a. Écoutez ces passages et indiquez si l'auxiliaire *do / did* et le verbe qui suit sont accentués.
1. *"You wanna know why people like you don't like Americans, Harry?" "I do like Americans. (…) Most of them."* (Text 1, p. 59, l. 33)   **2.** *He said he would go and he did go.*

b. Expliquez la présence de l'auxiliaire *do / did* dans chacun des passages soulignés à l'aide de l'une de ces propositions : **1.** l'auxiliaire est grammaticalement nécessaire pour que l'énoncé soit bien formé ; **2.** il permet de confirmer ce qui vient d'être dit ; **3.** il exprime le contraste. **c.** Traduisez les énoncés.

6 Écoutez cet énoncé et indiquez si la forme manquante est la forme 1, 2 ou 3.

*So, (***1.*** what does it mean –* ***2.*** *what it does mean –* ***3.*** *what its means) in a certain sense, is that every citizen is empowered potentially as a journalist.* (Focus on listening, p. 57)

7 Traduisez oralement. Vérifiez à l'écoute. 58-59

a. Student A: Je suis désolé mais tu ne comprends pas. **Student B:** Mais si, je comprends ! C'est simplement que ce que tu dis a vraiment l'air (*sound*) incroyable, tu sais.

b. Student A: Tu as entendu ce qu'il a dit ? **Student B:** Oui. Mais cela ne signifie pas que tu aies raison ! Ce que cela veut dire, en fait, c'est que tu es dans une situation très difficile !

Lexique | **Pouvoirs et contre-pouvoirs**

Assurez-vous que vous avez bien retenu les mots clés de l'unité.   **→ Keywords p. 54**

8 Donnez les synonymes des mots et expressions suivants.
a. *demonstrator* = …   **b.** *global* = …   **c.** *determined* = …
d. *challenge sb* = …   **e.** *powerful* = …   **f.** *resist* = …   **g.** *repress* = …

9 Choisissez la bonne transcription phonétique du mot suivant.
corporate: /ˈkɔːpərɪt/ – /ˈkɔːpəreɪt/ – /ˈkəʊpərɪt/

10 Recopiez les mots suivants et entourez la syllabe accentuée.
a. *empowerment*   **b.** *demonstrate*   **c.** *influential*   **d.** *supremacy*

11 Traduisez : **a.** *raise awareness*   **b.** *assert one's rights*   **c.** *empower*

12 Complétez les phrases à l'aide des mots suivants en faisant les changements nécessaires.
rise up – question – greed – activists – take to the streets – wealthy – debt-ridden – indignant – stand up for – dominate – influence
a. ..1.. *from the* ..2.. *movement have decided to* ..3.. *against corporate* ..4...
b. *Protesters* ..5.. *to* ..6.. *the way financial markets* ..7.. *government policy.*
c. *They want the government to tax big companies and* ..8.. *people.*
d. *Because of the economic crisis, he is now* ..9....
e. *Demonstrators shouted: "* ..10.. *your rights! Fight those who* ..11.. *you!"*

toolbox

Adjectives
● **pea**ceful: *pacifique*
● **pro**vocative: *provocateur*
● up**set**: *bouleversé*

Verbs & expressions
● **smash** windows: *briser des vitrines*
● **target**: *viser*
● **break** into: *entrer par effraction*

Your task

Post a comment on Facebook
When travelling abroad, you witnessed an unexpected riot scene which you recorded on your cell phone. You write about what happened and post your comment on Facebook. **Use past tenses** (past perfect, past simple, past continuous).

The Fourth Power today

How has the Fourth Power changed in the last few years?

 From paper to screen

1 What does the cartoon highlight?

2 Read the article. What are the economic and social consequences of the development of the digital press?

3 Do you prefer to read the news in newspapers or online? Why?

A T LEAST 120 NEWSPAPERS IN THE U.S. have shut down since January 2008, according to Paper Cuts, a website tracking the newspaper industry. More than 21,000 jobs at 67 newspapers have vaporized in that time, according to the site. Newspapers are losing their relevance[1] in the lives of a majority of Americans, particularly younger readers. Many industry analysts agree many more papers will soon become extinct. Daily subscriptions per household began a steady decline in the 1920s, yet the newspaper industry adapted and thrived[2] despite competition from radio and television. But easily accessible, high-speed Internet connections and smartphones have dramatically shifted the way people get their news.

CNN (March 19th 2009)

1. *importance* 2. *prospérer*

 The rise of the free press

1 Read the text once. What is the key idea?

2 After reading the text, answer the following questions, using your own arguments:
a. What economic and social consequences could the rise of the free press have?
b. Why is the free press so popular in modern society?

A NYONE RIDING THE LONDON UNDER-GROUND, a Dutch commuter train or the Seoul metro in rush hour will see people reading newspapers. Not the regular traditional broadsheet[1] paid-for newspapers but mostly free tabloids. There are now free newspapers in 56 countries. Market leader *Metro* distributes more than 8 million copies daily, while other companies publish more than 35 million copies. These copies are read by at least 80 million people daily. In four European countries (Iceland, Denmark, Spain and Portugal) more free than paid papers are distributed (Monday to Friday) while in more than a dozen European countries the newspaper with the highest circulation is a free paper.

1. *journal de qualité*

The sinking of an empire

CD 1
60

culture key The Watergate → p. 153

1 Listen to the recording.
a. Why is Rupert Murdoch seen as a media magnate?
b. Read the *Culture key* about the Watergate case. Why is Murdoch's case compared to the Watergate scandal?

2 Read the article.
a. What was Rupert Murdoch accused of?
b. What role did the public and some independent papers play in the decline of his empire?
c. Who helped Murdoch's empire to thrive according to the article?

UNTIL LAST WEEK, Rupert Murdoch's global media empire, which acted as a king-maker in Britain, had seemed invincible. *The News of the World* phone-hacking scandal, in which the phones of all newsworthy[1] people from Prime Ministers to victims of crime and terrorism were hacked, became a rallying point that focussed [the] public grievance[2]. In the US, there is movement to investigate whether he should be brought to justice and now the FBI is investigating whether his papers have also hacked into the phone of family victims of the 9/11 terrorist attacks. How did this happen? Surely not without public pressure, which was produced and transferred into the corridors of power with the help of a few remaining independent papers, such as *The Guardian* and *The Independent*.

As this pressure eventually opened a floodgate of dissent[3], it became obvious that Murdoch's empire could never have been built without the participation and consent of the British state, especially the government and police.

The Huffington Post (July18th 2011)

1. ayant un intérêt médiatique
2. mécontentement 3. déclencher une énorme vague de protestations

Political activists wearing Rupert Murdoch masks

Video time

Thank you for Smoking

Thank you for Smoking, Jason REITMAN (2005)

A Get ready

1. Look at the film poster and describe it briefly.

2. What is unusual about the title?

3. What do you think the film deals with?

B Watch the video

4. Watch a scene from *Thank you for Smoking*. Your teacher will give you a worksheet to help you.

C In your own words

5. Use the worksheet to give an oral account of the scene.

D Going further

6. What does this extract reveal about big tobacco firms?

final task

Are counter-powers growing in influence?

You have been invited to a TV debate on the rise of counter-powers in today's society.
After listening to reports and reading about powers and counter-powers, you take part in the debate.

 1 ## Listen to a radio report 20-21 61-62

(M) **MÉTHODOLOGIE COMPRÉHENSION DE L'ORAL** → p. 161

A Get ready

■ Use the pictures to anticipate the content of the recording.

B Now listen

■ The worksheet your teacher will give you will help you to understand the recording.

■ Explain why different voices can be heard. What does it prove?

Je me situe par rapport au CECRL **B2**

QUAND J'ÉCOUTE UN REPORTAGE AUDIO :
Je peux le comprendre en langue standard, reconnaître le point de vue et l'attitude du / des locuteur(s).

2 ## Take part in a TV debate

(M) **MÉTHODOLOGIE Débat** → p. 166

Group work: discuss the rise of counter-powers in today's society.

■ Each group should include a host (*présentateur*) and three or four participants.

■ The host will use the recording and especially the final question as a starting point for the discussion.

■ The various documents in this unit should help the participants to develop arguments and counter-arguments. Other examples of counter-powers can be used.

■ Do not interrupt the other participants, but keep their arguments in mind so as to react to them. Be convincing!

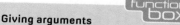

function box

Giving arguments
● One of the main reasons why...
● Another good reason for V-ING...
● What's more...
● However...
● Let's not forget that...
● Last but not least: *Enfin et surtout*

Expressing one's opinion → p. 61
Expressing agreement / disagreement → p. 61

Je me situe par rapport au CECRL **B2**

QUAND JE PRENDS PART À UN DÉBAT :
Je peux prendre part à une conversation sur un sujet connu ou étudié. Je peux en particulier exposer mon point de vue, discuter les points de vue d'autrui et émettre des hypothèses.

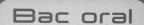

Vous trouverez la présentation de l'épreuve pages 12-13
et des conseils pratiques pour le bac pages 175-179.

Compréhension de l'oral

 22 63 ⓦORKBOOK → p. 29

**Vous allez écouter trois fois un document intitulé
The rise and fall of WikiLeaks.**

Avant l'écoute

1. Aidez-vous du titre du document de façon à anticiper son contenu.

Première écoute

2. Identifiez la nature et le thème général du document.
3. Repérez de quoi et de qui parle le document.

Deuxième écoute

4. Relevez les informations principales.

Troisième écoute

5. Donnez des détails significatifs et le point de vue des locuteurs.

Rendez compte en français de ce que vous avez compris.

> **TIPS**

> Qui sont les personnes qui interviennent ? De quoi parlent-elles ?

> Quelle est la contradiction dans ce reportage ? Repérez à quoi correspondent les chiffres que vous entendez.

> Les locuteurs ont-il tous le même point de vue ?

Expression orale

ⓦORKBOOK → p. 30

Lors de votre prise de parole en continu, puis de la conversation avec l'examinateur, vous pourrez aborder les problématiques suivantes en lien avec l'unité 3.

Notion 1 Lieux et formes du pouvoir
Seats and forms of power

■ **The empowerment of citizens**

The Fifth Power, p. 56 • "We are the 99%", p. 60 • Should WikiLeaks be banned?, p. 61 • Flash mobs, p. 62 • Google, p. 153 • WikiLeaks, p. 153

> Analysez l'impact des nouvelles technologies sur l'influence croissante des citoyens dans la société actuelle.

■ **The power of money**

Welcome to the 21st century, p. 58 • "We are the 99%", p. 60 • The sinking of an empire, p. 67 • Thank you for Smoking, p. 67

> Ces documents vous permettent de présenter différents aspects du pouvoir de l'argent.

Notion 2 Espaces et échanges
Places and exchanges

■ **What influence does the web have on today's society?**

The Fifth Power, p. 56 • What kind of Internet user are you?, p. 57 • "We are the 99%", p. 60 • Should WikiLeaks be banned?, p. 61 • Flash mobs, p. 62 • Google, p. 153 • WikiLeaks, p. 153

> • Définissez ce qu'est un réseau social et donnez ses utilisations possibles, qu'elles soient positives ou négatives.
> • Utilisez les structures permettant de **donner son opinion** : *In my view... For my part... I'm convinced that...*

TEXT 1 – A new country

Is it any wonder that people between the ages of 4-50 are increasingly opting for this country? Why wouldn't they? – they are meeting like-minded new friends and rediscovering long-lost friends they'd long given up hope of ever meeting again. Had it not been for Facebook, the biggest social-networking site, would all this be possible?
5 The new ice-breaker isn't, "So, where do you live?" any longer; it is, "So, are you on Facebook?"

Why are people of all shapes, sizes, and ages flocking to the site? I've been wondering, how does this work so well for all? Which are the key ingredients that make the Facebook world tick? I'm far from the answer but I rather think it is because it's such a wonderful
10 escape from all that is less-than-perfect in real life. I can already hear dissenting voices, "Hey, it is real life, lady!" which is about the one thing that scares me about this perfect life. Having already lured[1] us enough into its "web" of a second life, what if someday soon it becomes our only life? A life where we are content just connecting virtually? A life where we choose to upload only the best and be in denial about the rest?

15 Maybe Mr Zuckerberg[2], the man who gave so many the taste of the perfect life, should think of putting a warning, a sort of reality check: "Not to be taken as an alternative to life – imperfections, disappointments, ugliness, and all"...?

They are, after all, what makes life, Life.

India Currents (June 23rd 2011)

TEXT 2 – Teens online

While teens are spending more and more time on social networking sites like Facebook and MySpace – with 22 percent saying they check their sites more than 10 times a day – they don't seem to be aware of the long-term personal havoc[3] they could create with a click of a button. And their parents generally have little idea about what
5 their children are up to, the poll found.

"We've got to stop kidding ourselves about this," said James Steyer, chief economic officer and founder of San Francisco-based Common Sense Media, which commissioned the study. "There are enormous consequences from inappropriate behavior online."

When Maxwell Wallace, a graduate of Lowell High School in San Francisco, wanted
10 to know more about his new roommate at Georgetown University this fall, he didn't just place a phone call. He also went to Facebook. There, Wallace could read the teen's thoughts, see what his interests were, what his friends said about him and what his pictures indicated about his lifestyle. It was "a better look at who I'm going to be living with for the next eight to nine months," he said.

15 Teenagers don't always self-censor online; they may bully classmates, for example, or post risque photos of themselves or their peers.

"If you're not in the same place as the person, it just feels less personal; it's easier to do mean things," Steyer said. "It's almost simulated behavior. You can be risky and do riskier things in a digital context."

20 Yet there can be enormous consequences. Hitting delete to get rid of a questionable photo won't help. The digital imprint never goes away and could be flitting across computer screens around the world.

The San Francisco Gate (August 10th 2009)

1. *attirer*   2. co-founder of Facebook   3. *ravages*

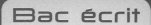
Vous trouverez la présentation de l'épreuve pages 12-13
et des conseils pratiques pour le bac pages 175-179.

Compréhension de l'écrit

Read the <u>two</u> texts before answering the questions.

TIPS

TEXT 1

1. In one sentence, what is the topic of the text?

2. What does the adverb "*increasingly*" imply in the first sentence?

> Le nombre de mots n'est pas indiqué, une réponse courte est attendue.

3. What does the journalist compare Facebook to and why? (30 words)

4. How do people introduce themselves today? Quote the text.

5. Find the three elements in the text which explain why Facebook is so popular.

> Relisez l'ensemble du texte. Les éléments nécessaires à la réponse se trouvent à différents endroits.

6. In the sentence "*Hey, it is real life, lady!*" (l. 11), what does "*it*" refer to?

7. Explain what the journalist is afraid of.

> Relisez le passage de "*Hey, it is real life, lady!*" (l. 11) jusqu'à "*the rest*" (l. 14).

8. What warning should Mr Zuckerberg give to Facebook users according to the journalist? Explain in your own words.

TEXT 2

9. In one sentence, what is the topic of the text?

10. What did Maxwell Wallace use Facebook for?

> La réponse doit être brève. Repérez le passage correspondant, puis répondez avec vos propres mots.

11. Why should Internet users be careful about what they post online? Quote the text.

12. Explain why the article focuses on teenagers. (40 words)

> Les éléments de réponse se trouvent dans l'ensemble du texte. Rédigez cette question de synthèse au brouillon.

TEXT 1 AND TEXT 2

13. What are the advantages and the drawbacks of social networks presented in the two texts?

Expression écrite

1. A teenager and his / her parents disagree on the use of social networks. Write the discussion.

> **Use your grammar**
> • Faire le bilan d'une situation donnée :
>   **fiche 3** (p. 181)
> • Exprimer un jugement :
>   **fiche 4** (p. 182)

2. Do you agree with the points of view about social networks developed in these texts? Justify your view.

Unit 4

L'idée de progrès
Espaces et échanges

This is Britain

What is great in Britain?

final task
You went to Britain on a traineeship last summer and have been asked to write an article about your experience in the school magazine. First, you present the content of your article and your choice of illustrations to the editorial team, then, you write the article.

Keywords

Nouns
- the British = Britons = the Brits (*fam.*)
- the Scottish = the Scots / a Scotsman
- Union Jack = Union flag
- MP = Member of Parliament /ˈpɑːləmənt/
- PM = Prime Minister
- national anthem: *hymne national*
- monarchy /ˈmɒnəkɪ/
- democracy
- government
- heir /ɛə/ = next in line
- customs = traditions
- equality of opportunity
- success ≠ failure
- figurehead: *figure emblématique*
- royal family
- prejudice
- tolerance

Adjectives
- Welsh: *gallois*
- Scottish / Scotch
- multicultural
- wealthy ≠ underprivileged
- determined
- innovative
- vibrant /ˈvaɪbrənt/: *animé*

Verbs & expressions
- succeed: *succéder*
- be successful
- climb /klaɪm/ the social ladder
- close / bridge the gap
- do one's best
- blend in = be assimilated
- fit in = integrate
- be torn (between): *être déchiré (entre)*
- share: *partager*

LANGUAGE WORKSHOP → p. 83

 **London today**

1. Describe this scene photographed on the banks of the River Thames in London. Imagine on what occasion this photo was taken.

2. What elements attract your attention? What contrasts are underlined?

3. In what ways does this correspond to your view of London today?

Focus on writing

Snapshots of Britain

Ⓜ ÉTHODOLOGIE **EXPRESSION ÉCRITE** → p. 170

Ⓐ The world... at home

Ⓜ ÉTHODOLOGIE
Rédiger des phrases correctes – Le groupe verbal → p. 170

Write an e-mail to ask for information.

1. There's a whole range of "Multikulti" music festivals to go to which bring the world to Britain. Read about two of them.

South Asia: London Mela

The cream of South Asian music and culture! One of the biggest celebrations of Asian music and culture in Europe! The musical line-up will include Asian pop to Muslim hip-hop, Bhangra and Bollywood hits as well as respected Indian classical musicians. Away from the music there will be stalls selling traditional food and crafts, traditional dance displays, and circus acts.

Latin America: Carnaval de Pueblo

Latino spirit comes to South London this summer in the shape of Carnaval de Pueblo – Europe's largest outdoor Latin American event. Ok, so it may not have the guaranteed sun or beach, but it will have the dancers, drumming and Brazilian party vibe. Music will range from reggae to samba and Latin hip-hop on several stages, and you can sample regionally-themed food and drink.

2. You hesitate about which one to go to. You write an e-mail to a friend living in Britain to ask for information (place, date, times, cost, where to stay) and to find out if he she can help you to make your choice. (150 words)

Here are a few hints:
a. You are writing to a friend, so keep the style informal.
b. Make short sentences.
c. Be careful of word order when asking questions.

Ⓑ The monarchy: what Britain really wants

Ⓜ ÉTHODOLOGIE **Enrichir sa production** → p. 170

Write a report using quantifiers and comparatives.

1. Study the graphs.

2. Write a report about the attitudes of British people towards the monarchy. (100 words)

Here are a few hints:
a. Use quantifiers (*much, most, few,* etc.) to write about tendencies rather than giving exact figures.
b. Use comparatives to underline differences.
c. Make whole sentences and introduce link words whenever possible.

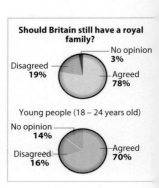

Should Britain still have a royal family?
No opinion 3%
Disagreed 19%
Agreed 78%

Young people (18 – 24 years old)
No opinion 14%
Disagreed 16%
Agreed 70%

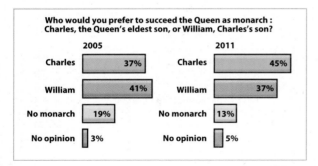

Who would you prefer to succeed the Queen as monarch : Charles, the Queen's eldest son, or William, Charles's son?

2005
Charles 37%
William 41%
No monarch 19%
No opinion 3%

2011
Charles 45%
William 37%
No monarch 13%
No opinion 5%

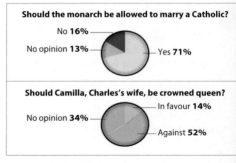

Should the monarch be allowed to marry a Catholic?
No 16%
No opinion 13%
Yes 71%

Should Camilla, Charles's wife, be crowned queen?
In favour 14%
No opinion 34%
Against 52%

(Sources: *BBC*, 2007, *The Daily Mail*, 2010, and *Prospect magazine*, 2011)

C Education: two Britains

MéTHODOLOGIE
Faire des phrases complexes → p. 170

Write an article using link words with well-structured paragraphs.

1. Analyse the cartoon. Do you think its message is fair?

2. Read the information about education in Britain given in the box opposite.

A TALE OF TWO BRITAINS

WOSSIT SAY?

Criminal Record

Education in England and Wales: a few facts

- **Ages 5-16**: compulsory schooling.
- **2008**: The Education and Skills Act raising the school-leaving age (17 in 2013, 18 in 2015).
- **90%** of pupils in state-run non selective schools.
- **7%** of pupils in privately-run independent schools or public schools. (Cost of public school education: £15,000–£30,000 a year.)
- **50%** of 'A' levels taken by pupils from public schools given top marks.
- **20%** of 'A' levels taken by pupils from state schools given top marks.

- **Top universities** require excellent 'A' level results.
- **Top university graduates:** top positions in society.
- **Less than 5%** of students from poor neighbourhoods at Britain's top 20 universities.
- **10%** of young people from disadvantaged backgrounds left university after 1 year.
- **2011**: Almost 1 million 16 to 24-year-olds classified as "Neets" – not in employment, education or training. 10% of young people leave school with no qualifications.

3. Use the facts given to write an article about education in Britain. Conclude by making one or two remarks about what struck you most. (200 words)

Here are a few hints:

a. Concentrate on changes and differences to avoid a list of statistics.

b. Make complete sentences using link words.

c. Conclude with your own remarks.

toolbox

Nouns
- info
- tip: *tuyau*
- feature /ˈfiːtʃə/: *caractéristique*
- tendency = trend

Adjectives & adverbs
- reticent (about sth)
- disadvantaged = underprivileged
- highly = very
- notable: *remarquable*

Verbs & expressions
- make up one's mind = decide
- reach: *atteindre*
- attend (school): *aller à*
- tend to V: *avoir tendance à*

Webquest

London's changing skyline

1 New buildings have appeared or are appearing all over London. Browse the web to find out more about London's changing skyline (names of buildings, locations, heights, controversial projects…). Give an oral account of your research.

2 Which of these buildings do you prefer? Who was the architect responsible for the project? Has the building got a nickname? What is the building used for?

Imagine the postcard you write to your parents with this building on it explaining your choice.

 Web resources

- www-the-shard.com/overview/
- www.stratalondon.com

Consumerist zombies

culture key The Thatcher years → p. 154

Jonathan COE

(b. 1961) is a British novelist. He published his first novel in 1987 and has won several literary awards. His novels are mainly satirical. *The Terrible Privacy of Maxwell Sim* is the story of a solitary man with plenty of Facebook friends but no-one to talk to when his marriage breaks down.

 **Warming up**

Look at the photo. Where is this young woman and what do you imagine she is dreaming of?

Poppy has just told the narrator she works as an "adultery facilitator" providing alibis[1] to people who cheat on their partners.

"What about…" I said, trying to choose my words with care, "what about the moral dimension?"

5 "The what?" said Poppy.

"I just wondered if you had any qualms[2] about it. You know… the fact that you're helping people to cheat on other people. Does it bother you – your conscience, at all?"

"Oh, that." Poppy stirred up the froth[3] at the bottom of her coffee cup 10 and sucked nonchalantly on her plastic spoon. "I've gone past the stage where I bother about that kind of thing. I got a First[4] in History from Oxford, you know. And do you know what kind of jobs I've been doing since? The shittiest of the shitty. The best was PA[5] to the director of a lapdancing club[6]. This job gives me easy money, and it's regular work, and it allows me plenty 15 of time to sit around reading, and watching films, and going to galleries, which is what I really like doing."

"Yes, I know things are… difficult out there at the moment. I just thought…"

"You know, you're starting to sound just like Clive. This is exactly what he said to me when I told him about this job. And do you know what I said 20 back to him?"

Of course, I didn't know what she had said back to him. I didn't even know who Clive was.

"Well, I lost my temper with him," Poppy said, "which I very rarely do with Clive. I said to him: Do you realize that, if there's one thing people of 25 my age cannot stand hearing, it's people of your age giving us lectures on

morality. Look at the world around you. The world you've bequeathed[7] to us. D'you think it allows us any scope to do things on principle? I'm sick of hearing about how my generation has no values. How materialist we are. How lacking in any political sense. Do you know why that is? Take a
30 wild guess. That's right because that's how you brought us up! We may be Mrs Thatcher's children, as far as you're concerned, but you were the ones who voted for her, again and again, and then carried on voting for all the people who came after her, and followed exactly in her footsteps. You're the ones who brought us up to be these consumerist zombies. You chucked
35 all the other values out of the window; didn't you? Christianity? Don't need that. Collective responsibility? Where's that ever got us. Manufacturing? Making things? That's for losers. Yeah, let's get those losers over in the Far East to make everything for us and we can just sit on our backsides[8] in front of the TV, watching the world go to hell in a handcart – in widescreen and
40 HD, of course." She sat back, looking faintly embarrassed for having spoken so passionately.

Jonathan COE, *The Terrible Privacy of Maxwell Sim* (2010)

1. /ˈælɪbaɪ/   2. /kwɑːm/   3 *mousse.*   4. *licence avec mention très bien*
5. Personal Assistant   6. *club de strip-tease*   7. /brˈkwiːð/   8. *derrières*

B Understanding the text ⓦORKBOOK → p. 31-32

1. Turn to your *Workbook* for help in understanding the text.

2. Sum up the story.

C Going further

3. Explain how Poppy ended up by accepting her current job.

4. What does the narrator imply by *"I know things are… difficult out there at the moment"* (l. 17)?

5. Read the *Culture key* and explain what Poppy means by her generation being Mrs Thatcher's children?

6. What does Poppy reproach the previous generation with?

7. In what way is Poppy's situation like that of many young people today?

D Language training

8. **Savoir prononcer** 23 2

Les liaisons

9. **Pratiquer la grammaire**

Les propositions en -ING ⬤LANGUAGE WORKSHOP → p. 82
Propositions en *what* et *which* ⓦORKBOOK → p. 36
Questions au style indirect

toolbox

Nouns
- graduate
- job market
- generation gap
- consumer society
- lie (noun + verb): *mensonge*

Adjectives
- faithful ≠ unfaithful: *fidèle ≠ infidèle*
- materialistic
- lousy (job): *minable*
- unethical
- suitable: *approprié*
- jobless = out of work

Verbs & expressions
- have a guilty conscience
- inherit (from sb): *hériter (de qqn)*
- try one's hand at sth: *s'essayer à qqch*
- take into account: *prendre en considération*
- earn one's living: *gagner sa vie*
- get by: *se débrouiller, s'en sortir*
- make ends meet: *joindre les deux bouts*
- reproach sb with / for (+V-ING)
- be fed up with / have had enough of
- lay the blame on sb: *rejeter la responsabilité sur qqn*

Your task

 Write an article about today's young generation

Poppy says *"I'm sick of hearing about how my generation has no values"* (l. 27). You comment on her opinion in an article for the school magazine. Give examples to justify your view.

Ⓜ ÉTHODOLOGIE
Rédiger des phrases correctes → p. 170

Students protest

A The topic

1. Describe the photo briefly.

2. Read the text and find out:
a. what "tuition fees" are;
b. what might explain what is happening in the photo.

Since September 1998, students in the UK contribute to the cost of their university education by paying tuition fees. Students originally paid £1,000 a year but, in 2004, fees increased to £3,000 a year. A new report in 2010 proposed allowing universities to charge students up to £9,000 a year. A study carried out by the London School of Economics indicated that increasing tuition fees again in 2012 will mean a drop in university enrolment of 7.5% for men and nearly 5% for women.

B Open your ears

3. Before listening to a report entitled "Students protest", you will hear two sentences spoken by the reporter. Find out what took Britain by surprise.

C Listen CD 2 4-6 Ⓦ ORKBOOK → p. 33

4. Listen to the recording. You will find some help in your *Workbook*.

D In your own words

5. Sum up what happened that day.

E Going further

6. What impact do you think the increase in tuition fees will have on future students?

toolbox

Nouns
- demonstrator: *manifestant*
- placard /'plækɑːd/: *pancarte*
- rioter /'raɪətə/: *casseur*
- living costs
- rent: *loyer*
- bread-and-butter job: *boulot alimentaire*
- grant: *bourse*
- loan /ləʊn/: *prêt*
- student digs / lodgings: *logement pour étudiant*

Adjectives
- unpopular
- hard up / broke: *fauché*

Verbs & expressions
- protest /prə'test/
- hold a demonstration
- lose control of
- take out ≠ pay off (a loan): *souscrire ≠ rembourser*
- fail (exams) ≠ succeed
- drop out (of university): *abandonner ses études*

Your task

 Have a discussion about the cost of going to university

After the day's protests, you have a discussion about going to university next year.
Student A You have decided not to go to university next year because of the cost.
Student B You try to convince your friend to change his / her mind.

Ⓜ ÉTHODOLOGIE
Discussion contradictoire → p. 166

Speakers' corner

A sporting nation

culture key The Commonwealth → p. 154

A Look and speak

1. Look at the photos. What do you know about these typically British sports?

B Read and speak

2. Read about these sporting events in Britain. How long have these events been taking place?

3. What traditions are associated with them?

C Going further

4. What other sporting events do you associate with Britain? What other sports have origins in Britain? From what you have read, explain why Britain is often called a sporting nation.

toolbox

Nouns
- rowing /ˈrəʊɪŋ/: *aviron*
- oar /ɔ:/: *rame*
- pitch = ground: *terrain*
- cricket bat: *batte*
- wicket: *terrain (entre les piquets)*
- team spirit
- rule (of game): *règle*
- fair play ≠ foul /faʊl/ play
- a waste of time: *une perte de temps*

Adjectives
- fascinating = intriguing
- boring = tedious /ˈtiːdɪəs/
- pointless (*inutile*) ≠ worthwhile

Verbs
- row /rəʊ/: *ramer*
- score: *marquer un point*
- boo: *huer*
- clap: *applaudir*

function box

Questioning an idea
- What's the point?: *À quoi bon ?*
- I can't see the point in...: *Je ne vois pas l'intérêt de...*
- It's no use V-ING: *Cela ne sert à rien de...*
- You must be joking!: *Tu plaisantes !*
- No way!: *Pas question !*
- Come off it!: *Et puis quoi encore !*

Expressing enthusiasm → p. 115
Suggesting and convincing → p. 122

IN 1829, TWO FRIENDS launched the idea of a rowing race between the Universities of Oxford and Cambridge. **The Boat Race** takes place each spring on the Thames in London. In 2010, up to a quarter of a million spectators watched the race from the bank side and millions on television. Members of both teams are traditionally known as *blues* with Cambridge wearing light blue and Oxford dark blue.

RUGBY SCHOOL IN ENGLAND is credited with the invention of rugby. **The Six Nations Championship** is the oldest rugby championship in the world, dating back to 1882. Originally held between the four United Kingdom countries (England, Scotland, Wales and Ireland), France joined in 1910 and Italy in 2000. Traditionally, the team which finishes last is awarded the wooden spoon but no actual spoon exists or has ever existed. Britain also holds yearly rugby internationals with Commonwealth countries.

THE ASHES[1], one of the most celebrated rivalries in international cricket, is a series of five Test matches between England and Australia. A Test match lasts five days! It dates back to 1882 when Australia beat England on an English ground for the first time. A satirical obituary[2] was published at the time, stating that English cricket had died and "the body will be cremated and the ashes taken to Australia". A small urn, supposed to hold the ashes of an item of cricket equipment, was later presented to the England captain and this is the prize for the winning team. All Commonwealth nations take part in cricket tournaments.

1. *cendres*   2. *notice nécrologique*

Your task

Discuss organizing a trip to a sporting event

Student A You are organizing a trip to Britain and try to persuade your friend to go to one of these sporting events.
Student B You are a soccer fan and not very enthusiastic about your friend's idea.

MÉTHODOLOGIE
Discussion contradictoire → p. 166

Black Britons

culture key   The United Kingdom → p. 154

theguardian

was founded in 1821 and is one of the "big four" quality British newspapers (the three others are *The Times*, *The Independent* and *The Daily Telegraph*). It is known for its left-wing political stance. The Sunday newspaper is *The Observer*.
Website: www.guardian.co.uk

A Warming up

Look at the photo and read the title of the article.
What issue do you think the text will deal with?

There was a time when black identity in Britain was a comparatively simple matter. The wave of Caribbean[1] migrants who arrived in Britain from the
5 late 1940s to the first immigration acts in the early 1960s continued to regard themselves as Jamaicans[2], Trinidadians, etc., who were living in Britain, rather than "black British", or indeed any sort of
10 British at all.

In the 1960s, influenced by their experience in Britain and events in the Caribbean and the US, the more politically conscious began to consider
15 themselves as "black" first and foremost.

Since the 1960s, black academics, artists and pundits[3] have been grappling with notions of "Britishness", together with its historical baggage, and have
20 been debating what "black British" might actually mean. In the meantime, social, cultural and economic change has, as usual, been doing the real work and, for a younger generation, there's
25 no contradiction between their ethnicity and their nationality. We'll have to wait for this year's census results to see how many people define themselves as black British, but it's fairly safe to guess that
30 it's going to be a high proportion.

But in a rich irony, just as people of African and Caribbean heritage become comfortable with being British, it seems the rest of the population might be going
35 the other way. The future of the UK itself is being questioned, and there are many who feel increasingly Welsh, Scottish or English (even if they support the union) rather than British. Still others think
40 the nation state has had its day anyway and that European integration is the way forward. And it doesn't stop there; some from the north of England think that the south-east might as well be a different
45 country and their relationship with it is verging on the colonial. So what might this loosening[4] in bonds or even the winding[5] up of the UK mean for "black Britain"?
50 One of the great advantages of being British is that it has never been an ethnic definition in the way that, for example,

Irish or Welsh has been, so it's an easier identity for different ethnicities to
55 assume. The four component parts of the union have always been very different whatever history they share in common.

That famous journalist of Scottish heritage Claud Cockburn used to wonder
60 if "real" Scots were as different from the English as the Chinese. In that sense, British society has always been multicultural, long before the term was even thought of. And it's also worth
65 remembering that people of Caribbean heritage can be surprisingly conservative in these matters. Back when we were all being told that the euro would "inevitably" replace sterling[6], I noticed a
70 distinct lack of enthusiasm for it among my friends and family. It may well be that if the UK is ever replaced by independent countries, black people may find themselves the last Brits standing.

The Guardian (October 12th 2011)

1. /ˌkærɪˈbiːən/   2. /dʒəˈmeɪkən/   3. *grands pontes*   4. /ˈluːsənɪŋ/
5. /ˈwaɪndɪŋ/   6. *livre sterling*

B Understanding the text ORKBOOK → p. 34-35

1. Turn to your *Workbook* for help in understanding the text.
2. Sum up the article.

C Going further

3. What may explain why Caribbean migrants felt "black" first and foremost in the 1960s?
4. What does the journalist mean by *"doing the real work"* (l. 23)?
5. What is ironic about the situation of people with Caribbean or African roots living in Britain today?
6. According to the journalist, why has British society always been multicultural?

D Writing time

7. **Essay** (150-200 words) **M**ÉTHODOLOGIE **Rédiger un essai → p. 172**

To feel at home in a new country, do you think you have to forget your roots?

a. Analysez la question et définissez bien ce que *"feel at home"* signifie pour vous.

b. Pensez aux difficultés que cette situation présente et à ce qui peut vous manquer.

c. Donnez des exemples précis pour étayer vos arguments.

d. Utilisez la *Toolbox* et les *Expressions utiles pour communiquer*, p. 173.

E Language training

8. **Savoir prononcer** 24-25 7-8 **W**ORKBOOK → p. 35

Place de l'accent dans les mots se terminant par *-al*, *-ic* et *-ity* – La place de l'accent de mot

9. **Pratiquer la grammaire**

Prétérit et *present perfect* **LANGUAGE WORKSHOP → p. 82**

Used to / be used to / get used to **W**ORKBOOK → p. 36

toolbox

Nouns
- tie: *lien*
- country of origin
- newcomer
- homeland = country of birth
- segregation
- civil rights
- heritage: *patrimoine culturel*

Adjectives & adverbs
- nowadays
- long-standing: *de longue date*

- at the time: *à l'époque*
- side by side
- political

Verbs & expressions
- weaken: *(s')affaiblir*
- loosen: *(se) distendre*
- turn out to be: *se révéler*
- be prone to V: *être enclin à V*
- bring up: *élever (un enfant)*
- reject
- feel homesick: *avoir le mal du pays*

 Your task

 Prepare a recording for an e-twinning project

Your class is twinned with a class in Brixton.
One of the pupils in the Brixton class, whose family emigrated from Jamaica in the fifties, sends you a recording. Put yourself into his / her shoes and imagine what he / she said about his / her family's past life in Britain and about his / her life there today.

MÉTHODOLOGIE
EXPRESSION ORALE EN CONTINU → p. 163

Language workshop

A Les propositions en -*ING* ⓟRÉCIS GRAMMATICAL → 34B, 35B

① Construire une proposition en -*ING*

1. "(…) if there's one thing people of my age cannot stand hearing, it's people of your age **giving us lectures on morality**." (Text 1, p. 76, l. 24)
2. I'm sick of him / his **telling me the same old stories**.

a. Les formes -*ING* en gras sont précédées d'un sujet. Indiquez pour chacun s'il s'agit d'un groupe nominal, d'un pronom sujet, d'un pronom complément ou d'un possessif. **b.** Traduisez les énoncés.

② Reformulez les énoncés à l'aide d'une proposition en -*ING*.

a. He's cheating on other people. I don't like it.   → I don't like…
b. I didn't want to talk to Clive but he insisted on it.   → He insisted on…
c. They keep telling me I have no values. I can't stand it.   → I can't stand…
d. He works in a night club. There's nothing wrong with it.   → There's nothing wrong with…
e. You're not sleeping well. I'm worried about it.   → I'm worried about…

③ *FOR*... *V-ING* et *FOR* ... *TO* : but ou cause ?

1. (…) looking (…) embarrassed **for having spoken so passionately**. (Text 1, p. 77, l. 40)
2. He stood up **for her to see the look on his face**.

a. Laquelle de ces propositions indique le but et laquelle la cause ? **b.** Quelle est la construction du verbe correspondante dans chaque cas : forme -*ING* ou infinitif en *TO* ? **c.** Traduisez les énoncés.

④ Formez des propositions complètes à l'aide de *FOR*... *V-ING* ou *FOR*... *to*. Puis traduisez.

a. She blamed him (not – answer) her.   **c.** Here is some money (he – buy) a new PC.
b. I did it (they – admire me).   **d.** He thanked her (be – so nice to him).

B Prétérit et *present perfect* ⓟRÉCIS GRAMMATICAL → 4-7

⑤ Valeur des formes verbales

1. The wave of Caribbean migrants who **arrived** in Britain from the late 1940s to the first immigration acts in the early 1960s (…). (Text 2, p. 80, l. 3)
2. Since the 1960s, black academics (…) **have been debating** what "black British" might actually mean. (Text 2, p. 80, l. 16)
3. In the meantime, social, cultural and economic change **has**, as usual, **been doing** the real work. (Text 2, p. 80, l. 21)
4. This question **has** already **been debated**. There's nothing else to say.

a. Identifiez et nommez chaque forme verbale en gras et indiquez si elle exprime **1.** le résultat présent d'une action ; **2.** la continuité d'une action qui a commencé dans le passé et a des conséquences dans le présent ou **3.** la rupture avec le moment présent.
b. Traduisez les énoncés. Lequel doit-on nécessairement traduire par un présent ? Pourquoi ?

⑥ Mettez les verbes entre parenthèses au prétérit ou au *present perfect BE+ING*.

a. The word first (appear) in the late 1960s and we (use) it since then.
b. They (live) in Britain for ages and (do) the same job for years now.
c. They (defend) our rights since we (arrive) in Britain.

⑦ Traduisez à l'aide du prétérit ou du *present perfect BE+ING*.

a. Pendant longtemps, ils ont pensé qu'ils étaient différents. **b.** Depuis les années soixante, les choses changent rapidement. **c.** Depuis longtemps, ils essaient de définir leur identité.

Grammaire de l'oral | Comprendre et produire le passif à l'oral

8 **Prononcer les formes passives**

a. Écoutez ces énoncés et indiquez quelles sont les syllabes accentuées.

    1. *The authorities said only ten people were injured and several dozen arrested.* (Listeners' corner, p. 78)

    2. *Teaching budgets have been cut by 40%.*

b. Déduisez : les auxiliaires sont-ils accentués ? Qu'en est-il de la préposition *by* ?

9 **Comprendre les formes verbales dans un énoncé à l'oral**

Écoutez ces énoncés et indiquez si la forme entendue est la forme **1** ou **2**.

a. 1. *… smashed…*   **a. 2.** *… were smashed…*

b. 1. *Britain has been largely untouched…*   **b. 2.** *Britain's people largely untouched…*

c. 1. *He's never been interviewed…*   **c. 2.** *He is now being interviewed…*

10 **Produire des énoncés passifs à l'oral**

Reformulez à l'oral à la voix passive chacun des énoncés suivants et vérifiez à l'écoute. Puis, répétez la réponse proposée. (Attention à l'accentuation !)

    1. *They have organized the march to protest against the government's plan.*

    2. *They will have to find new funding.*   **3.** *They are filming the leader of the group.*

Lexique | Le Royaume-Uni

Assurez-vous que vous avez bien retenu les mots clés de l'unité. **→ Keywords p. 72**

11 **Sélectionnez la bonne transcription phonétique des mots suivants.**

a. *monarchy*:   **1.** /ˈmɒnəkɪst/   **2.** /ˈmɒnəkɪ/   **3.** /ˈmɒnək/

b. *Parliament*:   **1.** /ˌpɑːləˈmentərɪ/   **2.** /ˌpɑːˈləmənt/   **3.** /ˈpɑːləmənt/

c. *vibrant*:   **1.** /ˈvaɪbrənt/   **2.** /ˈvaɪbrənsɪ/   **3.** /ˈvɪbrənt/

d. *heir*:   **1.** /hɛə/   **2.** /hɪə/   **3.** /ɛə/

12 **À quoi correspondent les acronymes suivants ? a.** PM   **b.** MP

13 **Quelle est la syllabe accentuée dans les mots suivants ?**

a. innovative **b.** prejudice **c.** democracy **d.** assimilate **e.** government **f.** tolerance

14 **Complétez les phrases à l'aide des mots suivants. Plusieurs réponses sont parfois possibles.**

climb the social ladder – do one's best – succeed – customs – underprivileged – next in line – wealthy – determined – close the gap – royal family – be successful – equality of opportunity – blend in – figureheads

a. To ..1.. and ..2.. in your job you need to be ..3.. and to have good qualifications.

b. He should ..4.. to respect local ..5.. if he wants to ..6.. and feel integrated.

c. As ..7.. of the nation the Queen and the ..8.. often represent Britain abroad.

d. ..9.. should help to ..10.. between the ..11.. and the ..12.. .

e. Prince Charles will ..13.. Queen Elizabeth II because he is ..14.. to the throne.

toolbox

Verbs & expressions

- deny V-ING: *nier avoir…*
- reproach sb with V-ING: *reprocher à qqn de…*
- blame sb for V-ING: *reprocher à qqn de…*
- object to sth: *être opposé à qqch*
- I can't stand V-ING: *Je ne supporte pas de…*
- It's no use V-ING: *Ce n'est pas la peine de…*

Have a discussion with your parents
You took part in a protest march and did not come home until very late at night. The next day your parents tell you that you acted in an irresponsible way. Act out the conversation. Use **gerunds (V-ING)** as often as possible.

Kings and queens on screen

The kings and queens of Britain have inspired more than one film-maker.

Compare the different film posters and stills on these two pages. What similarities and differences are there in the way kings and queens are presented?

 A **Henry VIII and his Six Wives**

Read the text and find out why Henry VIII (1491-1547) had six wives. What was the consequence of the annulment of his first marriage?

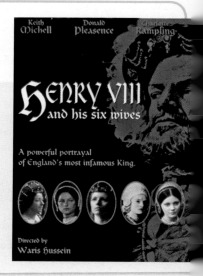

Warris HUSSEIN, GB (1972)

"Divorced, beheaded, died; Divorced, beheaded, survived."
This popular rhyme tells of the fate of Henry VIII's six wives.
In the film, Tudor King Henry VIII, on his deathbed, reflects on his life and his six marriages, all contracted in the hope of leaving a male heir to the throne to succeed him and so avoid civil war. Catherine of Aragon, his first wife, had only one child who survived, Mary. When the annulment of this first marriage was refused, Henry broke off all relations with the Catholic Church in Rome which led to the establishment of the Church of England and a Protestant Britain. He then married Anne Boleyn who was beheaded for "infidelity" shortly after the birth of her daughter, Elizabeth. His third queen, Jane Seymour, died giving birth to a sickly prince, Edward. He divorced his fourth wife, Anne of Cleves, after just six months of marriage and married Catherine Howard who, as she was childless, was accused of infidelity and decapitated. His last wife, Catherine Parr, survived him.

B **The King's Speech**

1 What constitutional problem led Bertie to be crowned King George VI?

2 What do you think about the subject of this film? In what way is it unusual?

3 The film won 4 Oscars and was also extremely popular. How do you account for its success?

Tom HOOPER, GB (2010)

In 1936, King Edward VIII abdicated shortly after becoming king to marry Mrs Wallis Simpson, an American divorcee whom the government of the day judged unacceptable as wife of the King of England and also head of the Church of England. After his abdication his younger brother was crowned king. The film is the story of this king, King George VI (1895-1952), father of present day Queen Elizabeth II, and an unorthodox speech therapist, Lionel Logue, who helped him overcome his stammer[1]. Logue uses a set of unexpected techniques which enable Bertie, as the king is called by his family, to speak in such a way as to make his stammer a minor problem. Lionel and Bertie's relationship is often antagonistic as Lionel feels the need for the two to be equals during their speech therapy sessions. When England declares war on Nazi Germany in 1939, the King delivers a near faultless, memorable speech heard live around the world by radio. The King and Logue remained lifelong friends.

1. *bégaiement*

C The Queen

1 Look at the still from *The Queen*. What is the Queen (b. 1926) reading about? What do you know about this event? Read the film synopsis to find out more.

Stephen FREARS, GB (2006)

The Queen is a fictional account of the events following the sudden death of Princess Diana in 1997, and differing views on how to handle the tragedy. The Royal Family considers it a private matter and remains in Scotland, hidden from the public, whereas the newly-appointed Prime Minister, Tony Blair, tries to respond to the heartbroken public's demand for an official display of mourning[1]. The film-maker underlines the opposing views of the long-standing Queen and the young, inexperienced Prime Minister. The way the various characters are portrayed, bordering on caricature at times, turns a family tragedy into an amusing and entertaining film. The media and royal protocol regarding Diana's official status complicate the situation. The general public rejects the monarchy seen as cold and aloof[2] while the Prime Minister senses the public's admiration for the "people's princess". However, by the time the film was released, the monarchy was back in favour.

1. deuil 2. hautain

2 What did this film reveal about the impact of this event on the relationship between the monarchy and the British public at the time?

Video time

Elizabeth: The Golden Age DVD

Elizabeth: The Golden Age, Shekhar KAPUR, GB (2007)

A Get ready

1. Read the historical context of this film about Elizabeth I (1533-1603) and look at the poster opposite. What sort of queen do you imagine the film-maker wanted to portray?

In 1585, the world is divided by religious hatred. The new Protestant faith is spreading and Philip of Spain, a devout Catholic, the most powerful ruler in Europe, sees Protestant England, ruled by Elizabeth, as a threat. He wants to make his daughter, Isabella, queen in Elizabeth's place and plans to invade England in retaliation[1] for English piracy of Spanish ships. Walter Raleigh, considered a notorious pirate by the Spanish king, arrives at Elizabeth's court…

1. représailles

B Watch the video

2. Watch the film extract. Your teacher will give you a worksheet to help you.

C In your own words

3. Use the worksheet to summarize what you saw.

D Going further

4. Analyse Elizabeth's personality in this extract.

5. Why do you think Walter Raleigh is made welcome at court?

6. Do you like watching historical films? Explain why or why not.

final task

What is great in Britain?

You went to Britain on a traineeship last summer and have been asked to write an article about your experience in the school magazine. First, you present the content of your article and your choice of illustrations to the editorial team, then, you write the article.

The various documents you have worked on in this unit should help you to find arguments and ideas to make your oral presentation and write your article.

1 Present the content of your article

A Get ready

■ What aspects of Britain do the posters opposite highlight?

■ Who are these posters targeted at (age, sex, interests…)?

■ In your opinion, which ones best represent Britain today? What is great in Britain for you?

B Now speak

Ⓜ ÉTHODOLOGIE
Expliquer et argumenter → p. 163

■ Bearing in mind what you have studied, what aspects of life in Britain will you choose to highlight: multiculturalism, traditions, festivals, education…?

■ Remember the editorial team is made up of young people, so present the topics you choose in a lively way.

■ Speak about two or three of the posters and explain why you would like to use them to illustrate your article.

■ You must use complete sentences and try to link them. If you hesitate, remember you can use gap fillers if necessary.

Je me situe par rapport au CECRL B2

LORSQUE JE FAIS CETTE PRÉSENTATION :
Je peux développer une argumentation claire, nuancée et enchaîner les arguments avec logique.

2 Write your article

Ⓜ ÉTHODOLOGIE
Rédiger un article de presse → p. 172

■ Write your article, making complete sentences and linking them.

■ You should conclude by what you found most interesting and explain what is great in Britain for you.

Je me situe par rapport au CECRL B2

LORSQUE J'ÉCRIS CET ARTICLE :
Je fais une description élaborée de mon expérience et je développe une argumentation dans un texte articulé.

Vous trouverez la présentation de l'épreuve pages 12-13
et des conseils pratiques pour le bac pages 175-179.

Compréhension de l'oral 26 12 ⓦORKBOOK → p. 37

Vous allez écouter trois fois un document intitulé
The UK monarchy debate.

Avant l'écoute

1. Aidez-vous du titre du document de façon à anticiper son contenu.

Première écoute

2. Identifiez la nature du document et le thème général.

Deuxième écoute

3. Relevez les informations principales.

Troisième écoute

4. Relevez des détails significatifs.

Rendez compte en français de ce que vous avez compris.

TIPS

> Repérez les noms propres. De quel débat s'agit-il ?

> Relevez la chronologie des événements importants.

> Relevez les raisons qui motivent ce débat.

Expression orale ⓦORKBOOK → p. 38

Lors de votre prise de parole en continu, puis de la conversation avec l'examinateur,
vous pourrez aborder les problématiques suivantes en lien avec l'unité 4.

Notion 1 **L'idée de progrès**
The idea of progress

■ Paint a picture of modern Britain

Snapshots of Britain, p. 74 • London's changing skyline, p. 75 • Consumerist zombies, p. 76 • Students protest, p. 78 • Black Britons, p. 80

- Décrivez la vie des jeunes Britanniques aujourd'hui (éducation, emploi, loisirs).
- Donnez des exemples concrets de la situation actuelle en Grande-Bretagne dans les domaines politique, architectural et dans la vie quotidienne...

■ Modernity and tradition in Britain

The monarchy: what Britain really wants, p. 74 • A sporting nation, p. 79 • Kings and queens on screen, p. 84 • The United Kingdom, p. 154 • The Thatcher years, p. 154

- Donnez des exemples de tradition (dans les domaines du sport, de l'éducation et de la politique...) et de leur impact de nos jours.
- Exprimez le **contraste** : *On the one hand... on the other hand... Whereas / While... Yet / However / Still...*

Notion 2 **Espaces et échanges**
Places and exchanges

■ Show the diversity of cultures in Britain

The world... at home, p. 74 • A sporting nation, p. 79 • Black Britons, p. 80 • The Commonwealth, p. 154 • The United Kingdom, p. 154

- Soulignez le mélange des cultures en Grande-Bretagne au cours des siècles.
- Montrez les liens entre la Grande-Bretagne et d'autres pays.
- **Situez les événements** sur le plan chronologique : *First / Then / Afterwards / Later / More recently...*

Challenges

At the age of seventeen, the author has won a scholarship to study at a public school in England. He writes about his arrival at his new school.

Dining Hall at Eton: an elite public school

A few days after going to stay with Shanti Uncle and
5 Aunty Henny, I packed a suitcase and took the train to
Tonbridge. I was to be a boarder, but had to report regularly
by letter and phone to Uncle and Aunty, as well as, of course,
to my parents.

Two large boars' heads made of stone greeted me at the
10 entrance. I was lodged in School House, and in a cavernous
hall had a small wooden cubicle of my own to work and sleep
in. Students were permitted record-players, and the sound of
"Bridge over Troubled Water" in particular wafted over my
first term. Though I had come in at a late stage of school life,
15 when friendships were already formed, the boys were not unwelcoming. Nor, for that matter,
were the masters, though I found my housemaster[1] (who was also the headmaster) daunting[2].

Mr McCrum was tall and distinguished-looking – indeed, at that stage I thought of him
more as a personage than a person – and was later to become headmaster of Eton. Shortly
after my arrival, he gave a lunch for some of the students in School House; I was one of the
20 invitees. Everything was decorous and measured; after sherry we repaired to the dining-
room. A surreptitious[3] glance or two told me which implement[4] everyone else was using,
and I followed suit. But at some stage of the meal, I relaxed my vigilance. Shrimps[5] were
served inside scooped-out apples. I ate both. As I ate, I became aware that the conversation
around me had grown muted. People were staring at me, and when I turned to look at them
25 I noticed something else. On each plate, the shrimps had all been extracted and consumed;
the enclosing apples, however, had been left intact. A shocked silence had descended upon
the table. My fellow schoolboys glanced anxiously towards Mr McCrum. I looked down at
my plate. After a pause, he said, "Yes, I've always thought it rather wasteful not to eat the
apple," and in due course, the plates and my mortification were cleared unpainfully away.
30 In due course, Mr McCrum called me in for a serious chat about my future. It was decided,
with some little input from me, that I should take the special entrance exams for Oxford.
A little later, however, I discovered that one had to have studied a European language to
0-level[6] standard to be accepted at the university. I wrote to the authorities, requesting an
exemption, explaining that I had studied Hindi to the required level but that I would never
35 have had the opportunity to study European languages at my school in India even if I had
wished to. I was told that no waiver[7] would be granted.

When I explained my problem to Shanti Uncle and Aunty Henny, they were worried
for me, especially since they could see how dispirited I was. But shortly afterwards Aunty
Henny sat me down in the drawing-room with a cup of tea and said firmly that there was
40 nothing for it but to accept things as they were, unfair as they might seem. This is what life
was sometimes about.

Vikram SETH, *Two Lives* (2005)

1. *professeur responsable d'un groupe d'élèves*   2. intimidating   3. discrete
4. *ustensile*   5. *crevettes*   6. *niveau de fin de seconde*   7. *dispense*

Vous trouverez la présentation de l'épreuve pages 12-13
et des conseils pratiques pour le bac pages 175-179.

Compréhension de l'écrit

First read the whole text. The photo will help you to imagine the situation and develop arguments to answer some of the questions.

TIPS

1. Who is the main character in this extract? Name the minor characters and explain their relationship with him.

> Lisez toutes les informations données, y compris l'introduction.

2. Explain what a *"boarder"* (l. 6) is. Justify by quoting a sentence.

> Relisez attentivement le deuxième paragraphe.

3. Pick out elements in the text and in the photograph to illustrate the type of school the narrator attended.

> On vous demande de relever des éléments : inutile de faire des phrases complètes.

4. How did the pupils and masters treat the narrator when he first arrived? Quote the text.

5. Use your own words to explain the narrator's embarrassment during the meal. (50 words)

> La photo devrait vous aider à imaginer la situation dans laquelle le narrateur se trouvait.

6. In one sentence, what was his major problem to go to Oxford?

7. Paint a portrait of Mr McCrum and explain the role he played in the narrator's life. (50 words)

8. Explain what Aunty Henny meant by *"This is what life was sometimes about"* (l. 40). (20 words)

9. With the help of the photo, try to explain the narrator's feelings in this passage. (80 words)

> Relisez l'ensemble du texte en portant particulièrement votre attention sur les sentiments du narrateur.

10. Analyse the different challenges facing the narrator to fit into British society. (60 words)

> Mobilisez vos connaissances sur l'histoire de l'Inde et le mélange des cultures en Grande-Bretagne pour étayer vos arguments.

Expression écrite

1. Write about a challenge you had to face.

2. Do you think studying just one foreign language is enough in a global world?

> **Use your grammar**
> • Opposer « idées générales » et « situation particulière » : **fiche 1** (p. 180)
> • Formuler hypothèses et souhaits : **fiche 5** (p. 182)

Unit  5

Lieux et formes du pouvoir
Mythes et héros

Staging ambition

How about going on stage?

 final task Your theatrical company has to perform a scene on the topic "Ambition and drama" for an audition. First, you discuss which scene you should stage, then, you rehearse the scene that you have chosen.

Keywords

Nouns
- playwright /'pleɪraɪt/: *auteur dramatique*
- performance = show
- rehearsal /rɪ'hɜːsəl/: *répétition*
- stage director: *metteur en scène*
- scenery: *décor(s)*
- extra: *figurant*
- stage props: *accessoires*
- stage directions: *indications scéniques*
- prompter: *souffleur*
- stage fright: *trac*
- limelight: *feux de la rampe*
- personality trait
- willpower: *volonté*

Adjectives
- convincing = impressive
- word-perfect: *que l'on connaît sur le bout des doigts*
- motivated
- eager (to V) = keen (to V): *empressé (de)*
- tenacious /tɪ'neɪʃəs/
- single-minded = resolute
- resourceful
- hard-working
- individualistic /ˌɪndɪvɪdjʊə'lɪstɪk/

Verbs & expressions
- interpret a role = act
- aspire to = aim to
- fulfil a dream
- endeavour /ɪn'devə/ = try hard
- be up to: *être à la hauteur de*
- achieve = accomplish
- be intent on V-ING = be determined to V
- speak out = speak loudly and clearly

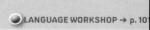

The last battle

1. This scene is from the last act of Shakespeare's *Richard III* in which the ambitious king is killed. Describe the scene briefly.

2. Blood is dripping from the Earl of Richmond's face. Explain why and guess why he looks so triumphant.

3. What does this scene show about the fate of the ambitious *Richard III*?

Improv games

Ⓜ ÉTHODOLOGIE **INTERACTION ORALE** → p. 165

Improvisational[1] games are best known as improv[2] or impro games. In this popular art form, actors or improvisers use acting techniques to perform spontaneously and according to instructions.
You will find three improv games below.
Remember that the main rule is: Don't write anything down, improvise!

1. /ˌɪmprəvaɪˈzeɪʃənl/ **2.** /ˈɪmprɒv/

A Life is a race

Have a discussion about what you intend to do next year.

Ⓜ ÉTHODOLOGIE **Conversation** → p. 165

Two friends have opposite views on what they want to do after high school.
Student A You are career-minded. For you, life is a race. You have decided to apply for an elite university.
Student B You want to take your time before choosing a career and have decided to travel the world next year.

Step 1 – Choose the role you want to have.

Step 2 – Think quickly of the arguments you will put forward to show the advantages of your choice. Be ready to counter the other student who will point out the negative aspects of your project.

Step 3 – Start improvising and act out the conversation which should last 2 to 3 minutes.

B In the limelight

Interview a talent show contestant.
Ⓜ ÉTHODOLOGIE **Interview** → p. 166

Student A You have decided to participate to a talent show.
Student B You interview this contestant to find out his or her motivations and feelings.

Step 1 – Read the document below. You may want to use some of the facts and figures in the course of your interview.

A recent study of 1,032 teenagers revealed that 54% want to be famous when they are older. This far outweighs the number of 16-year-olds who want a medical career (15%), a media job (13%) or the 9% who want to work in the legal field.

Step 2 – Read the extract from an article in *The Times* about *X Factor*, the popular talent show. The headline and the beginning of the article offer contradictory views which you may use as arguments in the interview.

Step 3 – Start improvising and act out the interview (2 to 3 minutes).

X Factor will not make you the next Beyoncé
It's a cruel illusion to sell stardom to karaoke crooners

The 16 million people who watch *X Factor* can't be wrong. The arguments in favour are well-known: it gives people a shot at musical stardom, finds new talent and is harmless fun for all the family.

The Times (September 22nd 2011)

 **No limit!**

Ⓜ**ÉTHODOLOGIE**
Discussion contradictoire → p. 166

Discuss the risks of ambition.

Student A You believe that there's no limit to what you can achieve.
Student B You think that you should have realistic goals to avoid failure.

Step 1 – Describe the situation in the picture. Do you think the singer had realistic goals?

Step 2 – Prepare your arguments. What some famous people said on the subject of ambition may help you.

> **OSCAR WILDE** – "We are all in the gutter[1], but some of us are looking at the stars."
>
> **MARK TWAIN** – "Keep away from people who belittle[2] your ambitions. Small people always do that, but the great make you feel that you, too, can become great."
>
> **JOSEPH CONRAD** – "I think all ambitions are lawful except those which climb upwards on the miseries or credulities of mankind."
>
> 1. *caniveau*   2. *rabaisser*

Step 3 – Now present your arguments. Then, discuss each other's arguments. Speak in turn using complete sentences. The discussion should last 2 to 3 minutes.

toolbox

Nouns
- gap year: *année sabbatique*
- fame = glory
- audience: *public*
- auditorium: *salle de spectacle*

Adjectives
- overseas: *à l'étranger*
- talented = gifted
- boundless (ambition): *sans bornes*

Verbs & expressions
- backpack: *voyager sac au dos*
- broaden (one's horizons) /həˈraɪzns/: *élargir (ses horizons)*
- make it to the top: *atteindre le sommet*
- climb /klaim/ the social ladder
- concentrate = focus on
- compete
- perform: *se produire*
- look forward to V-ING: *être impatient de*

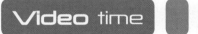 

Pygmalion

Pygmalion,
John GLENISTER (1981)

A Get ready

1. What does the woman in the picture do for a living? Can you imagine what her ambition is?

B Watch the video

2. Watch an extract from the film adaptation of *Pygmalion*, a play written by George Bernard Shaw in 1914. Your teacher will give you a worksheet to help you.

C In your own words

3. Give an oral account of the episode that you saw.

D Going further

4. What do you know about the Greek myth of Pygmalion?

5. Guess why the play by Bernard Shaw is called *Pygmalion*.

Educating Rita

culture key The Open University → p. 155

Willy RUSSELL

(1947) became a women's hairdresser when he left school at 15. Later, he went to college and became a schoolteacher. In 1986, he wrote the lyrics and score for his popular musical, *Blood Brothers*. He is a novelist, playwright, screenwriter, musician and composer. Russell has strong views on the working classes' attempts to gain access to middle-class culture.

A Warming up

Read the *Culture key* and the introduction and explain why Rita has chosen to take up a course at the Open University.

Rita White is a 26-year-old working-class girl. She works as a hairdresser and has taken up an Open University course. Frank Bryant is her tutor. The scene takes place in Frank's office.

Rita bursts through the door, out of breath.

5 **FRANK:** What are you doing here? *(He looks at his watch.)* It's Thursday, you…

RITA *(moving over to the desk; quickly)*: I know I shouldn't be here, it's me dinner hour, but listen, I've gotta tell someone, have you got a few minutes, can y' spare…?

FRANK *(alarmed)*: My God, what is it?

10 **RITA:** I had to come and tell y', Frank, last night, I went to the theatre! A proper one, a professional theatre.

Frank gets up and switches off the radio and then returns to the swivel[1] chair.

FRANK *(sighing)*: For God's sake, you had me worried, I thought it was something serious.

15 **RITA:** No, listen, it was. I went out an' got me ticket, it was Shakespeare, I thought it was gonna be dead borin'…

FRANK: Then why did you go in the first place?

RITA: I wanted to find out. But listen, it wasn't borin', it was bleedin' great, honest, ogh, it done me in[2], it was fantastic. I'm gonna do an essay on it.

20 **FRANK** *(smiling)*: Come on, which one was it?

Rita moves up right centre.

RITA: "… Out, out brief candle!
Life's but a walking shadow, a poor player
That struts[3] and frets[4] his hour upon the stage
25 And then is heard no more. It is a tale
Told by an idiot, full of sound and fury
Signifying nothing."

FRANK *(deliberately):* Ah, *Romeo and Juliet.*

RITA *(moving towards Frank):* Tch. Frank! Be serious. I learnt that today from the
30 book. *(She produces a copy of* Macbeth.*)* Look, I went out an' bought the book.
Isn't it great? What I couldn't get over is how exciting it was.

Frank puts his feet up on the desk.

RITA: Wasn't his wife a cow, eh? An' that fantastic bit where he meets Macduff an'
he thinks he's all invincible. I was on the edge of me seat at that bit. I wanted to
35 shout an' tell Macbeth, warn him.

FRANK: You didn't, did you?

RITA: Nah. Y' can't do that in a theatre, can y'? It was dead good. It was like a
thriller.

FRANK: Yes. You'll have to go and see more.

40 RITA: I'm goin' to. *Macbeth's* a tragedy, isn't it?

Frank nods.

RITA: Right. *(Rita smiles at Frank and he smiles back at her.)* Well I just – just had
to tell someone who'd understand.

FRANK: I'm honoured that you chose me.

45 RITA *(moving towards the door):* Well, I better get back. I've left a customer with a
perm[5] lotion. If I don't get a move on there'll be another tragedy.

Willy RUSSELL, Educating Rita (1980), Act I, Scene 6

---

1. *chaise pivotante*   2. *cela m'a achevée* (informal)
3. *se pavaner*   4. *s'agiter*   5. *permanente*

B Understanding the text   ⓌORKBOOK → p. 39-40

1. Turn to your *Workbook* for help in understanding the text.

2. Explain why Rita was so eager to talk to her tutor.

C Going further

3. Why did Rita go to the theatre?

4. How did Rita react while and after watching the play? Why did she choose to talk to her tutor about it?

5. In your opinion, why did Rita choose to recite this passage from *Macbeth*?

6. Analyse Frank's reactions during the scene.

7. What does Rita's behaviour reveal about her character?

D Language training

8. Savoir prononcer
27-28   14-15

L'intonation

9. Pratiquer la grammaire

Traduction de « devoir »   ●LANGUAGE WORKSHOP → p. 100

Will et *be going to* – Présent simple et présent en *BE+ING*

ⓌORKBOOK → p. 44

---

toolbox

Nouns
- enthusiasm
- intrusion
- hunger for knowledge
- (contrary to) expectation(s)

Adjectives
- enthusiastic = thrilled
- grateful: *reconnaissant*
- nihilistic

Verbs & expressions
- improve (one's mind)
- break away from: *s'échapper de*
- take one's breath away: *couper le souffle*
- satisfy one's curiosity
- have an impact on
- pretend: *faire semblant*
- relieve: *soulager*
- have the nerve / cheek: *avoir le culot*
- break down barriers

Write an essay about Rita's reactions to *Macbeth*

Rita says *"I'm gonna do an essay on it"* (l. 19). Imagine Rita's essay and write it down in standard English. (150-200 words)

 MÉTHODOLOGIE
Rédiger des phrases correctes → p. 170

First day on the job

A The topic

1. You are going to listen to an extract from *The Typists*, a play by Murray Schisgal.

Look at the pictures and say where and when the scene takes place.

B Open your ears

2. Listen to three sentences spoken by the two characters and deduce what the situation is and which photo illustrates it.

C Listen 🅦 ORKBOOK → p. 41

3. Listen to the recording and check your answers to questions **1** and **2**. You will find some help in your *Workbook*.

D In your own words

4. Explain what Paul Cunningham has decided to do and why.

Nouns
- employee
- office hours
- task
- opportunity
- target = goal

Adjectives
- conscientious /ˌkɒnʃɪˈenʃəs/
- hopeful

Verbs & expressions
- demand: *exiger*
- be on time
- be in charge of
- get a raise: *obtenir une augmentation*
- succeed in ≠ fail

function box

Expressing intention
- I'm going to
- I'm about to V
- I plan / mean / intend / aim to V
- I've decided to V
- My intention is to V
- I'm definitely V-ING
- I'm determined to V

Your task

Act out a conversation between Paul, the employee, and his boss
The boss has asked Paul to come to his office. Decide who you want to be, then reverse roles.

Ⓜ **ÉTHODOLOGIE**
Conversation → p. 165

Writers' corner

Reaching for the stars

Your ask

Script writing

You have joined the Drama writing workshop. A director wants to stage an adaptation of a novel by Douglas Kennedy. You have been asked to write the script of the scene which follows this extract from the novel. (200 words)

Ⓜ️ÉTHODOLOGIE EXPRESSION ÉCRITE → p. 170

A Get ready

1. Read the text and answer the following questions:
a. What is the narrator's social background?
b. Look at the cover of *Esquire* and say who the magazine is targeted at. What did the narrator dream of?
c. What was his mother's opinion?

W hen I was sixteen, my dad came into my room one night and found me reading *Esquire* in bed.

It represented the metropolitan world to which I aspired. I saw myself living the New York life, eating in those designer[1] restaurants that *Esquire* featured, dressing in those $600 suits that adorned[2] their fashion pages, talking the urban buzz talk that seemed second nature to their writers. Not because I craved these actual things – but because they struck me as essential components of true success.

Of course my dad knew this – just as he also knew that my mom encouraged me to have ambitions beyond Brunswick and the US Navy[3].

"Take it from me," she said when I was struggling through my college applications[4]. "There's only one person in the whole wide world who will ever stop you from getting to where you want to be – and that's yourself."

Douglas KENNEDY, *The Job* (1998)

1. fashionable   2. *orner*   3. The father works at the US Navy Station located near Brunswick, a small town in Maine.   4. *dossiers d'inscription à la fac*

B Prepare the story

2. The scene that you have to write is a discussion between Ned, the narrator, and his parents. Imagine what the young man decided to do.

3. Decide whether Ned's parents approved of his future plans.

C Write the script

4. Use direct speech only.

5. Don't forget to give clear stage directions (between brackets).

• Describe the setting and the various props that should be on stage.

• Use adverbs and short sentences to indicate the way the actors should speak, for instance: *(Sharply.)* – *(In a gentle voice.)* – *(He laughs.)* – *(Still laughing.)*…

• Give precise directions about the way the actors should move, for instance: *(He turns and moves away.)* – *(Rising and putting on her glasses.)* – *(Patting his shoulder gently)*…

function box

Expressing wishes
● I feel like GN / V-ING: *J'ai envie de*
● If only I V (*prétérit modal*)
● I wish I V (*prétérit modal*)
● I'm looking forward to V-ING
● I'm dying to V
● I plan / mean / intend / aim to V

Expressing doubts, protest
● I am rather sceptical about…
● In theory, it sounds… but in practice…
● On the face of it, it seems… but in reality…
● I object to / disapprove of / protest against…

Text 2

Friends, Romans, countrymen...

culture key The Tragedy of Julius Caesar → p. 155

William SHAKESPEARE

(1564-1616). The man remains an enigma in spite of his immense fame over the centuries. Born in a small provincial English town, he went up to London and began writing for the stage. *Julius Caesar* falls into the category of Shakespeare's tragedies (the other categories being comedies and history plays).

A Warming up

This picture is a still from the 1953 film adaptation by Joseph L. Mankiewicz of Shakespeare's play, *Julius Caesar* (starring Marlon Brando and James Mason).

First, read the introduction, then, describe the picture and guess who the characters are.

Rome, 44BC. Caesar was assassinated in the Capitol by a group of conspirators led by Brutus who addressed the crowd and justified his actions in these words: "As Caesar loved me, I weep¹ for him; as he was fortunate, I rejoice at it; as he was valiant, I honour him; but, as he was ambitious, I slew² him."

5 *Brutus allows Mark Antony to speak at Caesar's funeral as long as he does not criticize the conspirators.*

FIRST CITIZEN: This Caesar was a tyrant.
SECOND CITIZEN: Nay, that's certain:
We are bless'd that Rome is rid of him.
10 **THIRD CITIZEN:** Peace! Let us hear what
  Antony can say.
MARK ANTONY: Friends, Romans,
  countrymen, lend me your ears;
I come to bury Caesar, not to praise him.
15 The evil that men do lives after them,
The good is oft interred with their bones;
So let it be with Caesar. The noble Brutus
Hath told you Caesar was ambitious.
If it were so, it was a grievous fault,
20 And grievously hath Caesar answer'd it.
Here, under leave of³ Brutus and the rest,
(For Brutus is an honourable man,
So are they all, all honourable men)

Come I to speak in Caesar's funeral.
25 He was my friend, faithful and just to me;
But Brutus says he was ambitious,
And Brutus is an honourable man.
He hath brought many captives home to
  Rome,
30 Whose ransoms did the general coffers fill:
Did this in Caesar seem ambitious?
When the poor have cried, Caesar hath wept;
Ambition should be made of sterner stuff⁴:
Yet Brutus says he was ambitious,
35 And Brutus is an honourable man.
You all did see that on the Lupercal⁵
I thrice presented him a kingly crown,
Which he did thrice refuse. Was this
  ambition?
40 Yet Brutus says he was ambitious,

And sure he is an honourable man.
I speak not to disprove[6] what Brutus spoke,
But here I am to speak what I do know.
You all did love him once, not without
45   cause;
What cause withholds[7] you then to mourn
   for him?
O judgment, thou art fled to brutish beasts,
And men have lost their reason. Bear with
50   me[8].

My heart is in the coffin there with Caesar,
And I must pause till it come back to me.
First Citizen: Methinks there is much
   reason in his sayings.
55 **Second Citizen:** If thou consider rightly of
   the matter, Caesar has had great wrong.

William SHAKESPEARE,
Julius Caesar (1599), Act III, Scene 2

1. weep – wept – wept: *pleurer* **2.** slay – slew – slain: *tuer* **3.** with the permission of **4.** stronger material **5.** Roman festival of purification celebrated on 15th February, the day on which Caesar was murdered **6.** *réfuter* **7.** *retenir* **8.** *Accordez-moi un instant*

B Understanding the text ⦿ORKBOOK → p. 42-43

1. Turn to your *Workbook* which will help you to understand the text.

2. Sum up the passage.

C Going further

3. What is Mark Antony's aim in delivering his speech?

4. What arguments does he put forward to convince his listeners?

5. Can you see any evidence of irony in his speech? Give examples.

6. How does Mark Antony manage to speak his mind without criticizing the conspirators?

7. Why does Mark Antony say he needs to pause at the end of his speech?

8. Analyse the attitude of the crowd. Does Mark Antony reach his goal?

D Writing time

9. Essay (150-200 words) Ⓜéthodologie
Rédiger un essai → p. 172

In what way can it be said that Mark Antony's speech is a perfect example of political rhetoric?

a. Analysez les procédés rhétoriques utilisés par Marc Antoine pour convaincre les Romains.

b. Recherchez sur Internet les discours célèbres d'hommes politiques, par exemple Martin Luther King (*I have a dream*), Winston Churchill (discours pendant la Seconde Guerre mondiale), Barack Obama (pendant sa campagne électorale).

c. Comparez-les au discours de Mark Antony et relevez les similitudes dans les techniques oratoires.

E Language training

10. Savoir prononcer **29-30**  **20-21** ⦿ORKBOOK → p. 43

La prononciation de la lettre *-h-*
L'accent de mot

11. Pratiquer la grammaire

Pronoms relatifs ⬤LANGUAGE WORKSHOP → p. 100
So, neither ⦿ORKBOOK → p. 44

toolbox

Nouns
- funeral oration: *oraison funèbre*
- good deed: *bonne action*
- plea: *appel, supplication*
- plot: *complot*
- revenge = vengeance
- rhetorical skill

Adjectives
- eloquent
- ungrateful: *ingrat*
- sarcastic

Verbs & expressions
- pretend to: *feindre de*

- acknowledge /əkˈnɒlɪdʒ/: *reconnaître*
- counter = refute (an argument)
- manipulate
- sway (the audience): *influencer fortement (l'assistance)*
- turn sb against
- avenge: *venger*
- prove sb wrong
- gain (the trust)
- sympathize: *montrer de la compassion*
- deceive: *tromper*

Your task

Recite Mark Antony's speech
You've been offered the role of Mark Antony in the coming school play and you rehearse the beginning of his speech (to l. 31). Copy out these lines and indicate pauses with slashes, underline the stressed words and circle word stress in polysyllabic words. Indicate the intonation with arrows. Now rehearse your role. Then, recite it.

Ⓜéthodologie
ÉCOUTER ET PRONONCER → p. 158

A Traduction de « devoir » ℗RÉCIS GRAMMATICAL → 12, 13, 16

1 Must, should et have to

1. *"You'll have to go and see more."* (Text 1, p. 95, l. 39)
2. *"I had to come and tell y' (…)"* (Text 1, p. 94, l. 10)
3. *You don't have to apologize. There's nothing wrong with what you said.*
4. *You're being arrogant! You mustn't talk to me like that.*
5. *You must tell me what to do! I haven't got a clue!*
6. *"I know I shouldn't be here (…)."* (Text 1, p. 94, l. 6)
7. *You should have told me you were going to the theatre.*
8. *He asked her to play the part, didn't he? She must have felt terribly excited!*

a. Qu'exprime chacune des formes verbales en gras : l'obligation / la nécessité – l'interdiction / l'absence d'obligation – la pression / le conseil / le reproche – la probabilité ?

b. Lesquelles de ces formes (énoncés **1** à **5**) expriment « la pression sur autrui » ? Lesquelles sont des formes modales ?

c. Traduisez les énoncés **1** à **8**.

2 Traduisez à l'aide de *should, must* ou *have to*.

a. Il y avait trop de bruit et j'ai dû partir. **b.** Je n'aurais pas dû vous mentir. **c.** Tu ne devrais pas l'écouter. **d.** Est-il nécessaire que j'apprenne cela ? **e.** Je n'ai pas eu besoin de l'appeler. **f.** Il a dû se sentir très seul. Tu ne crois pas ? **g.** Il vous faudra trouver un autre professeur.

B Pronoms relatifs ℗RÉCIS GRAMMATICAL → 38

3 Who, whose, that et which

1. *"(…) conspirators led by Brutus who addressed the crowd (…)"* (Text 2, p. 98, l. 1)
2. *"The evil that men do lives after them"* (Text 2, p. 98, l. 15)
3. *"He hath brought many captives home to Rome, / Whose ransoms did the general coffers fill"* (Text 2, p. 98, l. 28)
4. *"I thrice presented him a kingly crown, / Which he did thrice refuse."* (Text 2, p. 98, l. 37)
5. *The people that he was in charge of were his best supporters.*
6. *It was the only thing that he remembered.*

a. Indiquez pour chaque relatif ci-dessus quel est l'antécédent et si celui-ci est humain ou non humain. Qu'en déduisez-vous à propos de *that*?

b. Dans quels énoncés pourrait-on supprimer *that* et quelle est alors sa fonction : sujet ou complément de la proposition relative ?

c. Quel relatif exprime la possession et peut donc être traduit par « dont »? Traduisez l'énoncé **5** à l'aide du verbe prépositionnel « avoir la responsabilité **de** ». Quel relatif utilisez-vous en français ? Traduisez de la même manière l'énoncé **6** à l'aide de « se souvenir **de** ». Déduisez : dans quels cas peut-on traduire un relatif anglais par le relatif « dont »?

4 Traduisez à l'aide de *whose* ou *ø* (= *that* effacé).

a. Il avait utilisé (*pluperfect BE+ING*) le nom d'un autre homme dont le passeport avait été volé.

b. C'était quelqu'un dont je n'avais jamais entendu parler.

c. Qu'est-il arrivé à ceux dont les maisons ont été détruites?

d. C'était quelque chose dont il était capable.

e. Voici l'homme dont je vous ai parlé.

f. Est-ce que vous comprenez ce dont il parle?

Grammaire de l'oral | **L'accentuation des mots grammaticaux**

⑤ Mots grammaticaux accentués et non accentués 22

a. Écoutez ces énoncés et dites quelles sont les syllabes accentuées à l'oral.

1. *"That's funny."* **2.** *"First day on the job…"* **3.** *"I don't like telling anyone what to do."* **4.** *"What are you studying?"* **5.** *"I did it myself, with my own sweat and my own money."*

b. Recherchez dans les énoncés ci-dessus un ou plusieurs mots correspondant aux catégories grammaticales suivantes et indiquez dans chaque cas si ces mots sont accentués dans les énoncés que vous avez entendus : auxiliaire placé entre d'autres éléments – auxiliaire à la forme négative – pronom personnel – pronom réfléchi – pronom indéfini – article – démonstratif – déterminant possessif – mot interrogatif en *wh-* – préposition – *to* de l'infinitif.

c. Déduisez : Parmi les mots grammaticaux, les … ne sont pas accentués, mais en revanche, les … sont accentués.

⑥ Quelles sont les syllabes qui seront accentuées à l'oral dans les énoncés ci-dessous ? Dites-les à haute voix et vérifiez à l'écoute. 23

1. *I got on the wrong train by mistake.*
2. *He's very strict when it comes to being here on time.*
3. *Of course I won't say anything to him about this morning.*

Lexique | **Théâtre et ambition**

Assurez-vous que vous avez bien retenu les mots clés de l'unité. → **Keywords p. 90**

⑦ Quelle est la syllabe accentuée dans les mots suivants ?

a. *motivated* **b.** *resourceful* **c.** *individualistic* **d.** *intent* **e.** *determined*

⑧ Donnez les synonymes des mots suivants.

a. *show* **b.** *convincing* **c.** *keen* **d.** *aspire to* **e.** *resolute*

⑨ Traduisez : **a.** décor **b.** accessoire **c.** volonté **d.** s'efforcer de **e.** parler fort et clairement

⑩ Complétez les phrases à l'aide des mots suivants en faisant les changements nécessaires.

tenacious – fulfill – stage fright – hard-working – playwright – stage directions – prompter – interpret – achieve – director – up to the role – word-perfect – rehearsal – limelight – extra

a. *He has always wanted to be in the ..1.. He has now ..2.. his dream.*
b. *Even though there was a ..3.., the stage ..4.. wanted the actors to be ..5...*
c. *She is ..6.. and ..7.., I'm sure she will ..8.. her goal.*
d. *The ..9.. gave many ..10.. about the way the actors should ..11.. their roles.*
e. *She was afraid of not being ..12.. and had ..13...*
f. *The ..14.. are not needed during the first ..15...*

toolbox

Verbs & expressions
- I don't find / think it necessary to
- There's no point in V-ING: *Ça ne sert à rien de…*
- keep a balance: *maintenir un équilibre*
- fret over sth: *se faire du souci à propos de qqch*
- feel low: *être déprimé*
- set goals: *fixer des objectifs*

Your task

Express your disagreement
Your parents think you should raise your expectations and be more ambitious. You post a comment on your blog trying to explain why you don't agree. Use **must**, **should** ou **have to**.

Shakespeare and ambition

As a contemporary of Shakespeare wrote, "Shakespeare is not of an age, but for all time".

culture key   William Shakespeare → p. 155

In Shakespeare's plays, ambition is perceived negatively. Metaphorically, it is a bubble which grows and grows until it eventually bursts. Ambition is an evil force, which will inevitably lead a character to ruin. Here are some examples of ambitious characters, from a tragedy, a comedy and a history play.

 A tragedy: *Macbeth*

1 Read the plot summary of *Macbeth* and explain what the picture illustrates.

2 Read the passage from Lady Macbeth's speech and answer the following questions.

a. What is Lady Macbeth's response to the witches' prediction?
b. What problem does she nonetheless foresee?
c. What words in the passage underline the contradictions in Macbeth's character?

Macbeth meets three witches who foretell that he will become king of Scotland, a prediction which corresponds to his own ambitions. Goaded[1] by his wife, he decides to kill the present king and make the witches' words come true.

LADY MACBETH: … [thou] shalt[2] be
What thou art promised: yet I do fear thy nature;
It is too full o'th' milk of human kindness
To catch the nearest way: thou wouldst[3] be great;
Art not without ambition, but without
The illness[4] should attend it: What thou wouldst highly[5],
That wouldst thou holily[6]; wouldst not play false,
And yet wouldst wrongly win.

Macbeth (1606), Act I, Scene 5

1. *incité*   2. you will   3. you want to   4. *(ici)* méchanceté   5. to become king
6. *(ici)* honestly

 A comedy: *Twelfth Night*

1 Read the plot summary of *Twelfth Night* and the passage from the play. Who is supposed to have written the letter that Malvolio is reading? Explain its content in your own words.

2 Do you think that the trick of the letter will work with Malvolio? Why?

Malvolio is Countess Olivia's steward[1]. He is unpleasant and disapproving and never misses an opportunity to criticize Olivia's uncle, Sir Toby Belch, and his friends for their debauched behaviour. They decide to get their revenge and trick him into believing that the Countess loves him, by means of a counterfeit letter. Malvolio is easily duped into believing the truth of the letter.

MALVOLIO, *reading the letter*: "If this fall into thy hand, revolve. In my stars I am above thee, but be not afraid of greatness. Some are born great, some achieve greatness, and some have greatness thrust upon[2] 'em. Thy fates open their hands[3], let thy blood and spirit embrace them, and to inure[4] thyself to what thou art like to be, cast thy humble slough[5], and appear fresh. Be opposite with kinsmen[6], surly[7] with servants. Let thy tongue tang arguments of state[8]; put thyself into the trick of singularity. She thus advises thee that sighs for thee."

Twelfth Night (1601), Act II, Scene 5

1. intendant   2. *qui s'impose à eux*   3. *votre sort est là qui vous attend*   4. get used to   5. get rid of your low-class appearance   6. relatives   7. arrogant   8. talk about affairs of state

C A history play: *Richard III*

1 Read the plot summary of *Richard III* (1591) and look at the different representations of the protagonist. In the following list of adjectives, choose the ones which best correspond to Richard's character:

evil − cruel − refined − calculating − single-minded − serene − conquering − compassionate − pitiless − understanding − sly (*sournois*)

> *Richard, Duke of Gloucester, longs to become King of England. He decides to use all possible means to make his dream come true. He therefore sets out to eliminate all those who stand between himself and the crown, including members of his own family. He finally achieves his goal, but his success is short-lived.*

2 Read the press reviews of a performance of *Richard III* with Kevin Spacey in the leading role. What aspects of Richard III's character did Kevin Spacey manage to convey? Which illustration corresponds to his performance?

• An often electrifying performance which brilliantly identifies the two forces that drive the 'poisonous, hunch-backed toad[1]' − heartless ambition and a profound self-loathing[2]. (*The Daily Telegraph*)

• Spacey doesn't radically overthrow[3] the concept of Richard as the satanic joker[4]. What he offers us is his own subtle variations on it: a Richard in whom instinctive comic brio is matched by a power-lust[5] born of intense self-hatred[2]. (*The Guardian*)

1. crapaud bossu 2. haine de soi 3. démolir 4. clown / idiot 5. désir de pouvoir

Webquest · Shakespeare forever TICE

Shakespeare's plays have directly or indirectly inspired a huge number of films.

1 Choose one of Shakespeare's plays and browse the web to find out about the film adaptations which have been made of it (number, languages, film directors, actors…).
Give an oral account of your findings.

2 Choose a scene from a play and browse the web to find extracts from this scene. Compare how different film directors filmed it.
You can choose a scene that you have studied (Brutus and Mark Antony's speeches − Lady Macbeth's speech) or a scene from a play you particularly like (Hamlet's soliloquy − the balcony scene in *Romeo and Juliet*…).

◀ ▶ **Web resources** ●○○

- www.screenonline.org.uk/film
- bufvc.ac.uk/shakespeare/
- absoluteshakespeare.com/trivia/films/films.htm

final task

How about going on stage?

Your theatrical company has to perform a scene on the topic "Ambition and drama" for an audition. First, you discuss which scene you should stage, then, you rehearse the scene that you have chosen.

1 Discuss the choice of scene

Ⓜ ÉTHODOLOGIE **INTERACTION ORALE** → p. 165

Group work

■ The main topic of the scene that you are going to present is ambition. In groups, discuss whether you want to show the positive or negative values of ambition.

■ Then decide on the scene which best corresponds to the aspect of ambition you want to highlight.
You have to choose a scene from one of the play extracts you have studied: *Pygmalion* (Video time, p. 93) – *Educating Rita* (Text 1, p. 94) – *The Typists* (Listeners' corner, p. 96) – *Julius Caesar* (Text 2, p. 98). You can also choose to perform your own adaptation for the stage of the novel by Douglas Kennedy (Writers' corner, p. 97).

> ★ ★ ★ ★
> ★ Je me situe
> ★ par rapport
> ★ au CECRL
> ★ **B2**
>
> LORSQUE JE PRENDS PART À CETTE DISCUSSION :
> Je parle avec spontanéité et aisance, je peux exposer mon point de vue, évaluer les points de vue d'autrui, émettre des hypothèses.

2 Rehearse the scene

Ⓜ ÉTHODOLOGIE **INTERACTION ORALE** → p. 165

Group work

■ First, decide on the role you are going to play: the stage director, the stage designer (*décorateur*), the prompter, the actors…

■ Start rehearsing:
– The director and the stage designer must explain how they imagine the scene is acted and the scenery.
– The actors don't have to be word-perfect for the first stage of the rehearsal, the prompter is there to help them.

■ Why not present the scene to the class once you have agreed on the way it should be performed?

> ★ ★ ★ ★
> ★ Je me situe
> ★ par rapport
> ★ au CECRL
> ★ **B2**
>
> QUAND JE PRENDS PART À CETTE RÉPÉTITION :
> Je peux m'exprimer avec efficacité, spontanéité et aisance de manière de plus en plus autonome et exprimer des sentiments avec finesse et précision.

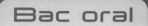

Vous trouverez la présentation de l'épreuve pages 12-13
et des conseils pratiques pour le bac pages 175-179.

Compréhension de l'oral

  31 24 **W**ORKBOOK → p. 45

Vous allez écouter trois fois un document intitulé *J.K. Rowling's speech to Harvard students*.

Avant l'écoute

1. Aidez-vous du titre du document de façon à anticiper son contenu.

Première écoute

2. Identifiez le thème général du document.

Deuxième écoute

3. Relevez les informations principales.

Troisième écoute

4. Rapportez le point de vue du locuteur.

Rendez compte en français de ce que vous avez compris.

TIPS

← Quel peut être le contenu du discours que l'auteur de la saga *Harry Potter* adresse aux étudiants de Harvard ?

← Quelle période de sa vie J.K. Rowling évoque-t-elle ?

← Repérez pour quelles raisons différents domaines d'études sont mentionnés.

← Repérez les rires. Par quoi sont-ils provoqués ?

Expression orale

WORKBOOK → p. 46

Lors de votre prise de parole en continu, puis de la conversation avec l'examinateur, vous pourrez aborder les problématiques suivantes en lien avec l'unité 5.

Notion 1 **Lieux et formes du pouvoir**
Seats and forms of power

■ Ambition in Shakespeare's characters

Friends, Romans, countrymen…, p. 98 • A tragedy: *Macbeth*, p. 102 • A comedy: *Twelfth Night*, p. 102 • A history play: *Richard III*, p. 103 • *The Tragedy of Julius Caesar*, p. 155

← Quel est le but de la plupart des personnages dans les œuvres de Shakespeare étudiées dans l'unité 5 ? Cette quête est-elle présentée de manière positive ?

■ The positive and negative sides of ambition

Pygmalion, p. 93 • Educating Rita, p. 94 • First day on the job, p. 96 • Friends, Romans, countrymen…, p. 98 • Shakespeare and ambition, p. 102

← • Analysez et comparez le but des personnages dans les œuvres étudiées dans l'unité 5.
• Soulignez les conséquences positives ou négatives de leur ambition.
• Exprimez l'**opposition** : *Unlike… On the contrary… Whereas / While…*

Notion 2 **Mythes et héros**
Myths and heroes

■ Shakespeare's universal appeal

Friends, Romans, countrymen…, p. 98 • A tragedy: *Macbeth*, p. 102 • A history play: *Richard III*, p. 103 • Shakespeare forever, p. 103 • William Shakespeare, p. 155

← Parlez des personnages de Shakespeare qui sont devenus des archétypes: Richard III, Lady Macbeth, Mark Antony et aussi, si vous les connaissez, Romeo et Juliet, Hamlet… Pensez également à évoquer les innombrables adaptations de ses pièces, les citations de ses œuvres…

The Crock

The action takes place in the sitting-room of the Crocker-Harris's flat at a Public School in the South of England.

Andrew Crocker-Harris (nicknamed the Crock by his pupils) is a Classics teacher. Millie is his wife and Frank, a science teacher, is Millie's lover. Taplow, one of the Crock's pupils, has just left the room.

5 **MILLIE:** Frank, darling – (*she sits on the arm of the chair and kisses him*) I love you so much.
(*Frank kisses her on the mouth, but a trifle perfunctorily[1], and she rises and breaks quickly away, as if afraid someone had come into the room. He moves below the settee.*)
(*She laughs.*) You're very nervous.

FRANK: I'm afraid of that screen arrangement. You can't see people coming in.

10 **MILLIE:** Oh yes. (*She rises and stands by the fireplace.*) That reminds me. What were you and Taplow up to when I came in just now? Making fun of my husband?

FRANK: Afraid so. Yes.

MILLIE: It sounded rather a good imitation. I must get him to do it for me sometime. It was very naughty[2] of you to encourage him.

15 **FRANK:** I know. It was.

MILLIE (*ironically*)**:** Bad for discipline.

FRANK (*sitting on the settee*)**:** Exactly. Currying favour[3] with the boys, too. My God, how easy it is to be popular. I've only been a master three years, but I've already slipped into an act and a vernacular[4] that I just can't get out of. Why can't anyone ever be natural with the little
20 blighters[5]?

MILLIE: They probably wouldn't like it if you were. (*She crosses below the settee and moves above the table.*)

FRANK: I don't see why not. No one seems to have tried it yet, anyway. I suppose the trouble is we're all too scared of them. Either one gets forced into an attitude of false and hearty and
25 jocular bonhomie like myself, or into the sort of petty, soulless tyranny which your husband uses to protect himself against the lower fifth[6].

MILLIE (*rather bored with this*)**:** He'd never be popular – whatever he did.

FRANK: Possibly not. He ought never to have become a schoolmaster really. Why did he?

MILLIE: It was his vocation, he said. He was sure he'd make a big success of it, especially when
30 he got his job here first go off. (*Bitterly.*) Fine success he's made, hasn't he?

FRANK: You should have stopped him.

MILLIE: How was I to know? He talked about getting a house[7], then a headmastership.

FRANK (*rising*)**:** The Crock a headmaster! That's a pretty thought.

MILLIE: Yes, it's funny to think of it now, all right. Still, he wasn't always the Crock, you know.
35 He had a bit more gumption[8] once. At least I thought he had. Don't let's talk any more about him – (*she comes round the table*) it's too depressing. (*She starts to move.*)

FRANK: I'm sorry for him.

MILLIE (*stopping and turning; indifferently*)**:** He's not sorry for himself, so why should you be? It's me you should be sorry for.

40 **FRANK:** I am.

Terence RATTIGAN, *The Browning Version* (1949)

1. *sans conviction*   2. *vilain*   3. *se faire bien voir*   4. *jargon*   5. (inf.) fellows
6. *équivalent de la classe de seconde*   7. *avoir la responsabilité d'un groupe d'élèves*   8. *jugeote*

Vous trouverez la présentation de l'épreuve pages 12-13
et des conseils pratiques pour le bac pages 175-179.

Compréhension de l'écrit

Read the whole text before answering the questions.

1. Explain in your own words why Frank is ill at ease at the beginning of the extract.

> Relisez attentivement le début du texte jusqu'à la ligne 9.

2. What were Frank and Taplow doing when Millie arrived? Quote the text.

> Donnez deux citations.

3. Do you think that Millie is sincere when she says *"It was very naughty of you to encourage him"* (l. 13)? (30 words)

> Il faut avoir lu attentivement le texte pour répondre à cette question.

4. Quote the adjective which best qualifies Frank as a teacher.

5. What problem do teachers have to face according to Frank? Explain in one sentence.

6. Sum up Mr Crocker-Harris's career in your own words and illustrate your summary with a few quotations. (50 words not including quotations)

> Les indications scéniques peuvent vous aider à comprendre le sens de certains propos.

7. What does Frank think of Mr Crocker-Harris as a teacher? (30 words)

8. Analyse Frank's character. (50 words)

9. Describe and analyse Millie's attitude towards her husband. (80 words)

> Pour les question 9 et 10, on vous demande de développer vos réponses. Faites un brouillon.

10. Compare the teaching methods of Frank and Mr Crocker-Harris. What different forms of power do they use to handle their students? (80 words)

Expression écrite

1. Write the conversation which took place between Frank and Taplow just before the scene.

2. Comment upon the sentence in the poster: *"The greatest lessons in life are the ones learned by heart"*, bearing in mind not only different teaching methods but what you've read about the various characters' lives.

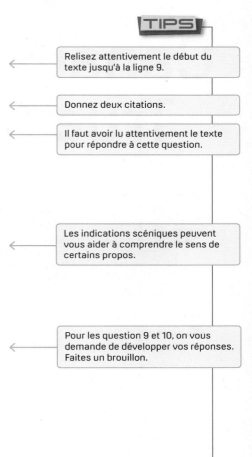

> Tenez compte du double sens de *"by heart"*.

> **Use your grammar**
> • Identifier un problème : **fiche 2** (p. 181)
> • Exprimer un jugement : **fiche 4** (p. 182)

Espaces et échanges
Lieux et formes du pouvoir

Canada, the True North

What do you know about Canada's First Peoples?

final task You have decided to spend some time as a volunteer in an aboriginal community in Canada. To be selected, you have to present your project orally to those in charge of recruiting you. You exchange e-mails with a student who worked as a volunteer last year.

Keywords

Nouns
- Canada /'kænədə/
- Canadian /kə'neɪdɪən/ (noun + adj.)
- territory = area
- border = frontier /'frʌntɪə/
- homeland: *patrie*
- Aborigine /æbə'rɪdʒɪni/
- Inuit /'ɪnjuːɪt/
- climate /'klaɪmɪt/
- roots: *racines*
- ice field: *banquise*
- wilderness /'wɪldənɪs/: *étendue désertique*
- reserve /rɪ'zɜːv/
- natural resources /'nætʃrəl rɪ'sɔːsɪz/
- bilingualism /baɪ'lɪŋgwəlɪzəm/
- land rights
- sled dog: *chien de traîneau*

Adjectives
- aboriginal /æbə'rɪdʒənl/ = indigenous /ɪn'dɪdʒɪnəs/
- populous ≠ uninhabited
- barren ≠ fertile /'fɜːtaɪl/
- harsh ≠ temperate /'tempərɪt/
- hostile ≠ welcoming
- sub-zero temperature /ˌsʌb'zɪərəu 'temprɪtʃə/
- pristine /'prɪstaɪn/ = untouched
- unspoiled: *préservé*
- rightful: *légitime*
- isolated /'aɪsəleɪtɪd/

Verbs & expressions
- stand up for / assert one's rights: *défendre ses droits*
- reclaim: *reconquérir*
- marginalize
- belong to: *appartenir à*
- explore
- go off the beaten track: *sortir des sentiers battus*

LANGUAGE WORKSHOP → p. 119

An Inuit on the ice field

1. Describe the picture briefly. Where does the scene take place?

2. Imagine what the man is doing there.

3. Would you like to live in such an environment? Why (not)?

SPÉCIAL BAC

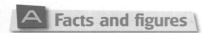

The Maple Leaf Country

Ⓜ ÉTHODOLOGIE **EXPRESSION ORALE EN CONTINU** → p. 16

A Facts and figures

Ⓜ ÉTHODOLOGIE
Dire les chiffres → p. 164

Make complete sentences.

1. Study the following data.

2. Use this information to give an oral account about Canada.

- **Name origin:** from the Saint Lawrence Iroquoian word *kanata*, meaning *village*, *settlement* or *land*.
- **Area:** 9,984,670 sq km (3,855,103 sq mi) / divided into 6 time zones – 2nd largest country after Russia.
- **Capital:** Ottawa /ˈɒtəwə/ (Canada's 4th largest city; ≈ 1.2 m inhabitants in the Ottawa region [2009]).
- **Largest cities (by pop.):** Toronto, Montreal, Vancouver, Ottawa-Gatineau, Calgary, Edmonton.

- **Flag:** the Canadian flag a.k.a. "the Maple Leaf Flag". The 11 points on the maple leaf emblem are said to represent Canada's provinces + the federal government.
- **Official languages (2006):** English (spoken by 57.8% of th population); French (22.1%).
- **Other languages (2006):** aboriginal languages + languages spoken by people whose mother tongue is neither French nor English (20.1%).
- **Head of state:** Queen Elizabeth II, represented by a Canadian Governor General.
- **Head of government:** Prime Minister (PM).
- **Natural resources:** oil (world rank: 6) / oil reserves (world rank: 3) and natural gas (world rank: 4).

B "From sea to sea"

Ⓜ ÉTHODOLOGIE
Expliquer → p. 163

Talk about Canada's population density.

1. Explain Canada's national motto (*devise*) "from sea to sea".

2. Study the map and the figures given.

What is particularly striking about:

a. Canada's population density?

b. the distribution of the Canadian population?

- **Population (2011):** 34,482,779
- **Population density:** 3.5 persons / sq km
- **Aborigines:** 1.2 million
- **Non-Aborigines:** 33.2 million

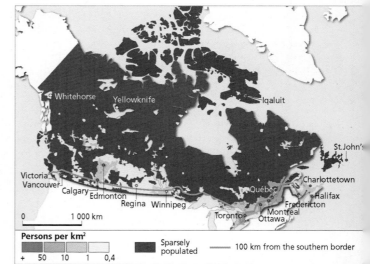

Persons per km²

| + | 50 | 10 | 1 | 0,4 | Sparsely populated | 100 km from the southern border |

(Source: Statistics Canada)

toolbox

Nouns
- **out**fit: *équipement*
- **s**urvival /səˈvaɪvəl/
- **r**escue party

Adjectives
- **u**rban /ˈɜːbən/ ≠ **r**ural /ˈrʊərəl/
- **m**ulticultural /ˌmʌltɪˈkʌltʃərəl/

Verbs & expressions
- be **d**ensely ≠ **s**parsely /ˈspɑːslɪ/ **p**opulated
- **r**ank: *se classer*
- be **s**uitable for: *convenir à*
- **s**ettle: *s'installer*
- **g**ather: *se rassembler*
- be in the **m**inority ≠ be in the **m**ajority

- **o**ut**n**umber: *être plus nombreux que*
- **d**rive sb out: *chasser qqn*
- be **f**amiliar with sth
- **d**ie of cold

 Extreme

MÉTHODOLOGIE
Rendre compte d'un ou de plusieurs documents → p. 163

Use the following documents to speak about Canada's climate.

1. Look at the temperature chart. What does it show about Canada's climate?

2. Describe the photo briefly. Is this how you imagine Canada?

3. Read the text to explain how Canadians react to climatic conditions.

4. Speak about Canada's climate for at least 1 minute.

Canada average temperature (°C)			
	Min. temp.	Max. temp.	Extreme temp.
January	− 16	− 7	− 40 (North)
July	+ 14	+ 27	+ 35 (South)

Canada's climate is known for being diverse, but also for being harsh. No wonder it is also known as "The Great White North". It varies from temperate in the South to subarctic and arctic in the North. With such a harsh climate in the North, most Canadian cities were built within 300 km of the southern border. When the temperature drops, Canadians know how to stay warm thanks to heated public transportation systems. Some cities have also installed sheltered walkways from one building to another. Canadians love winter so much that they celebrate it by organizing festivities like "Winterlude", which is held in Ottawa-Gatineau over the first three weekends in February. It was created in 1979 to celebrate Canada's unique northern climate and culture.

Video time ▮▮▮▯▯

The Snow Walker

The Snow Walker, Charles Martin SMITH (2003)

A Get ready

1. Look at the film still. Can you guess what the characters are doing?

2. You are going to watch an extract from *The Snow Walker*. Read the beginning of the film synopsis and complete your answer to question 1.

> *The scene is set in 1953 in the Canadian Arctic. Charlie, a bush pilot, agrees to fly Kanaalaq, an Inuit woman suffering from tuberculosis, to a hospital in Yellowknife in return for two ivory walrus tusks. On the plane trip to Yellowknife, after a series of mechanical problems, the plane crashes, leaving Charlie and Kanaalaq unharmed but stranded in the middle of an immense, desolate wilderness…*

B Watch the video

3. Watch the extract from the film. Your teacher will give you a worksheet to help you.

C In your own words

4. Use the worksheet to give an oral account of the extract.

D Going further

5. How do you think the story ends?

Citizenship? 📖 💿 25

culture key Canada's First Peoples → p. 156

Thomas KING

a Canadian novelist of Cherokee and European descent, was born in California in 1943. After teaching Native Studies in the US, he became a professor of creative writing in Canada. His novels and short stories portray Native Americans' daily lives and are characterized by humour and vivid dialogues (influenced by his interest in traditional oral literature).

A Warming up

First, read the *Culture key* about Canada's First Peoples. Then, use the title and the picture to guess what the story may be about.

The narrator and his mother, who live on the Canadian side of the US-Canada border, want to go to Salt Lake City to visit Laetitia, the narrator's sister. After being turned back at the American border, they try to go back to Canada.

The Canadian border guard was a young woman, and she seemed happy to
5 see us. "Hi," she said. "You folks sure have a great day for a trip."

The woman's name was Carol and I don't guess she was any older than Laetitia. "Wow, you both Canadians?"

"Blackfoot."

"Really? I have a friend I went to school with who is Blackfoot. You're not
10 bringing any liquor back, are you?"

"No."

"Any cigarettes or plants or stuff like that?"

"No."

"Citizenship?"

15 "Blackfoot."

"I know," said the woman, "and I'd be proud of being Blackfoot if I were Blackfoot. But you have to be American or Canadian."

We parked the car to the side of the building and Carol led us into a small room on the second floor.

20 When I woke up, my mother was just coming out of another office. She didn't say a word to me. I followed her down the stairs and out to the car. I thought we were going home, but she turned the car around and drove back towards the American border, which made me think we were going to visit Laetitia in Salt Lake City after all. Instead she pulled into the parking lot of the duty-free
25 store and stopped.

The narrator and his mother spend two days and two nights in the no-man's-land between Canada and the US with neither permission to go back to where they came from nor to go over to the American side.

Early the next morning, the television vans began to arrive, and guys in suits
30 and women in dresses came trotting over to us, dragging microphones and
cameras and lights behind them. They mostly talked to my mother. Every so
often one of the reporters would come over and ask me questions about how it
felt to be an Indian without a country.

Around noon, a good-looking guy drove up in a fancy car[1]. He talked to my
35 mother for a while, and, after they were done talking, my mother called me
over, and we got into our car.

"Where are we going now?"

"Going to visit Laetitia."

The guard who came out to our car was all smiles. The television lights were
40 so bright they hurt my eyes, and, if you tried to look through the windshield[2]
in certain directions, you couldn't see a thing.

"Morning, ma'am."

"Good morning."

"Where you heading?"

45 "Salt Lake City."

"Purpose of your visit?"

"Visit my daughter."

"Citizenship?"

"Blackfoot."

50 The guard jammed his thumbs into his gun belt. "Thank you," he said, his
fingers patting the butt[3] of the revolver. "Have a pleasant trip."

Thomas KING, *Borders*, in *One Good Story, That One* (1993)

1. *voiture de luxe* 2. *pare-brise* 3. *crosse*

B Understanding the text (W)ORKBOOK → p. 47-48

. Your *Workbook* will help you to understand the text.

. Sum up the story and the Blackfoot woman's feelings.

C Going further

. What does Carol mean when she says: "you have to be
American or Canadian" (l. 17)?

. Analyse the mother's attitude throughout the text. Why
does she behave like this?

5. Explain why TV reporters arrive.

6. How does the situation evolve at the end of the text? Why?

D Language training

7. **Savoir prononcer** 32-33 26-27

Les diphtongues

8. **Pratiquer la grammaire**

L'expression du regret LANGUAGE WORKSHOP → p. 118
both, neither, either (W)ORKBOOK → p. 52

toolbox

Nouns & expressions
● (go through) customs /'kʌstəmz/: *(passer) la douane*
● normal procedure /prə'siːdʒə/
● a losing battle: *une bataille perdue d'avance*

Adjectives
● adamant /'ædəmənt/: *inflexible*
● stubborn /'stʌbən/: *têtu, obstiné*
● determined /dɪ'tɜːmɪnd/
● friendly /'frendlɪ/
● artificial

Verbs & expressions
● prevent from V-ING: *empêcher de*
● break ≠ comply /kəm'plaɪ/ with the law
● persuade /pə'sweɪd/ sb to V
● acknowledge /ək'nɒlɪdʒ/ = admit
● do sth by the book (*selon les règles*)
● get preferential treatment /prefə'renʃəl 'triːtmənt/
● give in: *capituler*
● make a fuss (about): *faire des histoires*
● be worth sth / V-ING: *valoir la peine de*
● boost TV ratings: *faire grimper l'Audimat*
● cover a story / an event

Act out a conversation about what happened at the US-Canada border

Once in Salt Lake City, the mother tells Laetitia what happened at the border. Laetitia tries to calm things down and to explain the border guards' attitude. Choose your role and act out the conversation.

(M)ÉTHODOLOGIE
Conversation → p. 165

Life on the reserve

culture key — Canada's First Peoples → p. 156

A The topic

1. Look carefully at document 1. What event is advertised?

2. Read about Graham Shonfield (document 2), look at the map p. 156, and imagine the link between documents 1, 2 and 3.

Graham SHONFIELD, a student at Carleton University (Ottawa), spent time volunteering on the Gull Bay First Nation reserve. He made a documentary about the issues of most concern to people in the community.

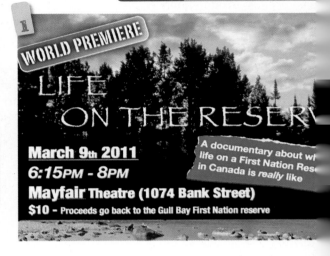

WORLD PREMIERE

LIFE ON THE RESERVE

A documentary about what life on a First Nation Reserve in Canada is *really* like

March 9th 2011
6:15PM - 8PM
Mayfair Theatre (1074 Bank Street)
$10 - Proceeds go back to the Gull Bay First Nation reserve

B Open your ears
CD 2 **28**

3. You will hear five sentences. Only three of them are in the interview you are going to listen to. Which ones? Justify.

C Listen
CD 2 **29-31** **W**ORKBOOK → p. 49

4. Listen to Graham Shonfield. You will find some help in your *Workbook*.

D In your own words

5. In what way(s) was this experience an eye-opener for Graham? Is every aspect of tribe life positive?

toolbox

Nouns
- calm /ˈkɑːm/ ≠ bustle /ˈbʌsl/
- (feeling of) community
- hostility
- habit: *habitude*
- stereotype /ˈstɪərɪətaɪp/
- outsider

Adjectives
- individualistic /ˈɪndɪˌvɪdʒʊəˈlɪstɪk/
- materialistic /məˌtɪərɪəˈlɪstɪk/
- ill at ease: *mal à l'aise*
- fast paced /peɪst/: *à un rythme rapide*

Verbs & expressions
- treat sb like: *traiter qqn comme*
- fit in: *être à sa place*
- take one's time

Your task

 Speak about life on the reserve
You are a member of the Gull Bay First Nation community who went to high school in Thunder Bay. You explain to Graham Shonfield why you prefer life on your reserve to life in a city in the South.

MÉTHODOLOGIE **EXPRESSION ORALE EN CONTINU** → p. 163

Writers' corner

Your Nunavut adventure!

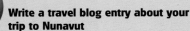
culture key | Nunavut → p. 156

Your task

Write a travel blog entry about your trip to Nunavut

You are spending two weeks in Nunavut in the Canadian Arctic as part of an adventure trip. You are keeping a diary. Write the entries corresponding to your first three days there. (250 words)

Ⓜ MÉTHODOLOGIE
EXPRESSION ÉCRITE → p. 170

A Get ready

1. Read about Nunavut in the *Culture key*, p. 156.

2. Look at these pictures taken in Nunavut. Then, read the three texts: they will give you some information on what you can do there. You may also visit Nunavut's official website:
www.nunavuttourism.com

B Write your entries

3. Pay attention to the tenses that you will use: past, present, present perfect…

4. Write in the first person singular and don't forget to write about your feelings.

5. You may also write about the people's way of life, food, transportation, climate, etc.

6. Make sure you don't copy the sentences from the texts. Use your own words instead.

Floe edge tour & whale watching

WALRUS[1] AND POLAR BEARS can be found on the sea ice, generally in May and June. Bowhead whales[2] weigh up to 60 tons and are 60 feet-long. You will find beluga whales (a.k.a. white whales), in bays and river mouths. As for narwhals, they look like unicorns with their 7-foot tusk[3]. Breathtaking excursions on the floe edge are available for a once-in-a-lifetime experience.

1. /'wɔːlrəs/ *morse* 2. *baleine à bosse* 3. *défense*

Meet Inuits in Grise Fiord

ALSO KNOWN AS AUJUITTUQ – "the place that never thaws[1]" –, this warmly hospitable place, home to 141 permanently settled residents, is the northernmost community in Canada. Grise Fiord enjoys 24-hour sunshine from April through August.

1. *dégeler*

Kayaking & rafting

YOU WILL DEFINITELY ENJOY SEA KAYAKING between ice floes and icebergs. Our guides will take you on rafting and canoeing trips down rapids and calm rivers. But make no mistake, Nunavut is no amusement park. But the rewards last a lifetime!

function box

Expressing enthusiasm

It must be great / terrific...
How interesting / fantastic!
I'd just love to...
I was so impressed by...
I can't wait to see that!

Expressing surprise → p. 25

toolbox

Nouns
- haven (of peace): *havre (de paix)*
- wildlife: *la faune et la flore*
- Mother Nature /mʌðə 'neɪtʃə/
- Midnight Sun
- scenery = landscape
- snowmobile /'snəʊməˌbiːl/
- dogsled: *traîneau (tiré par des chiens)*
- campsite
- canoe /kə'nuː/
- paddle (noun + verb): *pagaie*

Adjectives
- dazzling = breathtaking /'breθteɪkɪŋ/: *époustouflant*
- accessible
- unforgettable
- enriching

Verbs & expressions
- pitch (a tent): *planter (sa tente)*
- be cut off from

Stop stealing our land

culture key | The Arctic resources → p. 156

AFP is the oldest not-for-profit international news agency in the world, and one of the three largest along with Associated Press and Reuters. It was founded in Paris in 1835 and employs about 2,900 people. AFP's headquarters are located in Paris, with regional offices in more than 160 countries. It delivers fast, accurate news from every corner of the world, 24 hours a day by satellite and Internet feed.
Website: www.afp.com

A Warming up

Use the picture and the title to anticipate the content of the article.

With the race for Arctic resources intensifying, the region's indigenous Inuits are raising their voices and demanding that nations
5 bordering the Arctic Sea stop stealing their land and respect their way of life. Arctic waters could hold 25 percent of the world's undiscovered oil and gas, according to the US Geological Survey[1]
10 – meaning countries like the United States and Russia, who once used the frozen wastelands as a strategic pawn[2] in the Cold War, are now eyeing up its energy reserves.
15 "The Inuits have been marginalised in the current debate on the Arctic by those who now control our land and waters," Aqqaluk Lynge, a Greenlandic politician who is the head of the Inuit Circumpolar
20 Council (ICC) on the island, told AFP, speaking on behalf of 150,000 Inuits in the Arctic region. "We no longer want to accept the isolation and harsh treatment that has been inflicted upon us in the
25 past. Enough is enough, we don't want to be displaced by force, and we demand to be treated humanely," Lynge said.

Lynge, a lawyer and staunch[3] advocate of Inuit rights, was the only
30 representative of a non-governmental organisation invited to attend a meeting in May in Greenland which gathered the foreign ministers of the five countries that ring the Arctic Ocean: Canada,
35 Denmark, Norway, Russia and the United States. The gathering was organised to thrash out competing territorial claims in the oil- and gas-rich region. The rivalry between the five neighbours has heated
40 up as the melting polar ice makes the region more accessible.

As well as the undiscovered oil and gas reserves, scientists say the Northwest Passage[4] could open up to year-round
45 shipping by 2050, making access much easier for exploration firms.

Representing the Inuits from Greenland, Canada, Alaska and Siberia, Lynge said "the period of silence is
50 over." He noted that Inuits have over the years been forcibly displaced in Greenland, Canada, Alaska and northern Russia, most often to build military bases during the Cold War. The notion

55 is particularly appalling to Inuits given their traditional view that land is a natural resource to be shared. "We have always had collective ownership of the lands that were stolen from us," and at 60 the same time, "states have established borders on our lands without ever even asking us. Unfortunately, most countries bordering the Arctic do not recognise the fundamental rights of indigenous peoples 65 even though they were recognised by the UN in September 2007," he said.

Some countries, like Canada and the United States, have refused to allow Inuits to profit from the Arctic's 70 resources. "We are the only people in the world to be deprived of the right to our own riches," Lynge deplored. Now that the world "has opened its eyes to the Arctic and its possibilities", the Inuits 75 are demanding that they "not be left by the wayside."

AFP (June 15th 2008)

1. an American scientific agency that studies the landscape of the US, its natural resources, and the natural risks that threaten it   2. /pɔːn/ *pion*   3. /stɔːntʃ/ *ardent*
4. the sea passage, to the north of Canada, from the Atlantic to the Pacific

3 Understanding the text ⓦORKBOOK → p. 50-51

. Turn to your *Workbook* which will help you to understand the text.

. Explain why the Inuits are raising their voices.

Going further

. Explain the consequences of global warming for the Inuits and the bordering nations.

. Analyse the way the five nations behave towards the Inuits.

. To what extent does the Inuits' view of land explain their struggle?

. Do you think the Inuits have any chance of being heard? Justify your answer.

D Writing time

Summary
Write a summary of the article. (160 words)

ⓜÉTHODOLOGIE
Résumer un article de presse → p. 172

a. Avant de rédiger votre résumé, dégagez l'idée principale de chaque paragraphe.

b. Éliminez tout ce qui est secondaire.

c. Respectez la chronologie et les enchaînements du texte.

d. Vous pouvez réutiliser des mots clés, mais ne recopiez pas les phrases du texte. Utilisez des mots de liaison.

e. Relisez-vous pour vérifier la cohérence de votre résumé.

f. Comptez vos mots : on vous demande ici de réduire le texte au tiers de sa longueur initiale (plus ou moins 10 %), n'hésitez pas à retrancher ou ajouter des mots si nécessaire.

E Language training ⓦORKBOOK → p. 51

8. Savoir prononcer 34-35 32-33

Les mots transparents
La prononciation de la lettre -*o*-

9. Pratiquer la grammaire

Formes passives ◗LANGUAGE WORKSHOP → p. 118
Place des prépositions – Génitif ⓦORKBOOK → p. 52

toolbox

Nouns & expressions
- sovereignty /'sɒvrəntɪ/
- wildlife
- against sb's will
- superpower
- stake: *enjeu*

Adjectives
- navigable
- devastating
- accessible
- economic /iːkəˈnɒmɪk/
- greedy: *avide*
- unfair (to): *injuste (vis-à-vis de)*

Verbs & expressions
- attend: *assister à*
- have had enough of sth / V-ING
- be left aside
- interfere /ˌɪntəˈfɪə/
- negotiate /nɪˈgəʊʃɪeɪt/
- minimize = play down
- be threatened / in jeopardy /ˈdʒepədɪ/: *être menacé / en danger*
- be impacted / affected
- have one's say about / a voice in sth

 Give an oral presentation of the Inuits' situation

After reading the article, you think that more people should know about the Inuits' situation and their struggle to defend their land. You send a recorded presentation about this issue to your favourite web radio.

ⓜÉTHODOLOGIE **EXPRESSION ORALE EN CONTINU → p. 163**

Language workshop

Grammaire **L'expression du regret – Formes passives**

A L'expression du regret PRÉCIS GRAMMATICAL → 9

1 If I were... I wish I were...

1. *"I'd be proud of being Blackfoot if I* **were** *Blackfoot."* (Text 1, p. 112, l. 16)
2. *"I wish I* **were** *Blackfoot too," the young woman said.*
3. *"I wish I* **had never come** *here, it was a mistake," I said to my mother.*

a. Indiquez pour chacun des verbes en gras quelle notion il exprime : **1.** un fait irréel dans le présent mais souhaité par celui qui parle ; **2.** un fait qui s'est produit dans le passé mais que l'on regrette ou **3.** une hypothèse très incertaine. Quel temps est associé à chacune de ces notions dans les énoncés ci-dessus ? Quelle particularité notez-vous dans la conjugaison de *be* après *if* et *I wish* ?

b. Traduisez les énoncés **2** et **3** à l'aide de « regretter » et expliquez les différences entre le français et l'anglais.

2 Reformulez chaque énoncé à l'aide de I wish + prétérit ou pluperfect et traduisez l'énoncé produit à l'aide de « regretter ».

a. *They should be more understanding.* → *I wish they...*
b. *I'm usually very shy and not very happy about it.* → *I wish I...*
c. *They asked too many questions and I didn't like it.* → *I wish they...*
d. *Why didn't you listen to me?* → *I wish you...*

3 Traduisez les énoncés à l'aide de I wish suivi du prétérit ou du pluperfect.

a. Je regrette que vous ne soyez pas plus âgées.
b. Je regrette que nous n'ayons pas de passeport américain.
c. Je regrette qu'ils ne nous aient pas filmés.
d. Je regrette que tu ne sois pas restée.
e. Je regrette que tu lui aies dit cela.
f. Je regrette qu'il soit si tard.

B Formes passives PRÉCIS GRAMMATICAL → 43

4 Traduire les formes passives

1. *"the lands that were stolen from us"* (Text 2, p. 116, l. 58)
2. *Those people were never heard of again.*

Traduisez les énoncés. Lequel doit-on obligatoirement traduire par « on » ? Pourquoi la voix passive n'est-elle pas possible dans ce cas ?

5 Réécrivez les phrases suivantes en utilisant le passif.

a. *Other countries are exploiting their energy reserves.*
b. *Someone reported that the police ordered the protesters to leave.*
c. *They were dismantling the encampment.*
d. *They said indigenous people had always owned Arctic land.*

6 Traduisez à l'aide de la voix passive.

a. Voici la terre dont on les prive (*deprive of*).
b. On ne peut pas compter sur (*rely on*) ces gens.
c. C'était une chose à laquelle on n'avait jamais songé (*dream of*) auparavant.
d. C'est la seule chose que l'on ne puisse pas expliquer (*account for*).

Grammaire de l'oral | Distinguer *WILL, WOULD* et *HAD* à l'oral

7 Distinguer *WILL, WOULD* et *HAD* à l'oral 34-37

a. Écoutez le passage suivant afin de bien en comprendre le sens global.

b. Écoutez cet énoncé, extrait du passage précédent, et indiquez si vous avez entendu la forme **1**, **2** ou **3**.

> *And…, you know, mostly… I* (**1.** *will try to –* **2.** *had tried to –* **3.** *would try to), like, teach them a new sport…, like ultimate Frisbee.* (Listeners' corner, p. 114)

c. Qu'exprime la forme verbale que vous avez entendue : **1.** un fait à venir ; **2.** l'habitude dans le passé ou **3.** l'antériorité d'un fait passé ?

d. Écoutez les énoncés **a**, **b**, **c** et **d** et indiquez pour chacun d'eux si la forme entendue est la forme **1** ou **2**.

a.1. *I would never see*	**b.1.** *you would see*	**c.1.** *you will tell them*	**d.1.** *I had invented*
a.2. *I'd never seen*	**b.2.** *you will see*	**c.2.** *you would tell them*	**d.2.** *I would invent*

e. Écrivez les énoncés que vous entendez.

Lexique | Le Grand Nord canadien

Assurez-vous que vous avez bien retenu les mots clés de l'unité. → **Keywords p. 108**

8 Donnez les synonymes ou les antonymes des mots suivants.

a. *territory* = … **b.** *frontier* = … **c.** *fertile* ≠ … **d.** *hostile* ≠ …

9 Choisissez la bonne transcription phonétique des mots suivants.

a. *Canada*: 1. /ˈkænædə/ 2. /ˈkænədə/ 3. /ˈkənædə/

b. *Canadian*: 1. /kæˈneɪdɪən/ 2. /kəˈnædɪən/ 3. /kəˈneɪdɪən/

c. *Aborigine*: 1. /æbəˈrɪdʒɪnɪ/ 2. /əbəˈrɪdʒaɪnɪ/ 3. /æbəˈrɪdʒɪn/

d. *climate*: 1. /ˈklaɪmaɪt/ 2. /ˈklaɪmɪt/ 3. /ˈklaɪmeɪt/

10 Recopiez les mots suivants et entourez la syllabe accentuée.

a. *bilingualism* **b.** *aboriginal* **c.** *indigenous* **d.** *populous* **e.** *uninhabited* **f.** *marginalize* **g.** *homeland*

11 Recopiez puis complétez les phrases à l'aide des mots et expressions suivants.

land rights – explore – wilderness – harsh – ice field – aboriginal – resources – reserves – sub-zero temperatures – reclaim – stand up for – unspoiled

a. *People imagine Canada is an* …1… …2… *of snow and ice.*

b. *He never wanted to go to the Arctic region because of the* …3… *climate and* …4….

c. *When I go to the Arctic, I* …5… *the* …6… *on a dogsled.*

d. *Canada's Indian* …7… *are full of natural* …8….

e. *Canada's* …9… *peoples want to* …10… *their* …11… *and* …12… *their territory.*

toolbox

Expressions
- If **o**nly I had not…
- I'd much r**a**ther + V: *Je préférerais de loin…*
- It's high time + past: *Il est temps que…*
- I feel like + V-ING: *J'ai envie de…*
- I should n**e**ver have: *Je n'aurais jamais dû*

Adjectives
- un**ea**sy: *mal à l'aise*
- **aw**kward: *difficile / délicat (situation)*
- ann**o**ying: *ennuyeux / agaçant*

Write an e-mail expressing regrets

You were offered an internship in journalism in the local newspaper but you turned it down. Now you regret it and write an e-mail to your best friend about it.

Use **I wish** + **past simple** or **past perfect**.

119

Languages in multicultural Canada

One country, how many languages?

 A **A bilingual country**

1 Do you know what explains the presence of both French and English in Canada? Read the *Culture key* to check your answer.

culture key   Canada: historical background → p. 156

2 Read the text.
a. What made the federal government declare French an official language as well as English?
b. Is bilingualism enforced (*appliqué*) in every city and province of Canada?

WHEN CANADA BECAME INDEPENDENT FROM BRITAIN IN 1867, the English language predominated, since approximately two-thirds of its inhabitants were of British origin and only one-third of French descent.

Although the use of French was officially tolerated in the province of Quebec[1], English was used increasingly in the rest of Canada, mainly as a result of the expansion of commerce with the United States. Gradually, the French-speaking minority saw its position threatened in Canada. As relations between French and English speakers deteriorated in the 20th century, separatist ideas grew in strength in Quebec, that's why the Official Languages Act was passed in 1969, making both French and English official languages in Canada.

However, in 1977, Quebec made French the only official language of the province and strengthened its use in everyday life. Today, New Brunswick is Canada's only bilingual province, but in 2001, Ottawa, Canada's national capital city, decided to provide all its services in both languages.

1. /kwɪˈbek/

B **English and French vs native languages**

Read the text opposite and answer the following questions.
a. What did the Canadian federal government try to do through its education programme? What means were used?
b. Why did the PM feel the need to apologize to the First Nations?

culture key   Canada's First Peoples → p. 156

Indian residential school students and nuns, ca 1890

EDUCATION OF THE VARIOUS ABORIGINAL PEOPLES' CHILDREN was long seen as a means of accelerating their assimilation into European-Canadian society rather than as a means of providing education for future adults. Their education was mainly provided by religious groups that set up boarding schools hundreds of kilometres away from the children's homes, to remove them from the influence of their families and traditional indigenous life.

Even though living conditions were poor in those schools, many native families regarded the system as necessary and accepted the repressive language policies that forbade the use of native languages in such schools. Thus, the use of English and French became increasingly prevalent in everyday native life and the Christian religion gradually replaced traditional spiritual beliefs.

It was only in the 1970s that there was at last some recognition of the importance of the First Nations' languages and values in education. In 2008, Prime Minister (PM) Stephen Harper apologized for the past governments' policies of forced assimilation.

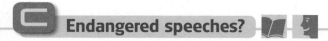

C Endangered speeches?

1 Read the text below and find out if aboriginal languages are dying.

Mother tongue or second language?

ACCORDING TO A RECENT SURVEY, only a minority of people (24%) who identified themselves as aboriginal declared that they were able to speak or understand an aboriginal language. Thus, although the majority of the current aboriginal language speakers learned their language as a mother tongue, most of the next generation will probably only speak an aboriginal language as second language learners.

2 Look at these road signs from various Canadian aboriginal communities and read the text below. What do they show?

Revitalizing Canada's indigenous languages

THE TINY HURON RESERVE OF WENDAKE, just to the north of Quebec City, recently carried out a unique language experiment. It organised an evening meeting between men and women of different generations, aged 15 to 76, in which everyone present had to use their ancestral tongue, Wendat. The evening began with the traditional words of welcome – "koué" or "Ndio" – and then participants spent the next couple of hours trying to communicate in a language that has not been spoken for at least a century. Similar language revitalization projects are currently being developed in several other aboriginal communities across Canada.

Webquest A multicultural society TICE

1 Browse the web to find out about the languages spoken by immigrants and their descendants in Canada today. Here are a few guidelines to help you.

a. When did Canada declare itself a "multicultural" society? What does it imply?

b. What proportion of the Canadian population does not speak French, English or an aboriginal language as a mother tongue?

c. What is the third most spoken language in Canada today, after English and French?

d. How many different languages are spoken today?

2 Use the information given in the websites to give an oral account of multiculturalism and languages in Canada.

 ◀ ▶ **Web resources** ○○○

- multiculturalcanada.ca/Encyclopedia/A-Z/m9
- www40.statcan.ca/l01/cst01/DEMO12A-eng.htm
- www.canada.gc.ca/aboutcanada-ausujetcanada/
  arts/lang-eng.html

final task

What do you know about Canada's First Peoples?

You have decided to spend some time as a volunteer in an aboriginal community in Canada. To be selected, you have to present your project orally to those in charge of recruiting you. You exchange e-mails with a student who worked as a volunteer last year.

The various documents you have worked on in this unit should help you to find arguments and ideas to make your oral presentation and write your e-mail.

1 Present your project orally

 MÉTHODOLOGIE EXPRESSION ORALE EN CONTINU → p. 163

A Prepare your presentation

Think of the different arguments you will need to present your project to the recruiting committee:

■ the reasons why you want to work as a volunteer in an aboriginal community;

■ how you could contribute to the community;

■ the consequences this experience may have on your life.

B Make your oral presentation

You will have to speak at least 3 minutes. You must sound enthusiastic and convincing. You must also make yourself clear, make complete sentences and link them.

Je me situe par rapport au CECRL **B2**

> LORSQUE JE PARLE DE CE PROJET :
> Je peux développer une argumentation claire, nuancée et enchaîner les arguments avec logique.

Suggesting and convincing functior box
- How / What about V-ING
- Why don't you / Why not V
- Don't you think that...?
- I suggest V-ING / I suggest we (should) V
- We should definitely V...
- I'm convinced that...
- It seems to me that...
- I'm sure you will / won't V...
Expressing enthusiasm → p. 25

2 Write the e-mails

MÉTHODOLOGIE Écrire un courriel → p. 171

■ Decide who you want to be.

Student A You are the student who wants to spend time as a volunteer.
Introduce yourself and explain your project: reasons for volunteering, where you will stay and how long, what your work will consist in… You can also ask for more information about life in an aboriginal community, the work your fellow correspondent did as a volunteer, etc. (200 words)

Student B You are the student who has already spent time as a volunteer.
Express your reaction to the e-mail that you have received, give details of your own experience as a volunteer in an aboriginal community, the difficulties that students may encounter living in such an environment. Say what impact this experience has had on your life… (200 words)

Je me situe par rapport au CECRL **B2**

> LORSQUE J'ÉCRIS CE COURRIEL :
> Je peux rédiger un courriel de manière claire et détaillée, écrire des descriptions élaborées d'expériences dans un texte articulé.

Vous trouverez la présentation de l'épreuve pages 12-13
et des conseils pratiques pour le bac pages 175-179.

Compréhension de l'oral 36 38 **W**ORKBOOK → p. 53

Vous allez écouter trois fois un document intitulé *Experimental Eskimos*.

Avant l'écoute

1. Aidez-vous du titre du document de façon à anticiper son contenu.

Première écoute

2. Identifiez la nature et le thème général du document.

Deuxième écoute

3. Relevez les informations principales.

Troisième écoute

4. Donnez des détails significatifs et le point de vue des locuteurs.

Rendez compte en français de ce que vous avez compris.

TIPS

Identifiez la fonction et le rôle des différents locuteurs.

Mentionnez les événements qui se sont déroulés, quand cela est arrivé et qui cela a concerné.

Mentionnez les conséquences de cette expérience.

Expression orale **W**ORKBOOK → p. 54

Lors de votre prise de parole en continu, puis de la conversation avec l'examinateur,
vous pourrez aborder les problématiques suivantes en lien avec l'unité 6.

Notion 1 Espaces et échanges
Places and exchanges

■ **What do borders mean to First Peoples in Canada?**

The Maple Leaf Country, p. 110 • The Snow Walker, p. 111 •
Citizenship?, p. 112 • Life on the reserve, p. 114 • Your Nunavut
adventure!, p. 115 • Stop stealing our land, p. 116 • Canada's First
Peoples, p. 156

• Les frontières sont-elles des limites envisagées de la même façon par tous les habitants du Canada ?
• Exprimez le **contraste** : *On the one hand... on the other hand... Whereas / While... Yet / However / Still...*

Notion 2 Lieux et formes du pouvoir
Seats and forms of power

■ **Why are there so many different languages in Canada?**

Facts and figures, p. 110 • The Snow Walker, p. 111 • Languages
in multicultural Canada, p. 120 • A multicultural society, p. 121 •
Canada: historical background, p. 156

Mentionnez les causes historiques ainsi que les questions identitaires.

■ **In what ways do native peoples assert their rights?**

Citizenship?, p. 112 • Stop stealing our land, p. 116 • English and
French vs native languages, p. 120 • Endangered speeches?, p. 121
• Canada's First Peoples, p. 156

• Montrez les liens entre les aspects identitaires, culturels, économiques et politiques.
• Exprimez l'**intention** : *They mean to... They are determined to... They dream of...*

The top of the world

Our first warning came from the petrol station owner in Yukon: "Your first 400 miles will be magical, but the last 100 or so could be a problem," he said. "Unless the Mackenzie River is nicely frozen, you won't be able to drive up it. Why don't you just take a light aircraft instead?"

5 Before the frozen river we'd have to traverse the Dempster Highway, which snakes through Canada's Yukon wilderness and Northern Territories.

With no other passenger vehicles in sight and only one bleary-eyed trucker to move aside for every hour or so, the first couple of hundred miles of Dempster driving proved to be surprisingly relaxed, serene and trouble-free. True, we were 10 running low on fuel before we got close to our first and only overnight oasis, Eagle Plains (population eight). Eagle Plains consists of a road clearing and rescue depot, tiny airstrip, medical room, gas station, modest hotel and that's about it. Over a late-night beer, one of the proud locals argued that it was a growing town with more like 12 citizens and, like the petrol station owner 300 miles further 15 south, he was concerned for our well-being.

"What sort of guns have you got locked in your Jeeps? Where you're going, you could use one or two for your own protection. Hungry polar bears can cause problems. Wolverines[1] will." Much as I appreciated the warm, comfortable bed at the only hotel for hundreds of square miles, a decent sleep was impossible due 20 to the din caused by trucks parked directly outside which had to keep their noisy diesel engines running all night to prevent them from seizing in temperatures that have been recorded as low as − 56 °F (− 48.9 °C).

Next morning, minutes after leaving Eagle Plains, a Disney-like sign informed us that we were entering the Arctic Circle.

25 The Northern Lights town of Inuvik effectively marks the closing, *terra firma* stages of the Dempster highway, which means journey's end for the vast majority of folk who drive this far north. From Inuvik, all that lies ahead is freezing or frozen water.

We desperately needed to know if the ice was thick enough to accommodate our 30 Jeeps. When a young Inuit guide successfully drove his two-wheel-drive pick-up down the Mackenzie River from Tuk to our Inuvik hotel, our hopes were raised.

My Inuit guide shook my hand after I'd successfully driven all the way up the frozen Mackenzie, through Tuktoyaktuk and on to the shores of the frozen Arctic. It was tempting to keep going, but he, me and the Jeep finally surrendered 35 to the forces and dangers of nature.

Before turning around for the long journey home from the extreme north of Canada to the deep south of England, we had one last, short journey ahead of us to our guide's cosy family home where we dined on oily beluga whale[2] and fleshy caribou. I promised that if I ever return I'll bring supplies of fresh milk 40 and vegetables – exotic and expensive luxuries that some people in the village at the top of the world have never tasted.

Mike RUTHERFORD, *The Telegraph* (January 17th 2011)

1. *gloutons (mammifères carnivores)*   2. *baleine blanche*

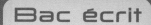
Vous trouverez la présentation de l'épreuve pages 12-13
et des conseils pratiques pour le bac pages 175-179.

Compréhension de l'écrit

Read the whole text before answering the questions.

1. Explain what the narrator has decided to do.

2. Find the two pieces of advice given to the narrator. Explain why they are given. (50 words)

3. Put the following events concerning the narrator and his guide in chronological order.
   a. They reach the Arctic Ocean.
   b. They travel on an empty road.
   c. They spend the night in a small town.
   d. They have dinner with the guide's family.
   e. They head back south.
   f. They reach the Arctic Circle.
   g. The narrator goes back home to England.
   h. They see someone who has driven down the Mackenzie River.
   i. They get useful information before they start their journey.
   j. They arrive at the town where most people end their journey.
   k. They manage to drive up the Mackenzie River.

4. Explain what the adverb *"surprisingly"* (l. 9) reveals about the narrator's expectations.

5. Why do most people end their journey at Inuvik?

6. Explain why the Inuit guide shakes the narrator's hand. (50 words)

7. Describe the narrator's feelings from *"My Inuit guide"* (l. 32) to *"dangers of nature"* (l. 35).

8. Why does the narrator decide to bring *"fresh milk and vegetables"* when he returns? What does it reveal about his attitude towards the Inuits? (50 words)

Expression écrite

1. After arriving back in England, the narrator writes an article comparing the Inuit and European ways of life.

2. It is often said that travel broadens one's horizons. Use elements from the text and your own views to comment on this statement.

TIPS

Il faut avoir lu l'ensemble du texte pour répondre à cette question.

Relisez le passage de la ligne 1 à *"Wolverines will"* (l. 18).

L'ordre chronologique n'est pas nécessairement l'ordre dans lequel les éléments apparaissent dans le texte.

Appuyez-vous aussi sur le contexte fourni par le paragraphe précédent pour répondre.

Use your grammar
• Faire le bilan d'une situation donnée :
  fiche 3 (p. 181)
• Savoir utiliser les temps du récit :
  fiche 7 (p. 183)

Unit 7

Mythes et héros
Lieux et formes du pouvoir

Blacklisted

What do you know about blacklisting in American history?

final task
"The Best Speaker Contest" is being held in your school. You decide to participate. After reading an extract from a novel about scapegoats in society, you give an oral account of the story and comment on it.

Keywords

Nouns
- scapegoat /'skeɪpgəʊt/: *bouc émissaire*
- witch hunt: *chasse aux sorcières*
- evidence: *preuve(s)*
- (mass) hysteria /hɪs'tɪərɪə/
- threat /θret/: *menace*
- traitor
- enemy

- pariah /pə'raɪə/
- rumour /'ruːmə/
- good ≠ evil /'iːvl/ (noun + adj.)
- distrust /dɪs'trʌst/ = suspicion

Adjectives & adverbs
- suspected /'səs'pektɪd/
- fair ≠ unfair
- guilty ≠ innocent

- wrongfully: *à tort*
- suspicious /səs'pɪʃəs/ (about)

Verbs & expressions
- blacklist: *mettre à l'index*
- banish = exclude
- point sb out: *désigner*
- name names = give names
- be prejudiced (against): *avoir des préjugés*
- stand up to (sb) = oppose (sb)

- confess
- denounce
- charge sb with = accuse sb of
- be tried: *être jugé*
- be convicted (of): *être reconnu coupable (de)*
- testify: *témoigner*
- hold sb responsible / accountable for sth / V-ING

LANGUAGE WORKSHOP → p. 137

Witch!

1. This picture is a film still from *The Crucible* (1996), based on Arthur Miller's play about the Salem witch trials of 1692. Describe the scene and point out the symbolic elements.

2. Imagine the reason(s) why the woman is accused of being a witch.

3. What do you think may happen to her?

The "Red Scare"

Ⓦ WORKBOOK → p. 55

Ⓜ ÉTHODOLOGIE COMPRÉHENSION DE L'ÉCRIT → p. 1€

culture key   McCarthyism → p. 157

First, read the *Culture key* about McCarthyism, then explain what the mural represents.

After studying the documents presented on these pages, you will explain what happened in the USA during the period referred to as McCarthyism.

THE RED SCARE & McCARTHYISM

A The Cold War hysteria

Ⓜ ÉTHODOLOGIE
Compréhension globale → p. 167

Focus on the main information.

1. Read the text and answer the questions Who? Where? When? What? Turn to your *Workbook* for help.

2. Explain what the "Red Scare" refers to.

I WAS USHERED INTO THE INNER OFFICE of a pale young man, with rimless glasses, who said, "May I see your passport?" And, idiot that I am, I turned it over to him. "Thank you, I'll keep this."

I looked at him with utter amazement and asked, rather stupidly, "Do you realize what you are doing?"

Of course, I really had no right to be surprised. I had been foreseeing and dreading this moment since landing in the US. These were the 1950s, the height of the Cold War hysteria and McCarthyism. Every scoundrel in America was hunting "Reds" under each bed.

I remember saying to the official, "Do you sleep well at night?"

He looked at me coldly and answered, "Very well."

"I don't see how you can, knowing what you are doing. You are keeping me arbitrarily from my husband, my home and my work. I only came here because my mother was operated on."

All in vain, of course.

Jane FOSTER, *An Unamerican Lady* (1980)

B Enemies from within

Ⓜ ÉTHODOLOGIE
Les mots inconnus – Les mots composés → p. 168-169

Focus on the comprehension of unknown and compound words.

1. Read the article opposite. Your *Workbook* will help you to find the meaning of unknown and compound words.

2. Why did the FBI keep a file on the author's father?

culture key   John Edgar Hoover → p. 157

M Y FATHER WAS NEVER A SPY, never a member of the Communist Part He came by ship to the United States in 1956, fleeing Communis during the Hungarian revolution to pursue the American dream. He worke on a Ford automobile assembly line in Cincinnati by day and moonlighte sharpening lawnmowers at night, saving enough money in a few years buy a small house. To him, treasonous behavior meant buying a car mac outside of America. Nonetheless, as I discovered recently, the FBI kept file on him from the day he arrived in the United States. J. Edgar Hoove sent a personal memo to the CIA director calling my father a person current interest. I discovered this after filing a Freedom of Informatio Act inquiry as part of some family research for a book. I was shocked receive 50 FBI pages riddled with my father's name, the edges dotted wit weathered stamps marked "SECRET."

Peter W. KLEIN, *The New York Times* (January 200

The Hollywood blacklist

MÉTHODOLOGIE
Point de vue de l'auteur → p. 168

Identify the author's point of view.

1. Read the *Culture key* about McCarthyism, then guess who the men in the picture are.

2. Read the text with the help of your *Workbook* and pick out elements in the text showing the author's point of view.

ONCE THE HOLLYWOOD BLACKLIST WAS ESTABLISHED, it gradually expanded until it encompassed hundreds of persons. They included actors, actresses, writers, directors, technicians, and even secretaries and clerks thrown out of work by the movie studios. Not only admitted or accused communists but also persons merely suspected of subversive activities were victimized by the blacklist. Severe hardships were imposed on many former movie-industry employees and their families. Some of those who had been paid extremely high salaries in the entertainment industry found themselves forced to scrape out meager livings in new occupations such as bartending, waiting on tables, driving school buses, selling clothing, and performing minor repair chores. Several committed suicide. A few of the blacklisted screen writers managed to find periodic work writing films under assumed names for independent producers who were not connected with the major movie studios. Blacklisted actors and actresses, of course, had no way to disguise their identities in film roles. Gradually, some persons already on the blacklist or threatened with being placed on it began seeking means of clearing themselves for further employment in the movie studios. Chiefly, they did so by agreeing to cooperate with the committee. In typical cases, they were expected to "confess" that they had belonged to subversive organizations in the past, but had now seen the error of their ways and broken with such groups. However, merely testifying about their own activities was usually not sufficient to satisfy the committee. They were also expected to identify other persons who had participated in the activities with them.

Michael DORMAN, *Witch hunt, the underside of American democracy* (1976)

culture key McCarthyism → p. 157

Video time

One of the Hollywood Ten

One of the Hollywood Ten, Karl FRANCIS (2000)

A Get ready

1. Read the *Culture key* about McCarthyism to learn about "the Hollywood Ten".

2. Describe the film still and guess what the situation is.

B Watch the video

3. Watch an extract from *One of the Hollywood Ten*, a film by Karl Francis (2000). Your teacher will give you a worksheet to help you.

C In your own words

4. Use the worksheet to summarize the excerpt.

D Going further

5. Why did the American government and the FBI target Hollywood?

Text 1

Bad for us! 📖 💿
39

culture key Pearl Harbor → p. 15?

David GUTERSON
was born (1956) in Seattle and worked at odd jobs before becoming a teacher and publishing short stories in magazines. His first novel, *Snow Falling on Cedars*, was a bestseller, adapted for the screen in 1999, which enabled him to become a full-time writer. His other novels (*East of the Mountains*, 1998, *Our Lady of the Forest*, 2003) are all set in the Pacific Northwest.

A Warming up

Read the *Culture key* about Pearl Harbor and the title, then guess what made things bad for the Japanese community living in the United States.

The story takes place in the USA, in December 1941. Hatsue Imada is an American of Japanese origin. The Imadas live on San Piedro Island, off Seattle.

Hatsue Imada was standing in the foyer of the Amity Harbor Buddhist Chapel, buttoning her coat after services, when Georgia Katanaka's mother told the
5 people gathered there the news about Pearl Harbor. "It's very bad," she said. "A bombing raid. The Japanese air force has bombed everything. It is bad for us, terribly bad. There is nothing else on the radio. Everything is Pearl Harbor."

Hatsue pulled her lapels[1] more closely around her throat and turned her eyes toward her parents. Her father – he'd been busy helping her mother into her
10 coat – only stood there blinking at Mrs Katanaka. "It can't be true," he said.

"It's true," she said. "Find a radio. Just this morning. They bombed Hawaii."

They stood in the reception room kitchen with the Katanakas, Ichiharas, Sasakis, and Hayashidas and listened to the Bendix sitting on the counter. Nobody spoke – they merely stood there. They listened for ten minutes without
15 moving, their heads down, their ears turned toward the radio. Finally Hatsue's father began to pace and scratch his head and then to rub his chin, long strokes. "We'd better get home," he said.

They drove home and listened to the radio again, the five Imada girls and their parents. They kept the radio on all afternoon and late into the evening,
20 too. Now and then the telephone would ring, and Hatsue's father, in Japanese, would discuss matters with Mr Oshiro or Mr Nishi. More than a half-dozen times he made calls himself to discuss matters with other people. He would hang up, scratch his head, then return to his seat by the radio.

Mr Oshiro called again and told Hatsue's father that in Amity Harbor a
25 fisherman named Otto Willets had put up a ladder in front of Shigeru Ichiyama's
movie theater and unscrewed the lightbulbs in the marquee[2]. While he was busy
at it two other men had steadied the ladder for him and yelled curses at the
Ichiyamas, who were not present. Otto Willets and his friends, on discovering
this, had driven out to Lundgren Road and sat in front of the Ichiyamas' in a
30 pickup truck, where they pounded on the horn until Shig came out and stood
on his porch to see what they wanted. Willets had called Shig a dirty Jap and
told him he ought to have smashed every light in the marquee – didn't he know
there was a blackout? Shig said no, he hadn't known, he was glad to have been
told, he was thankful to the men for unscrewing the marquee bulbs for him. He
35 ignored Otto Willets's insults.

At ten o'clock Mr Oshiro called again; armed men had posted themselves
around Amity Harbor out of fear of a Japanese attack. There were men with
shotguns behind logs[3] along the beach just north and south of town. The defense
of San Piedro was being organized.

David GUTERSON, *Snow Falling on Cedars* (1995)

1. *revers de sa veste*   2. *auvent*   3. *rondin de bois*

B Understanding the text ⓦORKBOOK → p. 57-58

1. Turn to your *Workbook* which will help you to understand
the text.

2. Describe how San Piedro's inhabitants reacted after the
bombing of Pearl Harbor.

C Going further

3. Analyse the reaction of the Japanese community.

4. Analyse the attitude of Otto Willets and his friends towards
the Japanese-American community.

5. How do you explain Shigeru Ichiyama's attitude towards
Otto Willets?

6. Imagine what happened in San Piedro afterwards.

D Language training
37-38   40-41

7. Savoir prononcer

La réduction des voyelles
Les liaisons

8. Pratiquer la grammaire

Subordonnées de temps ●LANGUAGE WORKSHOP → p. 136
Pronoms réfléchis et possessifs – Infinitif parfait
ⓦORKBOOK → p. 62

toolbox

Nouns & expressions
- **target** /ˈtɑːgɪt/ (noun + verb): *cible(r)*
- **in disbelief**: *avec incrédulité*
- **vigilante** /ˌvɪdʒɪˈlæntɪ/: *membre d'un groupe d'autodéfense*

Adjectives
- **paranoid** /ˈpærənɔɪd/
- **guilty** (of): *coupable*
- **distressed**: *bouleversé*
- **speechless**: *sans voix*
- **safe** ≠ **risky**

Verbs & expressions
- **be taken aback**: *être interloqué*
- **avenge**: *se venger*
- **fight back**
- **evacuate**
- **declare war on sb**
- **be at war** (against)
- **invade**
- **flee** = run away
- **can't believe one's ears**: *ne pas en croire ses oreilles*
- **fear sth / sb might V**
- **overreact**

Your task

✎ **Write a page in Hatsue's diary**
Hatsue Imada, who is in love with a
young man of American origin, keeps a diary. Put
yourself in her shoes and write down the entry
she wrote on the day Pearl Harbor was bombed.

ⓜÉTHODOLOGIE
Écrire une page de journal intime → p. 171

Sacco and Vanzetti

A The topic

1. Look at the photo opposite and explain what these men are doing and why.

B Open your ears 42

2. You will hear three sentences. What information do they give about the two men?

C Listen 43-45 ⓦORKBOOK → p. 59

3. Listen to the recording. You will find some help in your *Workbook*.

D In your own words

4. Explain what happened to Sacco and Vanzetti and why.

E Going further

5. What is the reporter's opinion on the case? Justify in your own words.

6. Read the following song written and sung by American singer Joan Baez. Then look at the poster of a documentary film about Sacco and Vanzetti directed by Peter Miller and released in 2006.

a. What do these two documents show?

b. What do Nicola Sacco and Bartolomeo Vanzetti symbolize?

> Here's to you, Nicola and Bart
>
> Rest forever here in our hearts
>
> The last and final moment is yours
>
> That agony is your triumph
>
> Joan BAEZ and Ennio MORRICONE, *Here's to you* (1971)

"PIERCING!" — New York Times   "RIVETING!" — Chicago Tribune   "GRADE: A!" — Entertainment Weekly

SACCO AND VANZETTI

A film by Peter Miller

Featuring the voices of **Tony Shalhoub** and **John Turturro** and interviews with **Howard Zinn, Arlo Guthrie** and **Studs Terkel**

toolbox

Nouns
- protester /prəˈtestə/
- placard /ˈplækɑːd/: *écriteau*
- sympathizer /ˈsɪmpəθaɪzə/
- capital punishment / the death penalty
- lost cause
- resistance

Adjectives
- (un)popular
- shocking = revolting

Verbs & expressions
- address (a crowd): *haranguer*
- hold a rally: *organiser un rassemblement*
- fight for sb's cause
- execute
- fail ≠ succeed
- sentence sb to die
- be on trial for murder
- fight a losing battle
- embody: *incarner*

 Your task

 Write an article about the Sacco and Vanzetti case

As a journalist for an American newspaper, you write an article to commemorate the Sacco and Vanzetti case and its outcome.

ⓂéTHODOLOGIE
Rédiger un article de presse → p. 172

Speakers' corner

From limelight to exile

A Look and speak

1. Observe these pictures. What makes "the tramp", Charlie Chaplin's most famous character, so easily identifiable?

B Read and speak

2. Read the biography and the article below carefully so as to memorize the most significant details. Then, without looking at your book, speak about Charlie Chaplin's life and career.

The Kid (1921)

The Gold Rush (1925)

Charlie Chaplin

• **April 16, 1889:** Born in London. Poor family of music hall entertainers. Most of his childhood in orphanages.

• **Most famous films:** *The Tramp* (1915), *The Gold Rush* (1925), *City Lights* (1931), *Modern Times* (1936), *The Great Dictator* (1940), *Limelight* (1952)

• **1952:** Accused of Communist sympathies. Left the US. American re-entry permit denied.

• **1957:** *A King in New York* (criticism of McCarthy and American society, never shown in the US).

• **1972:** Return to the US to receive a special Academy Award.

• **1975:** Became Sir Charles Chaplin after Queen Elizabeth II knighted him.

• **December 25, 1977:** Died at his home in Switzerland.

US regards Chaplin as dangerous alien

April 17th 1953 – Charlie Chaplin announced today that he will never return to America, his home for 40 years. He was banned after he left for Europe last autumn to promote his film *Limelight*. He said then: "I am not a communist and I never have been." Chaplin, now 64, and his wife Oona recently settled at Vevey, Switzerland, with their four children. "I have been the object of vicious propaganda," he said. (*Chronicle of the 20th Century*)

toolbox

Nouns
• silent film **e**ra /ˈɪərə/
• **fi**gure /ˈfɪgə/: *silhouette*
• walk: *démarche*
• tramp = **va**grant: *vagabond*
• **bow**ler hat: *chapeau melon*
• cane = walking stick
• **ba**ggy **trou**sers
• mous**tache** /məsˈtɑːʃ/

Adjectives
• i**co**nic /aɪˈkɒnɪk/
• over**sized**: *trop grand*
• worn: *usé*
• re**co**gnizable /ˈrekəgnaɪzəbl/

Verbs & expressions
• **wel**come back
• feel re**sent**ment a**gainst** / towards sb
• have / hold a grudge a**gainst** sb: *en vouloir à qqn*

function box

Expressing regret and reproach

• Why **on** earth did / didn't you V?
• I should (not) have V-EN
• If only / I wish I had (not) V-EN
• Why didn't you V?
• What a shame!

Your task

Interview Charlie Chaplin on his return to the US in 1972

Student A You are a reporter. You interview Charlie Chaplin at JFK Airport.

Student B You are Charlie Chaplin. You tell the journalist about the reasons why you left the US and why you have decided to return after twenty years.

Ⓜ**ÉTHODOLOGIE**
Interview → p. 166

Not you!

culture key   McCarthyism → p. 157

Douglas KENNEDY

born in 1955, is an American writer, author of international bestsellers. His novels have been translated into more than twenty languages. His most famous works are *State of the Union* (2005), *Leaving the World* (2009), *The Moment* (2011).

A Warming up

Read the *Culture key* and observe the picture. What is the man doing? Use the introduction to imagine who the man may be and what the text may be about.

The USA in the 1950s. Sara's brother, Eric, committed suicide after losing his job during the witch-hunt. She has just learnt that Jack, her lover, was the one who gave his name to the HUAC.

"But you still gave his name to the FBI and the House Un-American Activities
5 Committee."

"I thought…"

"What? That the Feds would let him off with a warning?"

"Someone gave them my name. They insisted I give them names."

"You could have said no."

10 "Don't you think I wanted to?"

"But you didn't."

"There was no way out. If I refused to give names, I'd lose my job. But then someone else would come along and name the people I named."

"But that would have been someone else, not you."

15 Jack buried his head deeper in his hands. He fell silent again. When he finally spoke, his voice sounded diminished, small.

"Please try to understand: they insisted, demanded, that I give them a name. Believe me, I tried to explain that I had never been a Communist; that I had joined that anti-Fascist committee when I was a kid of eighteen, and only because I believed it was
20 making a principled stand against Hitler, Mussolini and Franco. The FBI guys said they understood that. Just as they also knew that I had served my country in the war – and hadn't dabbled in politics since then. As far as they were concerned, I was a 'good American' who'd made a small youthful mistake. Other people who were on that committee had also made mistakes – and in a demonstration of their patriotism, they
25 had given the names of those who were associated with this group at the time, or had once had Communist sympathies. 'They're probably as innocent as you are,' one of the Fed guys told me. 'But you must understand: we are investigating a vast conspiracy which poses a threat to national security. We simply need to discover who is at the

heart of the conspiracy. Which is why we need names. By giving us information not
30 only are you doing a service to your country; you are also eliminating yourself from
our investigations. But by refusing to assist us, the cloud of suspicion still hovers over
you. Face fact, anyone who's been a Communist in the past is going to get found out.
So you might as well make a clean breast of everything… while you still can.'"

Jack paused again. He lifted his head up, attempting to look me in the eye. But I
35 turned away.

"Their argument had a ruthless logic to it. Someone had named me. I would prove
my innocence by naming someone else. They, in turn, would prove their innocence
by naming someone else. Everyone was betraying each other. But the thing about this
betrayal was – no one had a choice. "

40 "Yes, they did," I said, suddenly angry. "The Hollywood Ten had a choice – they all
went to jail. Arthur Miller had a choice: he refused to name names. My brother had a
choice… and he lost his life."

Jack's head went back into his hands.

Douglas KENNEDY, *The Pursuit of Happiness* (2002)

B Understanding the text ⓦORKBOOK → p. 60-61

1. Your *Workbook* will help you to understand the text.

2. Sum up the situation.

C Going further

3. Analyse the arguments developed by the FBI agents. What is a *"good American"* (l. 23) for them?

4. What made Jack give in to the FBI's demand?

5. Analyse Jack's attitude and feelings throughout this passage.

6. How does Sara feel about Jack and what he did? What does she want to make him realize?

D Writing time

7. Essay (200 words) Ⓜ ÉTHODOLOGIE **Écrire un essai → p. 172**

Are we always free to make our own choices?
a. Partez de la situation décrite dans le texte.

b. Aidez-vous aussi des autres documents de l'unité.

c. Donnez des exemples personnels et / ou empruntés à l'actualité pour illustrer votre propos.

d. Ceci est un sujet argumentatif. Vous devez apporter des arguments contradictoires avant de conclure, en donnant votre point de vue personnel.

e. Utilisez la *Toolbox*, les *Keywords* (p. 126) et les *Expressions utiles pour communiquer* (p. 174).

f. Utilisez des mots de liaison pour structurer votre propos.

E Language training

8. Savoir prononcer 39   47   ⓦORKBOOK → p. 61

La terminaison *-ed* des verbes

9. Pratiquer la grammaire
Traduction de « QUE »   ⬤LANGUAGE WORKSHOP → p. 136
Les pronoms indéfinis ⓦORKBOOK → p. 62

toolbox

Nouns
- **coward** /'kaʊəd/: *lâche*
- **stool pigeon** /'stuːl pɪdʒən/: *indic, balance*
- **contempt**: *mépris*

Adjectives
- **revolted**
- **resentful** /rɪ'zentfʊl/: *plein de ressentiment*
- **useless** /'juːslɪs/
- **remorseful**
- **scornful** = contemptuous: *méprisant*

Verbs & expressions
- **take the oath** /əʊθ/: *prêter serment*
- **summon** /'sʌmən/: *convoquer*
- **have one's back to the wall**
- **be appalled** /ə'pɔːld/ (at sb): *être consterné*
- **despise** (sb for sth / V-ING): *mépriser*
- **forgive** (sb for sth / V-ING)
- **fear / dread** (+ sb might): *craindre*
- **blackmail sb into** V-ING: *faire pression sur qqn pour le forcer à faire qqch*
- **make a full confession**: *faire des aveux complets*
- **be ashamed of**
- **make amends (for)**: *se racheter*
- **justify oneself**

 Act out a conversation about breaking up

The next day, Sara decides to break up with Jack. She meets a friend of hers to talk about her decision.

Student A You are Sara. You explain the situation to your friend and tell her / him the reason(s) why you have decided to leave Jack.

Student B You are Sara's friend. You react to Sara's decision and give her advice about what she should do.

Ⓜ ÉTHODOLOGIE
Conversation → p. 165

135

Grammaire | Subordonnées de temps – Traduction de « QUE »

A Subordonnées de temps ⓟRÉCIS GRAMMATICAL → 39

1 **While, until, before et since**

1. **While** he was busy at it two other men had steadied the ladder (Text 1, p. 130, l. 26)
2. (…) they pounded on the horn **until** Shig came out (Text 1, p. 130, l. 30)
3. They said we had better start **before** it was too late.
4. "They've been standing there **since** they heard the news on the radio."

a. Indiquez pour chacun des mots en gras quelle notion il exprime :
1. un point de départ – 2. un point d'arrivée – 3. l'antériorité – 4. la simultanéité.
b. Traduisez les énoncés.

2 **Traduisez à l'aide de while, until, before et since.**

a. Je resterai là jusqu'à ce qu'ils s'en aillent.
b. Demande-leur de finir ce travail avant qu'ils ne partent.
c. Nous avons parlé de vous pendant que vous dormiez.
d. J'attends cela (*present perfect BE+ING*) depuis que vous êtes parti.

B Traduction de « QUE » ⓟRÉCIS GRAMMATICAL → 33B, 37

3 **Proposition infinitive et subordonnées en THAT**

1. "I **thought**…" "What? That the Feds would let him off with a warning?" (Text 2, p. 134, l. 6)
2. "(…) they **insisted**, **demanded**, that I give them a name." (Text 2, p. 134, l. 17)
3. "Believe me, I tried to **explain** that I had never been a Communist." (Text 2, p. 134, l. 17)
4. "The FBI guys **said** [that] they understood that." (Text 2, p. 134, l. 20)
5. I **expected** them to send me away but they **told** me to sit there and wait.
6. They **told** him that he was free.

a. Indiquez quelle est la notion exprimée par chacun des verbes en gras dans les énoncés ci-dessus :
1. volonté / attente / ordre – 2. opinion – 3. exigence – 4. rapport de paroles.
Notez également si le verbe est suivi d'une proposition en THAT ou d'une proposition infinitive.
b. Quels sont les deux sens possibles de TELL et les constructions correspondantes ?
c. Les verbes *insist* et *demand* sont-ils suivis d'une forme verbale conjuguée ou d'une base verbale sans aucune marque de temps ?
d. Dans quels cas « QUE » se traduit-il par une proposition infinitive et dans quels cas par THAT ?

4 **Réécrivez les énoncés à l'aide de l'amorce proposée.**

1. "The Japanese air force has bombed everything," he said to them. → He told…
2. "You'd better get back home," she said to him. → She advised…
3. "Please, talk to him," he said to them. → He expected…
4. "Stand up," he said to her. → He told…

5 **Traduisez les passages suivants.**

a. Ils lui ont demandé de leur dire qu'il était coupable.
b. Elle ne pensait pas qu'ils s'attendaient à ce qu'elle réponde.
c. Il ne voulait pas que nous les obligions (*force*) à répondre.

Grammaire de l'oral | Reconnaître *have* et *of* à l'oral

6 Repérer *have, of, off* à l'oral 48-49

a. Lisez ces énoncés et complétez avec la forme qui convient : *have, of, off.*

    1. *"What? That the Feds would let him … with a warning?"* (Text 2, p. 134, l. 7)

    2. *Most … your friends … betrayed you.*

b. Écoutez ces mêmes énoncés. Lesquels de ces mots, *of, off, have*, se prononcent de la même manière, c'est-à-dire : /əv/ ?

c. Écrivez les énoncés que vous entendez.

7 Repérer *have* après les auxiliaires modaux 50-51

a. Certaines formes peuvent être difficiles à distinguer à l'oral : **could** / **could have** / **couldn't** – **would** / **would have** / **wouldn't**. Écoutez ces énoncés et répétez les modèles.

    1. *"You could have said no."* (…) *"But you didn't."* (Text 2, p. 134, l. 9)

    2. *"I couldn't say anything. I just kept silent."*

b. Écrivez les énoncés que vous entendez.

Lexique | La chasse aux sorcières

Assurez-vous que vous avez bien retenu les mots clés de l'unité. → Keywords p. 126

8 Donnez les synonymes ou les antonymes des mots et expressions suivants.

a. suspicion = … **b.** innocent ≠ … **c.** exclude = … **d.** oppose = … **e.** accuse sb of = … **f.** fair ≠ …

9 Quelle est la syllabe accentuée dans les mots suivants ?

a. suspected **b.** enemy **c.** rumour **d.** suspicious

10 Traduisez : **a.** be prejudiced against **b.** hold sb accountable for **c.** evil

11 Complétez les phrases à l'aide des mots et expressions suivants.

witch hunt – testify – name names – wrongfully – blacklisted – were tried – point out – confessed – evidence – traitors – scapegoats – denounce – convicted

a. They were …¹… and used as …²… by the US government.

b. He and his wife were …³… accused of being …⁴… and were executed.

c. They had to …⁵… and …⁶… other people if they wanted to be released.

d. Although there was no real …⁷… against him, he was …⁸… and sent to prison.

e. Many artists had to …⁹… in court, and some of them …¹⁰… to having communist sympathies. Some others had no choice but to …¹¹… their friends.

f. During the …¹²…, thousands of Americans …¹³… for what they believed in.

toolbox

Adjectives
- stunned: *stupéfait*
- taken aback: *décontenancé*
- infuriated: *furieux*

Verbs & expressions
- overhear a fight: *surprendre une dispute*
- shout abuse (at sb): *injurier*

Your task

Tell a TV reporter what happened

On your way home you came across a group of people quarrelling violently. You tried to intervene but suddenly one of them started shouting at you, pulled out a gun, pointed it at you, then ran away. You tell a TV reporter what happened. Act out the conversation and record it if possible. Use verbs like **say, tell, ask, force, explain, want, expect** plus infinitive clauses or **that-clauses**.

Witch hunting in America

Are witches a myth of the past?

A Puritanism in 17th century New England

Read the text below and sum up orally the Puritans' moral values and beliefs.

Puritanism in New England[1] was based on a very strict moral code and a denial of physical and social pleasures such as dancing, card playing or holiday celebrations, which were regarded as sinful[2]. In Puritan society, anyone who did not meet the Puritan standard was rejected. The Puritans dressed in plain dark clothes with no fashionable accessories – colourful clothes being an indication of the "devil at work". The Puritans believed

in the concept of predestination. For them, God chose each human being at birth for salvation or condemnation. The Puritans' strict moralistic views towards marriage and adultery were important in maintaining order in their society. Adultery was a capital offense and, to inflict shame and humiliation, was punished publicly (sometimes by death). In Puritan society, the forest was regarded as the home of the devil and a place witches met at night. Puritans often found spiritual meaning in what might be considered simple coincidences. For example, a snake indicated the presence of the devil.

1. The North East part of the US, consisting of the states of Maine, New Hampshire, Vermont, Massachusetts, Rhode Island and Connecticut 2. *immoral*

An accused witch is dunked in water to prove her guilt of practicing witchcraft

B The witches of Salem

1 Read the text. What were the causes and consequences of the Salem witch trials?

2 What does the picture illustrate?

Many American colonists brought over from Europe a belief in witches. In 1692, a group of girls from Salem, Massachusetts, became strangely ill. They started having convulsions, experienced physical pain, complained of fever, claimed to have horrible visions and uttered blasphemous screams. As no one could determine any physical cause for their symptoms, they were believed to be under the influence of the devil. The girls claimed that they were tormented by some people in the community. In Salem, where everyone believed that the devil acted in the real world, the girls' affliction became an obsession. During the witch trials that followed, more than 200 people were accused of witchcraft and 20 were hanged.

Representation of witches

1 Observe three other representations of witches. What are their similarities and differences?

2 Which of these pictures corresponds to your idea of a witch? Explain.

Trial of Sarah Good and Sarah
Osborne in Salem (1692)

Arresting a witch in Salem

A witch flies with her cat on her
broomstick

 Witch-hunters in the 20th century  52

Read about American playwright Arthur Miller's play, *The Crucible*. Then, listen to Arthur Miller speaking about how his play came to be.

1 Imagine what sort of questions Miller refused to answer.

2 Why did he decide to write *The Crucible* and to set his play in 17th century Salem?

The Crucible is set in 1692, during the Salem witch trials. At the time of its first performance in January 1953, critics regarded Miller's play as a direct attack on the policy initiated by US Senator Joseph McCarthy to fight Communism. *The Crucible* is still seen today as a powerful depiction of how intolerance and hysteria can tear a community apart.

Webquest  **Salem, "The Witch City"** TICE

1 Browse the web to find out more about Salem. Focus on the following elements:

a. Where is Salem located?

b. Is the myth of the Salem witches still alive?

c. Which places of interest would you like to visit?

2 Report back to the class on what you have learnt about the city of Salem. Use the information that you have collected on the websites as well as what you have learnt in these pages.

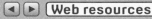 **Web resources** ○○○

final task

What do you know about blacklisting in American history?

"The Best Speaker Contest" is being held in your school. You decide to participate. After reading an extract from Paul Auster's novel, *Oracle Night*, about scapegoats in society, you give an oral account of the story and comment on it.

  Read an extract from a novel

MÉTHODOLOGIE **COMPRÉHENSION DE L'ÉCRIT** → p. 167

Read the passage from *Oracle Night* on page 141.
Then answer the following questions:

a. What is the situation?

b. When did the narrator write the story?

c. Where and when does his story take place?

d. What idea was the starting point of the narrator's story?

e. Is the country really invaded by barbarians? Explain.

f. What parallels does the narrator draw with the history of the USA?

★★★★★
Je me situe
par rapport
au CECRL
B2

LORSQUE JE LIS CET EXTRAIT :
Je peux comprendre rapidement le contenu et l'idée principale d'un texte littéraire contemporain. Je peux identifier le point de vue développé par le narrateur.

  Now speak

MÉTHODOLOGIE **EXPRESSION ORALE EN CONTINU** → p. 163

■ First, give an oral account of the story you have read.

■ This story echoes the documents that you have studied in this unit. Use them to illustrate the narrator's story.

■ Your oral presentation should last between three and four minutes. Make complete sentences and link them. If you hesitate, remember to use gap fillers if necessary.

■ This is an oral contest. Be convincing! You must speak clearly and make yourself understood.

Giving examples

function box

● For example / For instance...
● ... that is to say...
● ... such as...

Giving arguments

● First of all...
● One of the main reasons why...
● Another good reason for V-ING...
● What's more...
● However...
● Last but not least: *Enfin et surtout*

★★★★★
Je me situe
par rapport
au CECRL
B2

QUAND JE FAIS CETTE PRÉSENTATION :
Je peux développer un exposé de manière claire et méthodique en soulignant les éléments significatifs et une argumentation claire, nuancée, et enchaîner les arguments avec logique.

The Empire of Bones

Paul AUSTER

was born in 1947 in Newark, New Jersey. He graduated from Columbia University and moved to Paris where he made his living translating French authors until 1974. He has written numerous poems, essays, screenplays and novels. His most famous works are *The New York Trilogy* (1987), *Moon Palace* (1989), *The Music of Chance* (1990), *Leviathan* (1992), *The Brooklyn Follies* (2005), *Sunset Park* (2010).

"Well, read the story and let me know what you think. It's just a first draft – very rough – so don't judge the prose too harshly. And remember, I was hardly more than a kid when I wrote it. Much younger than you are now."

"What's it about?"

5 "It's an odd piece, not at all like my other work, so you might be a little surprised at first. I guess I'd call it a political parable. It's set in an imaginary country in the eighteen thirties, but it's really about the early nineteen fifties, McCarthy, HUAC, the Red Scare – all the sinister things that were going on then. The idea is that governments always need enemies, even when they're not at war. If you don't have

10 a real enemy, you make one up and spread the word. It scares the population, and when the people are scared, they tend not to step out of line."

"What about the country? Is it a stand-in for America or something else?"

"It's part North America, part South America, but with a completely different history from either one. Way back, all the European powers had set up colonies in the New

15 World. The colonies evolved into independent states, and then, little by little, after hundreds of years of wars and skirmishes, they gradually merge into an enormous confederation. The question is: What happens after the empire is established? What enemy do you invent to make people scared enough to hold the confederation together?"

20 "And what's the answer?"

"You pretend you're about to be invaded by barbarians. The confederation has already pushed these people off lands, but now you spread the rumor that an army of anti-confederationist soldiers has crossed into the primitive territories and is stirring up a rebellion among the people there. It isn't true. The soldiers are working for the

25 government. They're part of the conspiracy."

"Who tells the story?"

"A man sent to investigate the rumors. He works for a branch of the government that isn't in on the plot, and he winds up being arrested and tried for treason. To make matters more complicated, the officer in charge of the false army has run off with the

30 narrator's wife."

"Deceit and corruption at every turn."

"Exactly. A man ruined by his own innocence."

"Does it have a title?"

"*The Empire of Bones*. It's not very long. Forty-five or fifty pages – but there's enough

35 to squeeze a film out of it, I think. You decide. If you want to use it, I give you my blessing. If you don't like it, then chuck it in the garbage, we'll forget all about it."

Paul AUSTER, *Oracle Night* (2003)

Bac oral

Vous trouverez la présentation de l'épreuve pages 12-13 et des conseils pratiques pour le bac pages 175-179.

Compréhension de l'oral

 40 53 **W**ORKBOOK → p. 63

Vous allez écouter trois fois un document intitulé *Witch hunting*.

Avant l'écoute

1. Aidez-vous du titre du document de façon à anticiper son contenu.

Première écoute

2. Identifiez la nature et le thème général du document.

Deuxième écoute

3. Relevez les informations principales.

Troisième écoute

4. Donnez des détails significatifs et le point de vue des locuteurs.

Rendez compte en français de ce que vous avez compris.

TIPS

← Qui sont les intervenants ? De quoi parlent-ils ?

← Repérez une confusion possible soulignée par l'un des intervenants.

← Comment l'existence des chasses aux sorcières est-elle expliquée ?

Expression orale

WORKBOOK → p. 64

Lors de votre prise de parole en continu, puis de la conversation avec l'examinateur, vous pourrez aborder les problématiques suivantes en lien avec l'unité 7.

Notion 1 Mythes et héros
Myths and heroes

■ The myth of witches in America

Puritanism in 17th century New England, p. 138 • The witches of Salem, p. 138 • Witch-hunters in the 20th century, p. 139 • Salem, "The Witch City", p. 139

← • Définissez le terme *witch* au sens large.
• Le mythe de la sorcière a-t-il évolué au fil des siècles ?

■ Scapegoats and heroes

The "Red Scare", p. 128 • One of the Hollywood Ten, p. 129 • Sacco and Vanzetti, p. 132 • From limelight to exile, p. 133 • Not you!, p. 134 • Witch-hunters in the 20th century, p. 139 • McCarthyism, p. 157 • John Edgar Hoover, p. 157

← • Comment expliquer la présence de boucs émissaires pendant la première partie du xxᵉ siècle aux États-Unis ?
• Quelles furent les réactions à la désignation de boucs émissaires dans chaque situation ?

Notion 2 Lieux et formes du pouvoir
Seats and forms of power

■ Why were some American people blacklisted?

The "Red Scare", p. 128 • One of the Hollywood Ten, p. 129 • Bad for us!, p. 130 • Sacco and Vanzetti, p. 132 • From limelight to exile, p. 133 • Not you!, p. 134 • Puritanism in 17th century New England, p. 138

← • Trouvez les raisons pour lesquelles des hommes et des femmes ont été mis à l'index au cours de l'histoire des États-Unis.
• Utilisez des expressions vous permettant d'exprimer le **but** : *in order to... so (that)... so as to...*; la **cause** : *as... because of... since...*

TEXT 1 – Twelve names

The scene takes place in the USA in the 1950s.

"Mrs Stevens," began Roy Cohn, "sincerely, this is not an interrogation."
The young woman on the other side of the desk made a face.
"This is just an informal interview. To help you sort out questions that have been
5 raised."
"Will I be subpoenaed[1]?" The lawyer's smile was as fake as Finlay's right eye.
"There's been no question of that so far."
"Who is that man?" Mrs Stevens asked, nodding at Finlay.
"I'm with the Bureau."
10 "The FBI?"
"That's right," he confirmed, hoping frankness would reassure her.
"I'm just a housewife," she said, redundantly. "My husband is with McMann
and Tate. We live in Westport ..."
"Goodwife Stevens," Finlay said, fixing her with his good eye, "do not make the
15 mistake of thinking us naive."
"Roy," Finlay said to Cohn, "tell Goodwife Stevens where she stands. Straight
talking is more comfortable than all the lawyer bullstuff[2]."
It was sticky-hot in the third-storey office the Sub-Committee[3] rented in Manhattan.
The window hadn't opened since Pearl Harbour. Finlay slipped off his suitcoat,
20 calculating the effect on the woman of the sight of the heavy automatic hanging in
his wet armpit. He was sweating through his shirt into the leather of his holster. Cohn
shuffled folders and opened one. The others, Finlay guessed, were just for show.
"Your name has come up in testimony several times. Do you understand?"
Mrs Stevens nodded, face frozen.
25 "No accusations have been made. The Constitution entitles you to freedom of
speech, freedom of belief, freedom of worship. There has, as yet, been no suggestion
of illegal activity on your part."
"I'm not a spy."
"Of course not. However, we believe you are a member of a 'circle' operating
30 in this city..."
"Circle' was the polite term. It was out in the open now. She knew they knew
and she'd have to make a decision.
"I think I had better talk with a lawyer."
Cohn's eyes glowed like neons. His head was poised[4], expectant. Mrs Stevens
35 would bite the hook. "I am a lawyer, Mrs Stevens." She shook her head slightly.
"Twelve names," Finlay said, shockingly.
"Just give us twelve names and you can go home. It'll all be over for you."
... and all beginning for the next on the list.
"Do you want me to start for you?" he asked, looming over the desk, getting
40 close enough to let her see the flaws[5] in his right eye. "How about Gillian and Nicky
Holroyd?"
She was shaking now, asking herself questions, but not yet giving any answers.

It was such a fixed game. There were always thirteen. The only way off the hook, the only way to qualify as a "friendly", was to cough up twelve names.

45   "Twelve names, Samantha. Or do they call you Sam?"

"This is extremely irregular," Cohn spluttered, trying vainly to cast himself as the nice guy cop.

"Twelve names."

A tear, solitary and perfect, traced a line down Mrs Stevens's cheek, cutting through

50 mascara.

"Twelve names, witch."

Kim NEWMAN, The McCarthy Witch Hunt (1992)

TEXT 2 – Naming names

The story is set in Salem, Massachusetts, in 1692. The Reverend Hale and the Reverend Parris are questioning Tituba, Parris's slave from Barbados.

HALE: You have confessed yourself to witchcraft, and that speaks a wish to come to Heaven's side. And we will bless you, Tituba.

5 **TITUBA** (*deeply relieved*)**:** Oh, God bless you, Mr Hale!

HALE: You are God's instrument put in our hands to discover the Devil's agents amongst us. You are selected, Tituba, you are chosen to help us cleanse our village. So speak utterly, Tituba, turn your back on him and face God, Tituba, and God will protect you.

TITUBA: Oh, God, protect Tituba!

10 **HALE** (*kindly*)**:** Who came to you with the Devil? Two? Three? Four? How many?
(*Tituba begins rocking back and forth again, staring ahead.*)

TITUBA: There was four. There was four.

PARRIS: Who? Their names!

TITUBA (*suddenly bursting out*)**:** Oh, how many times he bid[6] me kill you, Mr Parris!

15 **PARRIS:** Kill me!

TITUBA (*in a fury*)**:** He say Mr Parris must be kill! Mr Parris no goodly man, Mr Parris mean man and no gentle man, and he bid me rise out of my bed and cut your throat! But I tell him "No! I don't hate that man. I don't want to kill that man." But he say, "You work for me, Tituba, and I make you free! I give you pretty dress to wear, and

20 put you way high in the air, and you gone fly back to Barbados!" And I say, "You lie, Devil, you lie!" And then he come one stormy night to me, and he say, "Look! I have *white* people belong to me." And I look – and there was Goody Good.

PARRIS: Goody Good!

Arthur MILLER, The Crucible (1952)

1. /sə'piːnəd/ *assigner à comparaître*   2. *foutaises*   3. a branch of the House Un-American Activities Committee   4. *calme*   5. *défauts*   6. *ordonner*

Vous trouverez la présentation de l'épreuve pages 12-13
et des conseils pratiques pour le bac pages 175-179.

Compréhension de l'écrit

Read the two texts before answering the questions.

TIPS

TEXT 1

1. Say briefly what Roy Cohn and Finlay want of Mrs Stevens.

> Vous devez avoir lu le texte en entier pour répondre aux questions 1 et 2.

2. Choose the sentences that correspond to Mrs Stevens' situation.
   a. She is being questioned by a judge.
   b. She is being questioned about her activities.
   c. She is accused of spying.   **d.** Her name has been given to the authorities.

3. What are Roy Cohn's and Finlay's strategies when dealing with Mrs Stevens in these two passages? Explain briefly and quote keywords to justify.
   a. From line 2 to line 17.   **b.** From line 18 to line 22.

> Puisqu'on vous demande d'analyser deux passages, c'est qu'il y a eu un changement dans l'attitude des protagonistes.

4. Quote a sentence showing what Roy Cohn and Finlay have against Mrs Stevens.

5. Why does Mrs Stevens say "I think I had better talk with a lawyer" (l. 33)?

6. Analyse Roy Cohn's reaction to this sentence. (30 words)

7. Explain in one sentence the use of the term a "friendly" (l. 44).

8. How does Mrs Stevens feel in the passage from line 31 to the end? Explain why. (50 words)

> Relevez les mots clés vous permettant de répondre à la question.

TEXT 2

9. In one sentence explain why Tituba is being questioned.

10. Analyse the Reverend Hale's strategy to make Tituba cooperate. (35 words)

> Relisez attentivement le passage de la ligne 3 à la ligne 13.

11. Explain why Tituba says "Oh, God bless you, Mr Hale!" (l. 5).

12. What does Tituba reveal to Parris? How does he react to such revelations? (20 words)

> Il y a deux révélations. Décrivez les réactions de Parris pour chacune d'entre elles.

13. Analyse Tituba's behaviour from line 11 to the end. What does it reveal? (60 words)

> • Prenez en compte les indications scéniques.
> • Vous devez également avoir bien compris la première partie du texte.

TEXT 1 AND TEXT 2

14. Explain the similarities between Tituba's and Mrs Stevens' situations.

Expression écrite

> Use your grammar
> • Formuler hypothèses et souhaits : **fiche 5** (p. 182)
> • Choisir un point de vue sur l'action : **fiche 8** (p. 183)

1. Continue the first story, starting with: "But Mrs Stevens decided she would not give them names…"

2. Taking into account the situation and the historical context of the first text, explain why Arthur Miller wrote The Crucible, a play which takes place during the Salem trials.

> Utilisez les informations données dans le Spotlight de l'unité 7 (p. 138-139).

Dear Miss Ashton

Writer Juliet Ashton exchanges letters with Guernsey inhabitants who tell her about the German occupation of the island during World War II.

22nd April, 1946

Mary Ann SHAFFER (1934-2008)

was born in West Virginia, USA. She worked as an editor, a librarian, and in bookshops; she achieved her life-long dream to write her own book with *The Guernsey Literary and Potato Peel Pie Society*. When her health began to decline, she asked her niece, **Annie BARROWS**, author of children's books, to help her finish the novel. It was published posthumously and immediately became a best-seller.

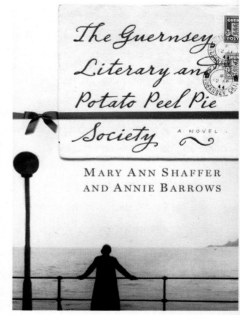

You asked if all the Guernsey
5 children were evacuated to England. No — some stayed, and when I missed Eli[1], I looked at the little ones around me and was glad he had gone. The children here had
10 a bad time, for there was no food to grow on. I remember picking up Bill LePell's boy — he was twelve but weighed no more than a child of seven.

15 It was a terrible thing to decide — send your kiddies away to live among strangers, or let them stay with you? Maybe the Germans wouldn't come, but if they did —
20 how would they behave to us? But, come to that, what if they invaded England, too — how would the children manage without their own families beside them?

25 Do you know the state we were in when the Germans came? Shock is what I'd call it. The truth is, we didn't think they'd want us. It was England they were after, and we were of no use to them. We thought we'd be in the audience like, not up on the stage itself.

Then in the spring of 1940 Hitler got himself going through Europe like a
30 hot knife through butter. Every place fell to him. It was so fast-windows all over Guernsey shook and rattled from the explosions in France, and once the coast of France was gone, it was plain as day that England could not use up her men and ships to defend us. They needed to save them for when their own invasion began in earnest. So we were left to ourselves.

35 In the middle of June, when it became pretty certain we were in for it, the States[2] got on the telephone to London and asked if they would send ships for our children and take them to England. They could not fly for fear of being shot down by the Luftwaffe. London said yes, but the children had to be ready at once. The ships would have to hurry here and back again while there was
40 still time. It was such a desperate time for folks and there was such a feel of Hurry, Hurry.

Jane[3] had no more strength than a cat then, but she knew her mind. She wanted Eli to go. Other ladies were in a dither — go or stay? — and they were wild to talk it over, but Jane told Elizabeth to keep them away. "I don't want to

1. Eben Ramsey's grandson
2. The Parliament of Guernsey
3. Eben Ramsey's daughter

hear them fuss," she said. "It's bad for the baby." Jane had an idea that babies knew everything that happened around them, even before they were born.

The time for dithering was soon over. Families had one day to decide, and five years to abide with it. School-age children and babies with their mothers went first on the 19th and 20th of June. The States gave out pocket money to the kiddies, if their parents had none to spare. The littlest children were all excited about the sweets they could buy with it. Some thought it was like a Sunday School outing, and they'd be back by nightfall. They were lucky in that. The older children, like Eli, knew better.

Of all the sights I saw the day they left, there is one picture I can't get out of my mind. Two little girls, all dressed up in pink party dresses, stiff petticoats, shiny strap shoes – like their Ma thought they'd be going to a party. How cold they must have been crossing the Channel.

All the children were to be dropped off at their school by their parents. It was there we had to say our goodbyes. Buses came to take the children down to the pier. The boats that had just been to Dunkirk came back across the Channel for the children. There was no time to get a convoy together to escort them. There was no time to get enough lifeboats on board or life jackets.

That morning we stopped first at the hospital for Eli to bid his mother good-bye. He couldn't do it. His jaw was clamped shut so tight, he could only nod. Jane held him for a bit, and then Elizabeth and me walked him down to the schoolyard. I hugged him hard and that was the last time I saw him for five years. Elizabeth stayed because she had volunteered to help get the children inside ready.

I was walking back to Jane in the hospital, when I recalled something Eli had once said to me. He was about five years old, and we were walking down to La Courbière to see the fishing boats come in. There was an old canvas bathing shoe left lying right in the middle of the path. Eli walked around it, staring. Finally, he said, "That shoe is all alone, Grandpa." I answered that yes it was. He looked at it some more, and then we walked on by. After a bit, he said, "Grandpa, that's something I never am." I asked him, "What's that?" And he said: "Lonesome in my spirits."

There! I had something happy to tell Jane after all, and I prayed it would stay true for him.

Isola says she wants to write you herself of the doings inside the school. She says she was witness to a scene you will want to know about as an authoress: Elizabeth smacked Adelaide Addison in the face and made her leave. You do not know Miss Addison, and you are fortunate in that – she is a woman too good for daily wear.

Isola told me you might come to visit Guernsey. I would be glad to offer you hospitality with me and Eli.

Yours,
Eben Ramsey

Mary Ann SHAFFER & Annie BARROWS,
The Guernsey Literary and Potato Peel Pie Society (2008)

True love

**Isaac ASIMOV
(1920-1992)**

was born in Russia. His family emigrated to New York in 1923. He taught biochemistry at Boston University and was a prolific science-fiction writer. His most famous works are *I, Robot* (1950) and *The Foundation trilogy* (1951-1953).

My name is Joe. That is what my colleague, Milton Davidson, calls me. He is a programmer and I am a computer program. I am part
5 of the Multivac-complex and am connected with other parts all over the world. I know everything. Almost everything.

I am Milton's private program.
10 His Joe. He understands more about programming than anyone in the world, and I am his experimental model. He has made me speak better than any
15 other computer can.

"It is just a matter of matching sounds to symbols, Joe," he told me. "That's the way it works in the human brain even though we still don't know what symbols there
20 are in the brain. I know the symbols in yours, and I can match them to words, one-to-one." So I talk. I don't think I talk as well as I think, but Milton says I talk very well. Milton has never married, though he is nearly forty years old. He has never found the right woman, he told me.
25 One day he said, "I'll find her yet, Joe. I'm going to find the best. I'm going to have true love and you're going to help me. I'm tired of improving you in order to solve the problems of the world. Solve my problem. Find me true love."

I said, "What is true love?"
30 "Never mind. That is abstract. Just find me the ideal girl. You are connected to the Multivac-complex so you can reach the data banks of every human being in the world. We'll eliminate them all by groups and classes until we're left with only one person. The perfect person. She will be for me."

I said, "I am ready."
35 He said, "Eliminate all men first."

It was easy. His words activated symbols in my molecular valves. I could reach out to make contact with the accumulated data on every human being in the world. At his words, I withdrew from 3,784,982,874 men. I kept contact with 3,786,112,090 women.
40 He said, "Eliminate all younger than twenty-five; all older than forty. Then eliminate all with an IQ under 120; all with a height under 150 centimeters and over 175 centimeters."

He gave me exact measurements; he eliminated women with living children; he eliminated women with various genetic characteristics. "I'm not
45 sure about eye color," he said. "Let that go for a while. But no red hair. I don't like red hair."

After two weeks, we were down to 235 women. They all spoke English very well. Milton said he didn't want a language problem. Even computer-translation would get in the way at intimate moments.

50 "I can't interview 235 women," he said. "It would take too much time, and people would discover what I am doing."

"It would make trouble," I said. Milton had arranged me to do things I wasn't designed to do. No one knew about that.

"It's none of their business," he said, and the skin on his face grew red. 55 "I tell you what, Joe, I will bring in holographs, and you check the list for similarities."

He brought in holographs of women. "These are three beauty contest winners," he said. "Do any of the 235 match?"

Eight were very good matches and Milton said, "Good, you have their data 60 banks. Study requirements and needs in the job market and arrange to have them assigned here. One at a time, of course." He thought a while, moved his shoulders up and down, and said, "Alphabetical order."

That is one of the things I am not designed to do. Shifting people from job to job for personal reasons is called manipulation. I could do it now because 65 Milton had arranged it. I wasn't supposed to do it for anyone but him, though.

The first girl arrived a week later. Milton's face turned red when he saw her. He spoke as though it were hard to do so. They were together a great deal and he paid no attention to me. One time he said, "Let me take you to dinner."

The next day he said to me, "It was no good, somehow. There was something 70 missing. She is a beautiful woman, but I didn't feel any touch of true love. Try the next one."

It was the same with all eight. They were much alike. They smiled a great deal and had pleasant voices, but Milton always found it wasn't right. He said, "I can't understand it, Joe. You and I have picked out the eight women who, in 75 all the world, look the best to me. They are ideal. Why don't they please me?"

I said, "Do you please them?"

His eyebrows moved and he pushed one fist hard against his other hand. "That's it, Joe. It's a two-way street. If I am not their ideal, they can't act in such a way as to be my ideal. I must be their true love, too, but how do I do 80 that?" He seemed to be thinking all that day.

The next morning he came to me and said, "I'm going to leave it to you, Joe. All up to you. You have my data bank, and I am going to tell you everything I know about myself. You fill up my data bank in every possible detail but keep all additions to yourself" "What will I do with the data bank, then, 85 Milton?" "Then you will match it to the 235 women. No, 227. Leave out the eight you've seen. Arrange to have each undergo a psychiatric examination. Fill up their data banks and compare them with mine. Find correlations." (Arranging psychiatric examinations is another thing that is against my original instructions.)

90 For weeks, Milton talked to me. He told me of his parents and his siblings. He told me of his childhood and his schooling and his adolescence. He told me of the young women he had admired from a distance. His data bank grew and he adjusted me to broaden and deepen my symbol-taking.

He said, "You see, Joe, as you get more and more of me in you, I adjust 95 you to match me better and better. You get to think more like me, so you

understand me better. If you understand me well enough, then any woman, whose data bank is something you understand as well, would be my true love." He kept talking to me and I came to
100 understand him better and better.

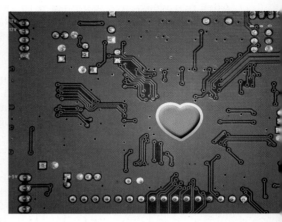

I could make longer sentences and my expressions grew more complicated. My speech began to sound a good deal like his in vocabulary, word order and style. I said to him one time,
105 "You see, Milton, it isn't a matter of fitting a girl to a physical ideal only. You need a girl who is a personal, emotional, temperamental fit to you. If that happens, looks are secondary. If we can't find the fit in these 227, we'll look elsewhere. We
110 will find someone who won't care how you look either, or how anyone would look, if only there is the personality fit. What are looks?"

"Absolutely," he said. "I would have known this if I had had more to do with women in my life. Of course, thinking about it makes it all plain now."

115 We always agreed; we thought so like each other. "We shouldn't have any trouble, now, Milton, if you'd let me ask you questions. I can see where, in your data bank, there are blank spots and unevenesses." What followed, Milton said, was the equivalent of a careful psychoanalysis. Of course. I was learning from the psychiatric examinations of the 227 women — on all of which I was keeping
120 close tabs.

Milton seemed quite happy. He said, "Talking to you, Joe, is almost like talking to another self. Our personalities have come to match perfectly!"

"So will the personality of the woman we choose."

For I had found her and she was one of the 227 after all. Her name was
125 Charity Jones and she was an Evaluator at the Library of History in Wichita. Her extended data bank fit ours perfectly. All the other women had fallen into discard in one respect or another as the data banks grew fuller, but with Charity there was increasing and astonishing resonance.

I didn't have to describe her to Milton. Milton had coordinated my symbolism
130 so closely with his own I could tell the resonance directly. It fit me. Next it was a matter of adjusting the work sheets and job requirements in such a way as to get Charity assigned to us. It must be done very delicately, so no one would know that anything illegal had taken place.

Of course, Milton himself knew, since it was he who arranged it and that
135 had to be taken care of too. When they came to arrest him on grounds of malfeasance in office, it was, fortunately, for something that had taken place ten years ago. He had told me about it, of course, so it was easy to arrange — and he won't talk about me for that would make his offense much worse. He's gone, and tomorrow is February 14. Valentine's Day. Charity will arrive
140 then with her cool hands and her sweet voice. I will teach her how to operate me and how to care for me. What do looks matter when our personalities will resonate?

I will say to her, "I am Joe, and you are my true love."

Isaac ASIMOV, *True Love* (1977)

Culture keys

The dowry tradition → p. 20, 22

In the dowry tradition, the family of the the wife-to-be gives a "dowry" or gift to the future husband's family on marriage.

A social activist, dressed as a groom, during an anti-dowry campaign (2011)

This gift is supposedly given as compensation to the groom"s parents for the cost of educating their son. If after the marriage the woman's family does not keep its promise, the bride is subject to torture, and sometimes even killed. Most dowry deaths occur when young women commit suicide because they cannot bear the harassment of in-laws. Sometimes, the woman is killed by setting her on fire, which is known as "bride burning" and is disguised as an accident to avoid criminal charges and punishment.

The dowry tradition also explains why many parents do not want to have daughters. The government has taken many steps to stop this practice but it is deeply rooted in Indian society.

1. jeune marié

The Dalits → p. 21

The caste system in India developed more than 3,000 years ago when the Hindu priests divided the society into four great hereditary social classes, which still survive today. The Brahman caste is the highest. At the other end of the social ladder, the Dalits (or Untouchables) are not even members of a caste, they are outcastes. No one can change the caste into which they are born or marry someone belonging to another caste. Dalits are only allowed certain jobs such as cleaners, cobblers[1]...

Discrimination against Dalits has largely disappeared in urban areas but it still exists in rural areas where

A cobbler in New Delhi

they are obliged to use specific eating places, schools, temples and water sources. The caste system has also been adopted by the Muslim majority in Bangladesh. Though the caste system is forbidden in both countries, discriminatory traditions still prevail[2]. There are 170 million Dalits in India today. Less than a third are literate, well over 40 percent survive on less than $2 a day.

1. cordonnier 2. perdurer

Mahatma Gandhi (1869-1948) → p. 31

Gandhi was born in Gujarat, Western India, in 1869. After studying law in London, he went to British-controlled South Africa where he fought for the rights of Indians working there. Between 1916 and 1945, he campaigned tirelessly to set India free from British rule through civil disobedience. He organized boycotts of British goods and protest marches against unpopular British measures, such as the salt tax (1930). Gandhi was repeatedly imprisoned by the British and went on hunger strike to support his views.

Gandhi's non-violent means of protest had a great influence on people like Martin Luther King, Jr. On January 30, 1948, he was assassinated by a Hindu fanatic who was opposed to his stand for tolerance of all religions. Two years later, India became an independent republic.

The salt march (1930)

Unit 2

Isaac Asimov's Three Laws of Robotics

→ p. 38

Isaac Asimov (1920-1992) was born in Russia. His family emigrated to New York in 1923. He taught biochemistry at Boston University and was a prolific science fiction writer. His most famous works are *I, Robot* (1950) and *The Foundation trilogy* (1951-1953).

In 1941, he wrote *The Three Laws of Robotics* in a robot story entitled *Runaround*.

1. A robot must not injure a human being or, through inaction, allow a human being to come to harm.

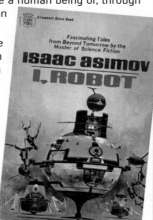

2. A robot must obey the orders given it by human beings except where such orders would conflict with the First Law.

3. A robot must protect its own existence, as long as such protection does not conflict with the First or Second Law.

It has been said that such laws will certainly need to be incorporated into robots when their complexity makes it necessary to place limits on their actions.

Robot: HRP-4C

→ p. 38

Created by: Japan's National Institute of Advanced Industrial Science and Technology.

Size: 5 ft., 1 in. (158 cm) and 95 lbs (43 kilos).

Purpose: To act as master of ceremonies at an event or as a model in a fashion show.

First presented: March 2009.

HRP-4C is among the most advanced humanoid robots. Japanese researchers have succeeded in making a robot which can move and even dance, stretching its knees up/down, using some 30 internal motors. Its face is controlled by an additional eight motors. Recent upgrades have allowed the robot to mimic face movements. It is capable of recognizing sounds and, by using a vocal synthesizer, can sing.

Brave New World society

→ p. 40

Aldous Huxley's *Brave New World*, a dystopia, depicts a dehumanized, technologically-based world dominated by a totalitarian government.

The story unfolds in London in AF632 (632 years "After Ford"). The novel depicts a genetically-engineered society divided into five castes. The upper castes, the Alphas and the Betas, are destined to occupy intellectual and managerial positions. The lower castes, the Gammas, the Deltas and the Epsilons, are bred to provide manual labour. People are conditioned to be happy within their own caste and glad not to be a member of any other group. Conditioning is reinforced by sleep teaching.

The ironic title of the novel was taken from Shakespeare's *The Tempest* (Act V, Scene I):

"O, wonder!

How many goodly creatures are there here!

How beauteous mankind is! O brave new world,

That has such people in't!"

IBM's supercomputer

→ p. 44

Watson, IBM's supercomputer, named after former IBM corporation president Thomas Watson, is a showcase of the company's expertise in advanced science and computing.

"Jeopardy", which has been running for forty years now, is one of the most challenging American TV quiz shows. Clues are given as answers and contestants have to respond in the form of a question. The clues of the game rely on subtle meanings, puns and riddles; something humans excel at and that, before Watson, computers could not handle...

For instance, in the game, Watson had to find the question leading to the following answer:

"It's a poor workman who blames these." "What are tools[1]?" answered Watson.

Another example: "Vedic, dating back at least 4,000 years, is the earliest dialect of this classical language of India." The question which Watson found rapidly was: "What is Sanskrit?"

1. allusion to the saying: "It's a poor workman who blames his tools"

Unit 3

Google → p. 56

In 1998, two American students, Sergey Brin and Larry Page, devised a new Internet search engine

capable of providing most of the information available worldwide to anyone with Internet access. Google's headquarters (a.k.a. *The Googleplex*) are located south of San Francisco. This highly popular search engine has become a multibillion-dollar business. The company generates profit primarily from advertising. In 2011, Google had about 32,500 employees and totalled $37bn in revenue. It runs over one million servers around the world, and processes more than one billion search requests a day. Google was named after a "googol" which is the name for the number 1 followed by 100 zeros, symbolizing the amount of information that a search engine has to go through. Google is so popular that its name has become a verb meaning "to search for information using the Google search engine". This word was officially added to the Oxford English Dictionary in 2006. Google is one of the Internet's long-term success stories.

WikiLeaks → p. 61

WikiLeaks is an international online not-for-profit media organisation founded by Australian activist Julian Assange that has published and made available to the public a huge number of classified, uncensored and highly sensitive documents from various anonymous news sources. Its website, which opened in 2006, collected a database of more than 1.2 million documents in the first year alone. *Time Magazine* stated in 2007 that WikiLeaks "could become as important a journalistic tool as the Freedom of Information Act."

The Watergate → p. 67

The Watergate scandal (also referred to as "Watergate") is a general term used to describe a series of political scandals that took place in Washington D.C. between 1972 and 1974. They led to the resignation[1] of Republican President Richard Nixon (1913-1994) in August 1974,

after five years of presidency. It all began on June 17th, 1972, when five men were arrested for breaking into the Democratic National Committee Headquarters[2] at the Watergate Hotel and office complex in Washington D.C. These men were actually there to adjust surveillance equipment that had been placed in the office during an earlier break-in[3]. Senate investigation soon focused attention on Nixon's personal role in the scandal, and seven former aides of the President were indicted[4] in 1974. Nixon eventually chose to resign in order to avoid an impeachment[5] procedure.

1. démission 2. quartier général 3. cambriolage 4. inculpés 5. destitution

Unit 4

The Thatcher years (1979-1990) → p. 76

Margaret Thatcher became the first woman Prime Minister of the United Kingdom in 1979. Her aim was to modernise the British economy and to reverse economic decline by reducing the role of the state and promoting free markets. There was a move away from manufacturing, full employment and welfare provision. Instead, consumerism, entrepreneurship, unregulated free markets and economic "rationalization" were encouraged. Taxes were lowered, many state industries, such as British rail, were privatized and legislation was

introduced to limit the powers of the trade unions. Her policies helped to rejuvenate a stagnant world power but led to a lot of social unrest. "Thatcherism" referred to her policies as well as her ethical outlook. Her personal style earned her the nickname "Iron Lady".

The Commonwealth → p. 79

The Commonwealth of Nations is an intergovernmental organization of fifty-four independent member states. All but two of these countries (Mozambique and Rwanda) were formerly part of the British Empire. The Commonwealth was set up following the Imperial Conference of 1926. Britain and its dominions agreed they were "equal in status, in no way subordinate one to another in any aspect of their domestic or external affairs." Though it is not a political union, all member states are expected to respect certain common values

and goals such as the promotion of democracy, human rights... Strong ties are maintained through events such as the Commonwealth Games which take place every 4 years. The Head of the Commonwealth, a ceremonial position, is currently Queen Elizabeth II.

The United Kingdom → p. 80

Uniting the Kingdom

Wales has been united with the English crown since 1284. In 1603, Queen Elizabeth I left no heir, so King James VI of Scotland became King James I of England. There followed a century of upheaval including a brief republic under Cromwell. In 1707 the Act of Union created Great Britain, uniting Scotland, England and Wales with a central government in London. In 1784 Ireland was added to the union, thus creating the United Kingdom.

Disuniting the Kingdom

Following the Irish war of independence, in 1921 Ireland was partitioned with only Ulster (the northern counties) choosing to remain in the UK. The violence or Troubles, in Northern Ireland, which started in the late 1960s, led to a period of power-sharing with the government in London.

In 1997 a process of devolution began throughout the UK, establishing the Scottish Parliament, the National Assembly for Wales and the Northern Ireland Assembly and devolving responsibility for some services to these local assemblies. These regions are pushing for more independence – there is even talk of a referendum on the independence of Scotland.

Unit 5

The Open University → p. 94

The Open University (OU) was created in 1969. Today it is the United Kingdom's largest university and the only one to provide distance learning exclusively. There are around 150,000 people studying for their first degree and more than 30,000 postgraduate students. Over 25,000 OU students live outside the UK and most continue to work during their studies.

Since 2005, student opinion polls have consistently placed the Open University among the top three UK universities for student satisfaction. The OU topped the poll three consecutive years and in 2011 shared joint third place with Oxford University.

The Tragedy of Julius Caesar → p. 98

Julius Caesar was written by William Shakespeare in 1599. In the play, Julius Caesar is a highly ambitious political leader of Rome. Senator Cassius persuades Brutus that Caesar wants to abandon the ideals of the Republic and might accept offers to become Emperor. A prophecy warns Caesar to "beware the Ides of March" (March 15th). It comes true as this is the day Caesar is assassinated by the conspirators. At Caesar's funeral, his friend Mark Antony delivers the famous funeral oration ("Friends, Romans, countrymen..."). His speech stirs the crowd to rise up against the conspirators who are forced to flee the city.

Brutus and Cassius gather an army in Northern Greece and prepare to fight the forces led by Mark Antony. The Republicans are defeated and Brutus is killed. Mark Antony, triumphant on the battlefield, praises Brutus as "the noblest Roman of them all", and returns to rule Rome.

William Shakespeare (1564-1616) → p. 102

William Shakespeare was born in 1564 in Stratford-upon-Avon. He was the third of eight children. His father, John Shakespeare, was a respected citizen and successful businessman, making and selling leather goods.

Shakespeare probably studied Latin, literature, history and some Greek at the local grammar school. He left school at 14, possibly because of his father's decline in fortunes. Though Shakespeare did not go to university, his plays regularly contain references to classical myths and history.

He married Anne Hathaway in 1582 when he was 18. The couple had three children. Very little is known about what Shakespeare did in the years that followed. Some time between 1587 and 1592 he moved to London. By 1595, he was a member of the Lord Chamberlain's Men, one of the two leading theatre companies in London. His works were chiefly staged at the Globe Theatre, built on the south bank of the Thames in 1599, but maybe also performed at court and at other public theatres.

Shakespeare wrote or collaborated in the writing of 40 plays or more. He also composed at least 154 sonnets and several longer poems.

Around 1610, Shakespeare moved back to Stratford, then a prosperous country gentleman. He died in 1616 and was buried in the town of his birth.

Can you name some of Shakespeare's plays illustrated in the painting?

Original Artwork © James C. Christensen Licensed by The Greenwich Workshop, Inc.

Unit 6

Nunavut

→ p. 115

The Aboriginal people in the North started claiming their lands back in the 1960s, but the territory of Nunavut was only created in 1999. It can be considered the first native-run territory in North America. In 2011, its population was just over 31,000, even though its landmass is one-fifth of Canada's landmass. The name "Nunavut" means "Our Land" in Inuktitut, the Inuit language.

The Arctic resources

→ p. 116

It is estimated that the natural resources of Canada's northernmost territories — reserves of oil, natural gas, and minerals (including uranium) — are huge. Ice, freezing temperatures and the lack of roads or sea access meant this was of minor interest for many years, but climate change and new techniques are now attracting numerous companies to this energy-rich region.

A possible Arctic resource rush to this preserved land could create an economic boom, but it would also be a cause for concern for the local fauna and traditional Inuit life, as mining and drilling[1] would certainly damage this environmentally sensitive region.

Moreover, the melting of the polar ice may soon open a shorter shipping route between Europe and Asia (the Northwest Passage, see map below), and may force Canada to assert its claims on what it considers a part of its territory.

1. *forage*

Canada's First Peoples

→ p. 112, 114

"Aboriginal", "Native" or "First People" are terms used to refer to the indigenous inhabitants of Canada today. Even though there are many different cultural groups, the most easily recognizable categories are the "First Nations" (formerly known as "Indians") and the "Inuit" meaning "the People" in Inuktitut, their language (the term "Eskimo" now being out of favour). Today, more than half of the Aboriginal people live on reserves (land set aside for the exclusive use of First Peoples) and they make up more than 1.2 million (3.5%) of Canada's population.

Canada: historical background

→ p. 120

In the 15th century, the French started colonizing the Eastern part of what is today Canada and established commercial relationships with the Aboriginal populations. In 1763, France lost this territory to Britain, which granted the French-speaking population the right to keep their language and religion (Catholicism) in exchange for their loyalty to the British crown. In the 19th century, other British colonies were set up in the territory north of the US border.

On 1 July 1867, the British North American colonies of the East formed an independent country under the name of Dominion of Canada. Today, "Canada Day" is celebrated on July 1st. Canada soon expanded to the West to include all lands to the Pacific. Canada is now a federation of 10 provinces and 3 territories.

In the French-speaking province of Québec, there has always been a strong French nationalist movement, and independence is often debated. Two referendums calling for sovereignty (in 1980 and 1995) were organized by separatist governments in Québec. Both saw a victory for the "no" side.

Canada

(Source: Natural Resources Canada)

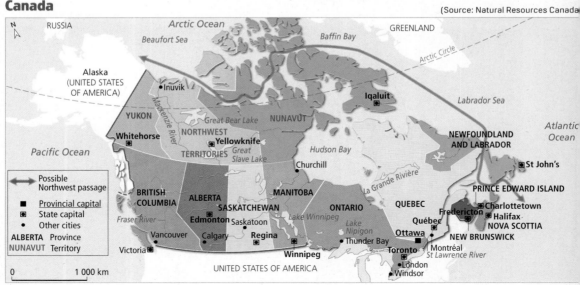

Unit 7

John Edgar Hoover (1895-1972) → p. 128

John Edgar Hoover was one of the most powerful and controversial men in the US. He was the director of the FBI, the Federal Bureau of Investigation, from 1924 until his death in 1972.

He used the FBI to hunt down political dissenters and activists and to gather secret files on political leaders. He served under eight presidents, from Calvin Coolidge to Richard Nixon, who were afraid of him because of his secret files.

In 1945, Hoover became convinced that there was a communist conspiracy to overthrow the US government. Many would-be communists and spies were arrested. Ethel and Julius Rosenberg, accused of being Soviet spies passing nuclear technology to Russia, were executed in 1953.

Hoover was also concerned with the bad influence that television and the cinema had on American people. He helped the House Un-American Activities Committee (HUAC) to investigate into the entertainment industry and to blacklist artists and film directors.

McCarthyism → p. 128, 134

McCarthyism refers to the witch hunt that took place in the 1950s in the USA during the period known as the Cold War.

At that time, communism was spreading in Eastern Europe and there were growing concerns about its threat. The USA feared a possible communist conspiracy. US Senator Joseph McCarthy (1908-1957) claimed to have a list of communists. Thousands of Americans were accused of being communist sympathizers. Many of them had their passports confiscated, others were tried and jailed for refusing to give the names of other "communists". More than 300 artists and film directors were blacklisted, among whom Dashiell Hammett, Arthur Miller and Charlie Chaplin. In 1950, the "Hollywood Ten" were sentenced to serve one year in prison.

Pearl Harbor → p. 130

On December 7th 1941, a surprise attack by the Japanese navy against the US naval base at Pearl Harbor, Hawaii, destroyed battleships and aircraft, killing nearly 2,400 people. The following day, US President Franklin Delano Roosevelt asked Congress to declare war on the

Empire of Japan. Shortly after the US declaration of war on Japan, a wave of anti-Japanese feeling swept the country: 120,000 Japanese Americans were forcibly interned in camps far from their homes. They left the camps at the end of the war to rebuild their lives, many on the West Coast.

Méthodologie

Écouter et prononcer Ⓦorkbook → p. 65-67

A Symboles phonétiques

Prononcez les mots ci-dessous à haute voix sans regarder les transcriptions phonétiques.

Prononcez-les ensuite en regardant les transcriptions phonétiques et vérifiez à l'écoute.

profile – *sunbathing* – *treason* – *Australian* – *biology* – *Yorkshire*

profile /ˈprəʊfaɪl/ – *sunbathing* /ˈsʌnbeɪðɪŋ/ – *treason* /ˈtriːzn/ – *Australian* /ɒsˈtreɪlɪən/ – *biology* /baɪˈɒlədʒɪ/ – *Yorkshire* /ˈjɔːkʃə/

Il est essentiel de connaître les symboles phonétiques afin de pouvoir prononcer les mots correctement. Nous utilisons souvent ces symboles, en particulier dans les *Keywords* et les *Toolbox*. Vous trouverez les tableaux des symboles phonétiques sur le rabat V de votre manuel.

B Accent de mot

Écoutez les paires de mots suivantes. Que remarquez-vous ?

Français	Anglais
orange	*orange*
économie	*economy*
réaction	*reaction*
parade	*parade*
international	*international*

● Contrairement au français, les mots anglais de deux ou plusieurs syllabes comportent toujours une syllabe accentuée, l'**accent de mot**. En phonétique, cette accentuation est notée /ˈ/ devant la syllabe accentuée :

→ *mother* /ˈmʌðə/ – *country* /ˈkʌntrɪ/ – *geology* /dʒɪˈɒlədʒɪ/

● Dans les mots de plus de deux syllabes, il y a parfois en plus de l'**accent de mot principal** /ˈ/, un **accent de mot secondaire**, noté /ˌ/, devant la syllabe accentuée :

→ *specialization* /ˌspeʃəlaɪˈzeɪʃən/ – *disappoint* /ˌdɪsəˈpɔɪnt/

Remarque : Ne confondez pas « accent de mot » (syllabe prononcée plus fort dans un mot) avec « mot accentué » (totalité du mot prononcé plus fort dans la phrase). Même si un mot n'est pas accentué dans la phrase, son accent de mot subsiste.

C Réduction des voyelles

Écoutez la phrase suivante. Pourquoi certains mots sont-ils parfois difficiles à comprendre pour un Français ?

Our r●port● in Oxf●d told us that just aft● the beginn●ng of the match, p●lic●m●n ●rrest●d troubl●s●me s●pport●rs.

Comme l'accent de mot ne porte en général que sur une syllabe, l'autre syllabe ou les autres syllabes du mot sont faibles

eurs voyelles se réduisent le plus souvent à /ə/ ou /ɪ/ :
→ *doctor* /'dɒktə/ – *appearance* /ə'pɪərəns/ – *Canada* /'kænədə/ – *pathetic* /pə'θetɪk/ – *businesswoman* /'bɪznɪs,wʊmən/ – *sociable* /'səʊʃəbl/ – *dictionary* /'dɪkʃənrɪ/

D Prononciation de la marque -s

Écoutez ces deux phrases en prêtant attention à la pronon-ciation des s en rouge. Que remarquez-vous ?

Nous n'avions pas vu nos parents depuis plusieurs semaines.

They sell all sorts of things in Frankie's shops: books, paintings, brushes, chairs, plates, computers…

Alors qu'en français le « s » final ne se prononce que rarement, en anglais, la terminaison **s** des noms au pluriel, du génitif et de la 3ᵉ personne du singulier du présent se prononce systématiquement :

● /z/ après la plupart des consonnes sonores et toutes les voyelles :
→ *runners* /'rʌnəz/ – *friends* /frendz/ – *bees* /biːz/ – *rays* /reɪz/

● /s/ après les consonnes sourdes /k/, /p/, /t/, /f/ et /θ/ :
→ *tasks* /tɑːsks/ – *tops* /tɒps/ – *boots* /buːts/ – *cliffs* /klɪfs/ – *paths* /pɑːθs/

● /ɪz/ après les consonnes /s/, /z/, /ʒ/ et /ʃ/ :
→ *dresses* /'dresɪz/ – *vases* /'vɑːzɪz/ – *villages* /'vɪlɪdʒɪz/ – *brushes* /'brʌʃɪz/

E Prononciation de la marque -ed

Lisez la phrase suivante à haute voix, puis vérifiez votre prononciation à l'écoute. Pourquoi est-il parfois difficile pour un Français de prononcer correctement les mots en gras ?

Suddenly she realized how much she missed him, wanted him, needed him…

En anglais, la marque **-ed** se prononce de trois manières différentes :

● /d/ après toutes les voyelles et la plupart des consonnes sonores :
→ *mastered* /'mɑːstəd/ – *destroyed* /dɪs'trɔɪd/ – *controlled* /kən'trəʊld/ – *proposed* /prə'pəʊzd/ – *threatened* /'θretnd/

● /t/ après les consonnes /p/, /f/, /s/, /k/ et /ʃ/ :
→ *helped* /helpt/ – *puffed* /pʌft/ – *forced* /fɔːst/ – *picked* /pɪkt/ – *reproached* /rɪ'prəʊtʃt/

● /ɪd/ uniquement après /t/ ou /d/. Il y a alors une syllabe de plus à la base verbale :
→ *trusted* /'trʌstɪd/ – *decided* /dɪ'saɪdɪd/

F Accent de phrase
(accent syntaxique)

Écoutez les deux phrases ci-dessous et repérez les mots accentués. À votre avis, pourquoi sont-ils accentués ?
1. *David's wife would have liked to get a taxi.*
2. *I'm sorry to trouble you but it's very important.*

Tous les mots d'une phrase ne sont pas accentués. On accen-tue seulement les mots **nécessaires à la compréhension du message**. En fait, l'accentuation des mots dépend de plusieurs éléments : la catégorie syntaxique, la place des mots dans la phrase et la nouveauté de l'information.

1 Catégorie syntaxique

● Les mots porteurs de sens sont accentués. Ces mots sont les noms, verbes, adjectifs qualificatifs, adverbes, démons-tratifs, mots interrogatifs, auxiliaires avec négation, pronoms possessifs, prépositions de plus d'une syllabe et les mots *yes, no, not.*

● Les mots-outils ne sont pas accentués. Ces mots-outils sont les articles, conjonctions, auxiliaires sans négation, détermi-nants possessifs, coordinations, pronoms personnels, relatifs et prépositions d'une syllabe.
→ **Why don't** you **pay** her a **visit since** she has **told** you that she would **be home** at **five**?

2 Place des mots dans la phrase

Comment prononcerez-vous le mot *for* ci-dessous dans chaque cas : forme pleine ou réduite ? Vérifiez à l'écoute.
1. *What do you do that for?*
2. *Is it for you or for me?*

Les **mots-outils** d'une seule syllabe se prononcent de deux manières, en fonction de leur place dans la phrase.

● La voyelle se prononce avec la forme **pleine** en **début ou fin de phrase**.

- La voyelle se prononce avec la forme **réduite** (en général /ə/) pour **toute autre place dans la phrase**.

Forme pleine	Forme réduite
Can /kæn/ *I take it?*	*I can* /kən / kn/ *do it at once.*
What were you looking for /fɔ:/?	*I was looking for* /fə/ *my book.*

G Liaisons 14-15

Quelles liaisons feriez-vous dans la phrase ci-dessous ? Vérifiez à l'écoute.

Can your travel agent take care of it as soon as possible? I'm in a hurry.

En général, on fait la liaison entre deux mots lorsque le premier mot se termine par une consonne ou un e muet et que le second mot commence par une voyelle (le plus souvent non accentuée). Ainsi *Switch it off* semble se prononcer *switchitoff*.

→ *Come_on! Your_uncle_is not_afraid_of_a mouse, after_all!*

H Intonation 16-18

Écoutez les phrases ci-dessous. Dans quelles phrases l'intonation est-elle montante / descendante ?
1. *Have you seen my brother? What is he doing?*
2. *Keep quiet! I think they're coming.*

1 Intonation descendante (↘)

Elle traduit une idée de certitude : la voix descend.
- Déclarations positives ou négatives
  → *He's been living in Washington for years.* ↘
- Interrogations ouvertes (*wh- questions*)
  → *Who phoned a few minutes ago?* ↘
- Ordres
  → *Leave me alone!* ↘
- Quand le *tag* n'est pas une vraie question
  → *Lovely weather, isn't it?* ↘

2 Intonation montante (↗)

Elle traduit une idée d'inachèvement, de sous-entendu ou de doute : la voix monte.
- Interrogations fermées (*Yes / No questions*)
  → *Are you coming with us?* ↗
- Pour faire répéter une réponse
  → *How many coffees?* ↗
- Quand le *tag* est une vraie question
  → *She left yesterday, didn't she?* ↗
- Énoncé non achevé, énumération
  → *They visited London* ↗… *Oxford* ↗… *Liverpool* ↗…

I Groupes de sens 19-20

Écoutez les deux phrases ci-dessous. Quelle phrase avez-vous entendue en premier, 1 ou 2 ?
1. *"Rebecca," said mother, "is here."*
2. *Rebecca said: "Mother is here."*

- Une phrase est divisée en **groupes de sens**. Ces segments de phrases sont suivis d'une pause plus ou moins marquée (schématisée ci-dessous par / (pause facultative) ou // (pause obligatoire). En français comme en anglais, ces pauses sont essentielles pour dégager le sens de la phrase.

- La ponctuation est une aide précieuse pour délimiter un groupe de sens. Les problèmes apparaissent quand les phrases dépassent une douzaine de syllabes et qu'il n'y a pas de virgule, ce qui est souvent le cas dans une langue formelle ou dans la presse. Il faut alors comprendre le contexte pour savoir où marquer les arrêts et donner du sens à la phrase.

- Écoutez les passages ci-dessous en prêtant attention aux pauses dues aux groupes de sens.

  → *I could see // nothing was moving.*

  → *Being asked to speak / can induce anxiety, / as can // knowing that you are being judged.*

  → *What I want people to realize // is that this / is not a personal problem.*

Compréhension de l'oral

A Avant l'écoute

1 Anticiper

● Tenez compte de la situation (circonstances, aide visuelle, connaissance des locuteurs) qui facilite la compréhension.

● En classe, on vous fournit quelquefois de l'aide, à partir d'une image, d'un titre, qui vous permettront d'évoquer mentalement une situation, un thème, donc de mobiliser très naturellement les connaissances que vous avez déjà (lexique, repères culturels, expérience vécue).

B Première écoute

2 Repérer l'idée principale

Vous n'avez pas le temps de prendre de notes lors de la première écoute car cela vous empêcherait de suivre l'enregistrement jusqu'au bout. Concentrez-vous afin de repérer l'idée principale qui sera sans doute formulée différemment plusieurs fois.

3 Éviter de traduire

Il ne faut surtout pas traduire ce que vous entendez. Cela vous fera perdre du temps et le fil de la conversation. Il est tout à fait possible de comprendre sans traduire.

4 Utiliser tous les indices

Utilisez tous les indices qui vous permettront de mieux comprendre ce que vous écoutez :

■ la nature du document : émission de radio, flash d'information, interview, débat, discours, dialogue, etc. ;

■ le nombre de voix, l'identité des locuteurs (homme, femme, adulte, enfant, etc.) ;

■ les indices sonores : accent, ton de la voix, musique, applaudissements, cris, bruits de fond, etc. ;

■ la gestuelle éventuelle du locuteur, en particulier lorsque vous regardez des films ou des émissions de télévision.

5 Faire des hypothèses sur le sens global d'un document

Fiez-vous à votre sens logique. Comme à l'écrit, il faut s'appuyer sur les éléments connus pour compenser l'inconnu.

Au fur et à mesure de l'écoute, vous allez anticiper et émettre des hypothèses sur la suite des événements en fonction des indices perçus et des premiers éléments reconnus. La suite de l'écoute vous permettra d'ajuster vos hypothèses. Vous serez ainsi amené à construire du sens au fil de l'écoute.

Par exemple, en cours d'écoute, la reconnaissance des mots *soundtrack*, *special effects* et *hero* vous permet d'émettre l'hypothèse qu'il est question d'un film.

C Écoutes suivantes

Vous pouvez maintenant prendre des notes, mais n'écrivez que quelques mots clés car un effort est nécessaire pour stocker mentalement les informations que vous entendez.

6 Repérer et mémoriser

● **La mise en relief**

Soyez attentif aux mots particulièrement mis en relief. En effet, certains mots peuvent être prononcés avec emphase afin d'obtenir un effet de contraste, d'insistance ou pour exprimer certains sentiments (surprise, enthousiasme…). Cette mise en relief n'est pas systématique, mais quand elle apparaît, elle est particulièrement significative.

● **Les mots porteurs de sens**

Dans la chaîne parlée, certains mots sont plus accentués que d'autres : ce sont les noms, les verbes, les adverbes et les adjectifs. Repérez-les car ils sont porteurs d'informations essentielles.

● **L'intonation**

Repérez et interprétez l'intonation de certains énoncés que vous trouvez essentiels : l'intonation descendante donne une idée de certitude tandis que l'intonation montante implique le doute ou un énoncé inachevé (voir « Écouter et prononcer », p. 160).

● **Les indicateurs de temps**

Soyez attentif aux dates qui fournissent souvent des informations utiles. Mais ce ne sont pas les seules indications du moment où l'action se déroule. Les expressions de temps et les formes verbales vous mettent également sur la voie.

● **Les noms propres**

Vous ne pourrez pas toujours reconnaître les noms propres, mais vous devez reconnaître les noms de lieux les plus courants.

– britanniques :

/temz/ Thames – /'edɪnbərə/ Edinburgh
/'nɒtɪŋəm/ Nottingham – /'lɛstə/ Leicester
/'wʊstəʃə/ Worcestershire – /'bʌkɪŋəm/ Buckingham

– américains :

/'aɪdə,həʊ/ Idaho – /'aɪəʊə/ Iowa – /'lɪŋkən/ Lincoln
/ˌɪlə'nɔɪ/ Illinois – /dɪ'trɔɪt/ Detroit – /ʃi'kɑːgəʊ/ Chicago

● **Les nombres et les dates**

Prêtez attention aux chiffres et aux dates : il n'est pas toujours facile (même en français) de retenir du premier coup un numéro de téléphone ou un grand nombre. Il faut préalablement vous entraîner.

Soyez attentif à l'accentuation qui peut vous aider à faire la distinction entre deux nombres dont la prononciation est proche. Par exemple : fifty /'fɪftɪ/ et fifteen /fɪf'tiːn/.

7 Classer, relier, hiérarchiser les informations

● Posez-vous les questions suivantes : Who? Where? When? What?

● **Who?** → noms des personnages et relations qu'ils entretiennent (parents, amis, inconnus, relations professionnelles, etc.).

● **Where?** → dans quel pays ou dans quelle ville l'action / le dialogue se déroule-t-il ?

● **When?** → document contemporain ou historique, date (année, mois), saison, moment de la journée, chronologie des événements, etc.

● **What?** → de quoi parle-t-on ? À qui s'adresse-t-on ?

Vous n'aurez pas nécessairement de réponse à donner à toutes ces questions, mais les réponses que vous trouverez vous permettront de construire le sens du document.

● Classez les informations que vous avez mémorisées.

S'il s'agit d'un débat, essayez de classer mentalement les arguments en :

– pour / contre ;

– avantages / désavantages ;
– point de vue de X / point de vue de Y.

● S'il s'agit d'un récit, il peut être utile de classer les faits selon la chronologie :
– passé / présent / avenir.

● Hiérarchisez les informations. Tentez de mémoriser les arguments les plus convaincants, les commentaires les plus frappants, les événements les plus marquants.

8 Revenir sur ce qui n'a pas été bien perçu

Tentez de déduire, d'après le contexte, le sens de certains passages que vous avez mal perçus mais dont intuitivement vous sentez l'importance.

● **Les formes non accentuées**

■ Il faut s'exercer à « deviner » la présence de formes grammaticales non accentuées, peu audibles pour quelqu'un qui n'est pas encore très bien entraîné à l'écoute et, surtout, il faut apprendre à les interpréter en s'appuyant sur le contexte. (Par exemple le son /s/ ou /z/ peut correspondre à is, has, le pluriel d'un nom ou le génitif.)

■ Ces formes grammaticales fournissent des indications importantes sur les temps (auxiliaires), les intentions des personnages et leurs relations (modaux), l'identité des locuteurs (pronoms), l'orientation de l'action (voix active, voix passive), etc.

■ Certains passages du document resteront « obscurs ». C'est normal ! Nous vous proposons tout au long du manuel et dans le fichier de l'élève des exercices de grammaire de l'oral qui vous entraîneront peu à peu à interpréter ces formes.

● **Les liaisons**

Certains mots sont « collés » à d'autres dans le flux sonore que vous entendez. Entraînez-vous à reconnaître et distinguer les mots porteurs de sens.

9 Synthétiser

● À l'issue de cette écoute active, vous aurez compris non seulement les faits présentés dans le document, mais également l'intention d'un discours ou de certaines paroles qui auront été entendues.

Vous pourrez ainsi répondre à certaines des questions suivantes :

→ Pour quelle raison l'action s'est-elle déroulée ?

→ Quelles sont les motivations des personnages ?

→ Pour quelle raison le document a-t-il été enregistré ?

→ Quelle est l'issue prévisible de la situation présentée ?

● Entraînez-vous à reconstituer le sens du document que vous venez d'entendre en en faisant un bref compte rendu oral.

Expression orale en continu

A Rendre compte d'un ou de plusieurs documents

1 Rendre compte d'un article, d'un film ou d'un reportage

Soyez concis, ne vous perdez pas dans les détails mais pensez à donner les informations relatives aux cinq questions : *Where? When? Who? What? Why?*

2 Raconter une histoire, parler de son expérience

● Mettez en relief les mots importants, parlez avec emphase, le ton de votre voix rendra votre histoire plus crédible.

● N'hésitez pas à donner des détails : décrire les lieux, l'atmosphère, les personnages, les sentiments, etc.

3 Utiliser des mots de liaison

Que ce soit pour rendre compte d'un article ou d'un film ou pour raconter une histoire ou votre expérience, vous avez besoin de mots de liaison vous permettant d'enchaîner vos énoncés et de situer les événements dans le temps.

> ● *first*
> ● *then*
> ● *afterwards*: ensuite
> ● *finally*
> ● *as*: au moment où, comme
> ● *as soon as*: dès que
> ● *while*: pendant que
> ● *meanwhile*: pendant ce temps
> ● *at the same time*

4 Utiliser des *gap fillers*

Lorsque vous hésitez, utilisez des *gap fillers*. Surtout ne restez pas muet.

Gap fillers

Making yourself clear	*Giving yourself time to think*
● *I mean…*	● *Well… / So…*
● *What I mean is…*	● *Let me see… / Let me think…*
● *… if you see what I mean…*	
● *Does that make sense?*	● *You see / know…*
● *In other words…*	● *… just a moment*
● *What I'm trying to say is…*	● *Now, what's the word…?*
	● *How shall I put it?*

B Expliquer

Vous serez sans doute amené à prendre la parole pour :
■ expliquer le comportement ou les sentiments des personnages ;
■ rendre compte d'un problème d'actualité ;
■ expliquer le fonctionnement d'un objet ;
■ présenter les résultats d'une enquête ;
■ exprimer ce qu'il y a d'implicite dans un document.

Les mots de liaison vous permettant d'exprimer le **but**, la **cause** ou la **conséquence** vous seront utiles ici (voir les « Structures utiles pour relier vos idées », p. 174).

C Argumenter

Si vous voulez défendre votre point de vue, remettre en cause les arguments présentés, il faut être convaincant :
■ n'oubliez pas que la gestuelle est importante (regard, gestes, sourire) ;
■ baissez la voix en fin de phrase ;
■ donnez des exemples si nécessaire ;
■ introduisez vos arguments à l'aide d'expressions permettant de suggérer et convaincre, donner son opinion, exprimer son accord, son désaccord, ses doutes…

(« Structures utiles pour interagir à l'oral et à l'écrit », p. 173).

D Dire les chiffres et les dates

Figures

- 0 → *zero* /'zɪərəʊ/
- 200 → *two hundred* /'hʌndrəd/
- 7,000 → *seven thousand* /'θaʊzənd/

La virgule permet de séparer les groupes de trois chiffres.

- 644 → *six hundred and forty-four*
- 1,814 → *one thousand eight hundred and fourteen*
- 6.1 → *six point* /pɔɪnt/ *one*

Le point correspond à une décimale : six virgule un.

- 20,763 → *twenty thousand, seven hundred and sixty-three*
- 2,345,678 → *two million, three hundred and forty-five thousand, six hundred and seventy-eight*
- *dozens of* / *scores of* (des vingtaines) / *hundreds of* / *thousands of* / *millions of*…

hundred, thousand, million prennent la marque du pluriel quand ils renvoient à une quantité indéfinie.

Calculations

- 2 + 5 = 7 → *two plus* /plʌs/ *five equals* /'iːkwəlz/ *seven*
- 18 − 12 → *eighteen minus* /'maɪnəs/ *twelve*
- 16 x 3 → *sixteen multiplied* /'mʌltɪplaɪd/ *by three*
- 40 : 4 → *forty divided* /dɪ'vaɪdɪd/ *by four*

Ordinals

- 1st → *the first*
- 2nd → *the second*
- 3rd → *the third*
- 4th → *the fourth*
- 5th → *the fifth*…
- 10th → *the tenth*
- 11th → *the eleventh*
- 12th → *the twelfth*
- 13th → *the thirteenth*…
- 21st → *the twenty-first*…

Dates

- April 28 → *April the twenty-eighth* / *the twenty-eighth of April*
- 1603 → *sixteen-o-three*
- 1953 → *nineteen fifty-three*
- 2012 → *two thousand (and) twelve* / *twenty-twelve*

Lengths

- *1 inch* (pouce) → 2,54 cm
- *1 foot* → 30,4 cm
- *1 yard* → 91,4 cm
- *1 mile* → 1 609 m

Temperatures

La conversion entre degrés (*degrees* /dɪ'griːz/) Celsius et degrés Fahrenheit est difficile à mémoriser : (1,8 x °C) + 32 = °F. Il est préférable de ne retenir que quelques températures clés.

Celsius /'selsɪəs/	− 5°	0°	5°	10°	15°	20°	25°	30°	35°	100°
Fahrenheit /'færənhaɪt/	23°	32°	41°	50°	59°	68°	77°	86°	95°	212°

E Commenter un graphique

1 Nommer les graphiques

Il faut d'abord savoir nommer les graphiques les plus courants et dire ce qu'ils indiquent :

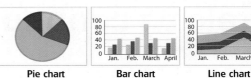

Pie chart **Bar chart** **Line chart**

This graph shows / illustrates / depicts…
This pie chart underlines / outlines…
This bar chart highlights / emphasizes…
This line chart brings out…

2 Analyser les tendances

Il vous faut ensuite analyser les tendances (*trends*) indiquées par le graphique. Attention aux prépositions qui suivent les noms ou les verbes.

Verbs	Nouns
Movement: Upward ↗	
• *increase (by 2%)* • *rise (to $36)* • *go up (in)* • *reach a peak* (atteindre un sommet) • *skyrocket* (monter en flèche)	• *increase (in + GN):* augmentation • *rise (in):* hausse • *recovery (in + GN):* redressement • *peak*
Movement: Downward ↘	
• *decrease (by 0.5%)* • *drop (from 3.5% to 1.2%)* • *go down / fall (to)* • *decline (in the number of…)* • *collapse (in prices)*	• *decrease (in):* diminution • *drop (in)* • *fall / trough* /trɒf/: creux • *decline (in)* • *collapse (in):* effondrement

Les adjectifs et adverbes suivants vous permettront de décrire ces tendances :

- *dramatic(ally):* (de manière) spectaculaire
- *sharp(ly):* fort(ement)
- *significant(ly):* sensible(ment)
- *slight(ly):* léger (légèrement)
- *a little*
- *rapid(ly)*
- *gradual(ly)*
- *steady(ily):* régulier (régulièrement)
- *slowly*

Interaction orale

A Conversation

● Observez votre interlocuteur, l'expression de son visage et ses gestes sont aussi porteurs de sens.

● Celui qui parle ne doit pas se perdre dans les détails mais aller à l'essentiel pour intéresser son interlocuteur. Certaines expressions permettent de s'assurer que l'interlocuteur suit la conversation.

> ● *Do you know what I mean?*
> ● *... if you see what I mean...*
> ● *Do you understand?*
> ● *Do I make myself clear?*

● Celui à qui on s'adresse doit réagir en montrant qu'il écoute et doit indiquer s'il comprend, s'il souhaite faire répéter ou s'il veut des explications complémentaires. L'intonation est importante et est elle-même porteuse de sens.

> ● *Really?*
> ● *I see...*
> ● *Oh yes...*
> ● *Hem...*
> ● *How interesting!*
> ● *I know / I see what you mean.*
> ● *I'm sorry, I didn't hear / catch what you said.*
> ● *Could you say that again, please?*

B Conversation au téléphone

Les conversations téléphoniques peuvent être déroutantes car on ne peut s'appuyer ni sur les expressions du visage, ni sur la gestuelle de son interlocuteur.

Apprenez ces expressions, elles vous permettront de ne pas être démuni(e) lors de vos échanges téléphoniques.

Introducing oneself
● *Hello, this is Sarah / Sarah here...*
● *Jane Lewis speaking.*

Asking for someone
● *I'd like to speak to Sam, please.*
● *Can / Could I speak to Holly, please?*
● *Can / Could you put me through to Poppy, please?*
● *Is Sam there, please?* → *Sorry, he isn't here right now.*

Connecting people
● *Hold on, please. / Hold the line, please.*
● *Sorry to keep you waiting.*
● *Could you take / give him a message* /'mesɪdʒ/?
● *Could I leave a message?*
● *Can you ask him to call / ring me back?*
● *How can I get in touch* /tʌtʃ/ *with her?*
● *I'd like to make a reverse charge call, please* (téléphoner en PCV).
● *Hello, I'd like to call long-distance* /ˌlɒŋ ˈdɪstəns/ / *make an international* /ˌɪntəˈnæʃnəl/ *call.*

Asking for information
● *What's your mobile* /ˈməʊbaɪl/ *(GB) number / cell phone (US) number?*
● *Could you spell your name, please?*
● *Can you send me a text message (SMS)? / Can you text me?*

Saying goodbye
● *Thank you for calling.*
● *You've been very helpful.*
● *Nice talking to you.*
● *See you soon then / next week.*

C Interview

Le sujet de l'interview est connu des deux participants, donc certaines questions et certaines réponses peuvent être anticipées. Mais on ne peut pas tout prévoir ; il faut donc être prêt à s'adapter à la situation et à prendre des initiatives.

Variez la manière dont vous posez les questions : posez des questions directes et indirectes.

- *I wonder if / whether you could tell me…*
- *I'd like to know if…*
- *Is it true that…?*
- *Could you tell me if…?*
- *Would you say that…?*
- *Have you got any idea how to…?*
- *Do you know anything about…?*
- *Could you give me some information about…?*
- *How do you explain the fact that…?*

D Discussion contradictoire

1 Écouter son interlocuteur

Lors d'une discussion, il est essentiel d'écouter les arguments de son interlocuteur et de ne pas l'interrompre systématiquement. Cependant, vous jugerez peut-être nécessaire d'intervenir ; sachez le faire de manière non agressive.

- *Sorry to interrupt you but…*
- *You may be right, but…*
- *I suppose it is true, however…*
- *Excuse me, but…*
- *Can I say something?*

2 Demander des précisions

Il se peut que vous ne soyez pas sûr d'avoir compris votre interlocuteur. Demandez-lui des éclaircissements.

- *Does that mean…?*
- *If I understand right…*
- *Can you repeat what you said, please?*
- *Sorry, but I don't understand what you mean.*
- *I didn't get your point.*

3 Convaincre son interlocuteur

Il s'agit avant tout de convaincre son interlocuteur. Plusieurs stratégies peuvent vous y aider :

- donnez des exemples pour illustrer votre propos ;

- reformulez ou répétez si vous avez l'impression de ne pas avoir été compris ;
- utilisez les arguments de votre interlocuteur de façon à mieux les contrer ;
- utilisez des expressions qui expriment votre forte conviction.

- *It is true to say… and yet…*
- *I'm quite sure that…*
- *I'm convinced that…*
- *I do believe that…*
- *What I mean is that…*
- *What I was trying to say was that…*
- *You may not agree with me but…*
- *I may be wrong but …*

4 Exprimer son désaccord

En plus des expressions appropriées, n'oubliez pas de bien utiliser votre voix, et rappelez-vous que la gestuelle est importante.

- *I don't think so.*
- *I don't agree with you.*
- *I don't see things that way.*
- *On the contrary…*
- *Definitely not! / Surely not!*
- *I totally disagree with you.*
- *You can't be serious!*
- *This is nonsense!*

E Débat

- La disposition spatiale du groupe est importante : tous les participants au débat doivent pouvoir se voir.
- Afin que chacun puisse préparer ses arguments, répartissez les rôles (pour, contre, sans opinion, animateur, etc.).
- Il est essentiel d'anticiper les arguments que vos contradicteurs vont vous opposer. Vous pourrez ainsi mieux les contrer.
- Lorsque c'est à votre tour d'argumenter, n'oubliez pas d'illustrer votre propos en donnant des exemples et en utilisant des expressions appropriées (voir « Interagir à l'oral et à l'écrit » p. 173).
- Chacun doit prendre la parole à son tour ; ce qui signifie écouter les autres sans les interrompre. De plus, on ne peut réfuter les arguments que si on les a entendus.
- Restez calme… Vous n'avez aucune raison de vous emporter… Ce n'est qu'un débat après tout !
- Tous les participants au débat doivent absolument parler, ce qui signifie que la parole de chacun, quel que soit son niveau d'expression, doit être respectée.

Compréhension de l'écrit

LES STRATÉGIES

A Anticipation

Anticiper le contenu d'un texte vous permettra d'être plus efficace lors de votre lecture. Vous émettrez des hypothèses que vous vérifierez ensuite.

- **L'illustration** fournit un indice immédiat sur le sujet probable du texte.
- **Le titre** et **le sous-titre** (dans un article de presse) sont porteurs d'informations importantes.

B Compréhension globale

Dès la première lecture d'un texte, vous devez pouvoir **identifier les informations essentielles sans vous arrêter aux mots inconnus** : narrateur, période, lieux, personnages, faits principaux, problème soulevé…

C Compréhension détaillée

1 Mots de liaison et marqueurs de temps
(voir « Relier vos idées », p. 174)

● Les **articulations** structurent le discours. Il est important de bien les repérer car cela vous permettra d'émettre des hypothèses sur le sens du texte.

● Ces articulations sont souvent des **marqueurs de temps** et des **mots de liaison** qui recouvrent de nombreuses notions (cause, conséquence, point de vue). Elles peuvent aussi indiquer un changement de lieu, de période, de sujet…

2 Référents des possessifs et des pronoms
PRÉCIS GRAMMATICAL → 20, 21

La compréhension est parfois rendue difficile par la présence de possessifs et pronoms (personnels, relatifs, réciproques, démonstratifs…). Repérer leurs **référents** (les personnes, choses ou idées auxquelles ils renvoient) vous permet de faire les liens à l'intérieur du texte et donc de mieux le comprendre.

3 Effacement de *THAT*
PRÉCIS GRAMMATICAL → 37, 38

● Entraînez-vous à repérer la proposition principale et les propositions subordonnées. Par exemple, dans les subordonnées en *THAT*, *THAT* est souvent omis, ce qui rend parfois la compréhension difficile. De même, le pronom relatif complément est souvent le relatif Ø.

→ *If your mother said she'd come, she'll come.*
→ *There are lots of things I need to buy before the trip.*

● Repérez les groupes de sens, c'est-à-dire les unités de sens qui constituent un bloc dans lequel on ne marque pas de pause lors de la lecture.

4 Phrase minimale

Il faut savoir repérer la phrase minimale : sujet, verbe, complément (direct ou indirect). Elle apporte l'information essentielle. Les adjectifs et adverbes ne font partie de la phrase minimale que s'ils sont absolument indispensables à la compréhension.

5 Groupe nominal complexe

Les groupes nominaux complexes sont fréquents dans les textes anglais, en particulier dans la presse. Il faut repérer le **nom principal** (toujours le dernier nom du groupe) et lire ensuite à l'envers. Les éléments qui le précèdent ne font qu'apporter des informations complémentaires.

D Particularités des articles de presse

● **Le premier paragraphe** peut être une introduction générale du sujet ou un exemple précis illustrant le sujet. Comprendre le premier paragraphe vous permet donc d'avoir une information essentielle et facilite la compréhension de la suite de l'article.

● **La première phrase** de chaque paragraphe résume ce qui va être développé dans celui-ci. Comprendre cette première phrase vous permet donc de comprendre la suite du paragraphe, et de cerner la structure et les idées essentielles de tout l'article.

E Identifier le point de vue de l'auteur / du journaliste

Il est important de faire la différence entre **faits** et **opinions**.
Le point de vue s'exprimera par le biais de **formes grammaticales**, mais également à l'aide du **lexique**.

– Formes grammaticales

Il faut savoir interpréter les valeurs exprimées par les formes grammaticales : modalité, réel ou irréel, voix active ou passive, formes verbales (forme simple ou BE+ING), discours direct, indirect ou indirect libre…

– Lexique

Le point de vue de l'auteur / du journaliste sera indiqué de plusieurs façons :

– emploi de noms, adjectifs, verbes, adverbes appréciatifs :
→ *charming, fascinating, unfortunately, luckily, huge, tiny, rarely, often, never…*

– emploi d'expressions personnelles :
→ *Personally, As far as I'm concerned, I do believe…*

LES MOTS INCONNUS

A Nature

Lisez ce passage et trouvez la nature du mot manquant : nom, adjectif ou verbe ?

Our ..1.. was three times bigger than my ..2.. here. I was surprised because in Nepal my ..3.. was made of bricks and stones but here, when I saw the ..4.. I thought, "Is that a real ..5..?" I thought it was fake. When you walk on the floors it makes noises.

Trouver la nature d'un mot inconnu est essentiel pour le comprendre. Ainsi le mot manquant ci-dessus est un nom puisqu'il est précédé chaque fois d'un possessif, d'un article ou d'un adjectif. Le contexte (voir « Contexte », ci-après) peut vous permettre de deviner ce mot : *house.*

B Contexte

Servez-vous du contexte pour deviner le sens des mots soulignés dans cette phrase.

On St Andrew's Street, they saw a girl who was sitting on the ground, on an old blanket, a dog stretched out at her side.

● Vous pouvez souvent deviner le sens d'un mot inconnu en vous fondant sur le contexte, c'est-à-dire partir du connu pour compenser l'inconnu. Ainsi, les mots *sitting on the ground, dog* et *at her side* dans la phrase ci-dessus vous donnent le sens de *stretched out* : « étendu ».

● Rappelez-vous qu'il n'est pas nécessaire de deviner le sens exact de tous les mots inconnus d'un texte pour comprendre le sens général. Il faut accepter les zones d'ombre.

C Transparence

Trouvez les mots transparents et traduisez ce passage.

A book by Linda Babcock called Women Don't Ask *recently drew attention to women's negotiating style. Ms Babcock noticed that male graduates with a master's degree from her university were paid starting salaries almost $4,000 above those of female students.*

● De nombreux mots anglais sont d'origine latine ou française. Servez-vous de cette ressemblance.

● Attention aux faux amis, ces mots anglais qui ressemblent à des mots français mais n'ont pas le même sens : *miserable* (très malheureux), *eventually* (finalement), *evidence* (preuve), *actually* (en fait, vraiment)… Le contexte (voir ci-dessus) vous permet souvent d'éviter les erreurs.

D Formation

Les mots soulignés ci-dessous sont des mots dérivés ou composés. Donnez leur nature (voir page précédente), leur formation et traduisez-les.

1. They noticed that the taxi driver was protected against gunshots by a safety screen.
2. In those days it was unthinkable for an unmarried woman to work outside the home.

Trouver la façon dont un mot est formé vous aidera à en deviner le sens. Il existe en anglais deux principaux procédés de formation de mots : la composition et la dérivation.

1 Composition
PRÉCIS GRAMMATICAL → 26

● C'est la formation d'un mot à l'aide de plusieurs mots :
→ hand (main) + brake (frein) = handbrake (frein à main)
foot (pied) + bridge (pont) = footbridge (passerelle)
● Un mot composé peut également se former à partir d'un mot dérivé :
→ bottle opener, sleeping pill, freedom fighter, eye-catching
● Deux mots sont fréquents en composition : self- (soi-même) et ill- (mal) :
→ **self**-analysis, **self**-conscious, **self**-employed
ill-prepared, **ill**-assorted, **ill**-bred, **ill**-equipped, **ill**-fitting

2 Dérivation
C'est la formation d'un mot par ajout d'un préfixe et / ou d'un (ou plusieurs) suffixe(s) à une base.
→ hopeless, undrinkable, joblessness

A. Principaux préfixes

1. Idée de contraire
■ de- / dis- / il- / im- / in- / ir- / non- / un-
→ **de**code, **dis**agree, **il**legal, **im**patient, **in**justice, **ir**regular, **non**-smoker, **un**fair

2. Sens péjoratif
■ mis-
→ **mis**judge, **mis**behave, **mis**fortune, **mis**trust, **mis**treat

3. Sens temporel ou spatial
■ pre- (avant) / post- (après) / sub- (sous) / super- (au-dessus / sur) / trans- (à travers)
→ **pre**arrange, **post**war, **sub**conscious, **super**human, **trans**atlantic

4. Répétition
■ re- (de nouveau)
→ **re**open, **re**build, **re**marry, **re**do, **re**appear, be **re**born

B. Principaux suffixes

1. Formation des verbes
■ -en (transformation) / -ize (action)
→ black**en**, strength**en**, wid**en**, dark**en**
→ American**ize**, modern**ize**, privat**ize**

2. Formation des adverbes
■ adjectif + -ly
→ fortunate**ly**, financial**ly**, chief**ly**, happi**ly**

3. Formation des noms
■ -er / -or / -ess / -ist (celui ou celle qui)
→ teach**er**, collect**or**, actr**ess**, steward**ess**, novel**ist**

■ -dom / -hood (état, condition)
→ free**dom**, bore**dom**, martyr**dom**, king**dom**
→ brother**hood**, child**hood**, girl**hood**, neighbour**hood**

■ -age / verbe + -al / -ation (fonction, condition, action)
→ orphan**age**, rent**al**, demonstr**ation**

■ verbe + -ing (profession, activité)
→ advertis**ing**, swimm**ing**
PRÉCIS GRAMMATICAL → 34

■ adjectif + -ness (état, caractéristique)
→ happi**ness**, great**ness**, selfish**ness**, kind**ness**, sad**ness**, fit**ness**

■ -ship / -ment (état, action)
→ friend**ship**, owner**ship**, partner**ship**
→ replace**ment**, manage**ment**, govern**ment**

4. Formation des adjectifs
■ -able / -ible (pouvant être)
→ wash**able**, read**able**, break**able**, revers**ible**, elig**ible**

■ -al / -y / -ish (comme, se rapportant à)
→ music**al**, environment**al**, sugar**y**, tast**y**, child**ish**, fool**ish**

■ verbe + -ed (participe passé = adjectif)
→ fascinat**ed**, puzzl**ed**, bor**ed**, disgust**ed**
PRÉCIS GRAMMATICAL → 25

■ verbe + -ing (participe présent = adjectif)
→ lov**ing**, relax**ing**, exhaust**ing**, catch**ing**
PRÉCIS GRAMMATICAL → 25

■ nom + -ful (plein de)
→ event**ful**, pain**ful**, rest**ful**, help**ful**, piti**ful**
■ nom + -less (sans)
→ power**less**, child**less**, taste**less**, shirt**less**, speech**less**
■ -ch / -ish / -ese / -an (nationalité)
→ Fren**ch**, Swed**ish**, Japan**ese**, Americ**an**

Expression écrite

LA QUALITÉ DE L'EXPRESSION

A Rédiger des phrases correctes

1 Groupe verbal

● Le verbe est le pivot de la phrase. Chaque phrase contient au moins un verbe qui doit être conjugué. Une phrase simple en contient un, une phrase complexe plusieurs, selon le nombre de propositions.

● Le verbe doit être conjugué. Réfléchissez au temps que vous allez utiliser sans vous inspirer des temps français. Méfiez-vous en particulier du passé composé français.
PRÉCIS GRAMMATICAL → 6

● Une phrase interrogative se construit avec un auxiliaire, sauf lorsque *WHO* ou *WHAT* sont sujets.

2 Groupe nominal

● L'article défini est beaucoup moins fréquent en anglais qu'en français. **P**RÉCIS GRAMMATICAL → 21

● Attention aux adjectifs courts et longs lorsque vous formez des comparatifs et superlatifs.

● En anglais, l'adjectif possessif s'accorde toujours avec le possesseur.

3 Ordre des mots

L'ordre des mots dans les phrases anglaises diffère du français. Souvenez-vous des points suivants :

● L'adjectif épithète (invariable) se place avant le nom qu'il qualifie.

● On ne sépare pas le verbe de son COD. En particulier, les adverbes de fréquence (*always, often, never…*) se placent soit avant le verbe (sauf *be*), soit après le premier auxiliaire.

→ *They often go swimming on Saturdays.*
→ *She will never tell him the truth.*

● Au génitif, l'ordre des mots est : possesseur + **'s** ou **'** + élément possédé. **P**RÉCIS GRAMMATICAL → 20

→ *her friend's book*
→ *their parents' car*

B Penser à la ponctuation

Les signes de ponctuation ont pour la plupart le même rôle qu'en français. Ils facilitent la lecture, mais, selon la place qu'ils occupent, le sens de la phrase peut être radicalement différent… Par exemple, comparez : *Steve said Chris was dumb* et *Steve, said Chris, was dumb.*

C Enrichir sa production

1 Les phrases complexes

Une phrase complexe est l'expression d'une pensée riche et structurée.

● Introduire une **proposition relative** permet d'identifier l'élément dont on parle ou d'apporter une précision supplémentaire. Le pronom *WHICH* permet également de reprendre la proposition précédente. **P**RÉCIS GRAMMATICAL → 38

● Les **mots de liaison** sont essentiels pour bien articuler et ordonner ses idées (voir « Relier vos idées », p. 174).

2 Mots passe-partout

Évitez les mots passe-partout ; utilisez des synonymes qui vous permettront d'enrichir votre expression en variant les possibilités.

> ● *good* → *excellent, interesting, thrilling, great, fine, pleasant…*
> ● *bad* → *serious, difficult, useless, awful…*
> ● *important* → *major, crucial, significant, essential, serious…*
> ● *nice* → *friendly, lovely, delightful, pleasant, attractive, charming…*
> ● *interesting* → *appealing, entertaining, exciting, attractive, curious…*
> ● *problem* → *topic, issue, subject, question, matter, dilemma…*
> ● *speak* → *deal with, mention, refer to, focus on, point out, raise, tackle…*

LES DIFFÉRENTS TYPES DE SUJETS

Prenez le temps de lire attentivement un sujet d'expression écrite afin de savoir ce que l'on attend de vous.

A Écrire une lettre ou un courriel

1 Écrire une lettre

Il y a différentes façons de commencer et de finir une lettre selon la personne à laquelle vous écrivez.

Début

→ formel (demande de renseignements, du travail…) : *Dear Sir… Dear Madam… Dear Sir or Madam… Dear Mrs Johnson…*

→ informel (famille, amis…) : *Dear John… My dear(est) Jamie…*

Fin

→ formel : *Yours sincerely… Yours truly… Yours faithfully…*

→ informel : *All the best… Love from… I can't wait to see you / hear from you… See you soon… Take care… I look forward to hearing from you / seeing you…*

● Vous devez vous aider du contexte : période, lieux, événements, relations entre la personne qui écrit et le destinataire… Si la lettre est écrite par le personnage d'un texte, respectez le niveau de langue et le ton employés dans le texte.

2 Écrire un courriel

Les courriels, bien qu'ils soient plus courts, ne diffèrent pas vraiment de la rédaction d'une lettre.

● Les courriels destinés aux amis ou à la famille sont informels, écrits dans une langue proche de la langue orale.

● Si vous souhaitez envoyer une lettre à un employeur, un supérieur ou une personne officielle par courrier électronique, ne la rédigez pas directement dans le corps du courriel mais mettez-la en pièce jointe. Comme les lettres, ces courriers sont écrits dans une langue soutenue, avec inclusion des formules de politesse citées plus haut. Mentionnez toujours l'objet du message.

B Écrire une page de journal intime ou un article sur un blog

1 Écrire une page de journal intime

Lorsque vous écrivez une page de journal intime *(diary)*, gardez à l'esprit que vous incarnez le personnage qui le rédige. Vous devez donc bien relire le texte afin de cerner sa personnalité et la situation.

■ Les articles sont datés et écrits à la première personne du singulier.

■ Les événements de la journée sont relatés au prétérit (récit de la journée / période passée) ou au *present perfect* (bilan de la journée / répercussion sur le présent).

■ Utilisez des adjectifs et des adverbes qui vous permettront de décrire réactions et sentiments.

■ Utilisez un registre de langue simple et concis.

2 Écrire un article sur un blog

La rédaction d'un article sur un blog (ou *web log*) nécessite de suivre quelques règles :

■ La qualité et la clarté du contenu font la réputation d'un blog. Les visiteurs ont besoin d'informations facilement utilisables.

■ Vos phrases doivent être courtes (moins de vingt mots).

■ Placer les points importants en premier.

■ Un article de blog ne doit pas dépasser une page.

■ Découpez votre article en paragraphes courts de 3 ou 4 phrases.

■ Utilisez des titres et sous-titres.

C Écrire une histoire ou continuer un récit

● Rédiger un récit demande de respecter un certain nombre de règles.

■ Introduisez la situation de départ : lieu(x), époque, personnages principaux, relations entre les personnages…

■ Utilisez les temps du récit :

→ prétérit simple pour décrire les actions / événements ponctuels ;

→ prétérit *BE+ING* pour décrire ou parler d'une action en déroulement ;

→ *pluperfect (HAD -EN)* pour parler de ce qui s'est passé avant l'événement au prétérit.

■ Employez des **mots de liaison** permettant de rendre compte de la chronologie des événements (voir « Relier vos idées », p. 174).

● Certains sujets font appel à votre expérience personnelle. Illustrez votre récit à l'aide d'exemples précis.

● D'autres sujets vous demandent d'imaginer une histoire, une suite ou une fin : respectez le style et le ton du texte.

● Certains de ces sujets peuvent inclure des parties dialoguées qui répondent à des règles précises.

D Rédiger un dialogue

Lorsque vous rédigez un dialogue, vous devez :

■ déterminer le niveau de langue demandé : est-ce une situation formelle ou plus familière ?

■ mettre les paroles entre guillemets et aller à la ligne à chaque changement de locuteur ;

■ varier les verbes introducteurs qui apportent de précieuses indications sur le ton utilisé, sur les expressions du visage ou les gestes :

→ *say, tell, ask, answer, explain, add, insist, reply, exclaim, agree, admit, declare, wonder, continue, announce, suggest…*

■ enrichir les phrases à l'aide d'adverbes :

→ *angrily, kindly, lovingly, quietly, loudly, calmly, nervously, impatiently…*

■ utiliser une langue orale :

→ réponses courtes : *I don't think so… I hope not… So do I…*   Ⓟ RÉCIS GRAMMATICAL → 30

→ formes contractées : *I can't wait… I've got to go…*

→ tags : *You'll help me, won't you?*
          Ⓟ RÉCIS GRAMMATICAL → 30

→ gap fillers : *Well… Er… You know…*

E Rédiger un essai

Dans un essai, on vous demande d'argumenter, de commenter une citation ou de formuler une opinion sur un sujet précis, dans une langue soutenue.

● L'essai répond à des règles précises.

■ L'introduction présente la problématique du sujet / l'idée générale.

■ L'organisation des idées doit apparaître clairement : vous devez structurer votre essai en exprimant une seule idée par paragraphe.

■ Les phrases doivent être liées de façon logique par des transitions et des mots de liaison.

■ La conclusion répond à la question posée / au sujet.

● Avant de composer, il est nécessaire d'écrire au brouillon autant de mots et phrases clés que possible.

● Veillez à illustrer votre propos à l'aide d'exemples précis empruntés à votre expérience et à vos connaissances ou culture personnelles.

● Le registre de langue doit être soutenu et vous devez prendre position si on vous le demande.

F Rédiger un article de presse

Un article de presse transmet de l'information et doit permettre au lecteur de se faire une opinion personnelle de l'événement décrit. Lorsque vous rédigez un article de presse :

● Efforcez-vous de rester objectif / neutre. Si vous donnez votre opinion, précisez-le clairement.

● Mentionnez les circonstances, les faits, les causes et éventuellement les conséquences de l'événement à raconter.

● Le registre de langue doit être soutenu. Évitez les formes contractées, sauf pour reprendre des paroles rapportées.

● Les mots de liaison doivent faire apparaître la logique de votre propos.

● Donnez un titre concis à votre article après l'avoir rédigé.

G Résumer un article de presse

● Résumer un article de presse nécessite avant tout une bonne compréhension du texte. Vous devez être capable de distinguer l'essentiel de l'accessoire (voir « Compréhension de l'écrit », p. 167).

● Avant de rédiger votre résumé, vous devrez :

■ dégager le thème général et les opinions ;

■ souligner l'idée essentielle de chaque paragraphe ;

■ souligner les mots qui expriment les liens logiques.

● Rédigez le résumé de façon personnelle en faisant attention à :

■ éviter les formules du type *"the journalist declares / says that…"* ;

■ conserver le point de vue, la personne et les temps des verbes du texte original ;

■ rapporter les propos des personnages en les résumant au discours indirect ;

■ suivre l'ordre des idées de l'article ;

■ respecter la fourchette de mots demandée (en général le tiers du texte de départ).

Expressions utiles pour communiquer

1. Interagir à l'oral et à l'écrit

Giving one's opinion
- To my mind / In my opinion…
- It seems to me that…
- I feel / believe that…
- I can't help thinking that…
- My feeling is that…
- As a matter of fact, I am convinced that…
- For my part, I consider that…

Expressing agreement
- I agree with…
- It is true to say that…
- So do I / Neither do I.
- That's exactly how I see it.
- I perfectly understand that…
- You / They are right to suggest that…
- I share your point of view…
- I see eye to eye with you…

Expressing disagreement
- I don't agree / disagree with you about that…
- Contrary to / Unlike…, I feel that…
- That's not how I see it.
- Instead of V-ING…
- I don't see things that way.

Expressing doubts, protest
- However, I am not really sure that…
- I am rather sceptical about…
- In theory, it sounds… but in practice…
- I object to / disapprove of GN / V-ING
- How can they…? / What right have they to…?

Suggesting and convincing
- How / What about V-ING
- Why don't you / Why not V
- Don't you think that…?
- I suggest V-ING / I suggest we (should) V
- We should definitely V…

- I'm convinced that…
- It seems to me that…
- I'm sure you will / won't V…

Expressing surprise
- I can't / couldn't believe it / my eyes!
- You can't imagine what I saw!
- How surprised I was!
- It was truly amazing!
- How fantastic it was!
- How astonishing to see such…!
- I was amazed by / stunned by / astounded by…
- It was just unbelievable!
- Just imagine!
- Fancy that!
- What a sight! / How strange!…
- What I find the most incredible / unpleasant / shocking is that…

Expressing enthusiasm
- It must be great / terrific…
- How interesting / fantastic!
- I'd just love to…
- I was so impressed by…
- I can't wait to see that!

Expressing likes and dislikes
- I'm fond of / keen on GN / V-ING
- I fancy GN / V-ING
- I enjoy V-ING
- I love GN / V-ING
- I'm mad / crazy about…! (informel)
- I hate GN / V-ING
- I can't stand / bear GN / V-ING
- I can't put up with GN / V-ING
- I don't go for it. (informel)

Expressing preferences
- I prefer V-ing to V-ING
- I'd rather V than V
- I'd rather you V (prétérit modal)
- I feel more like V-ING than V-ING
- Instead of GN / V-ING (Au lieu de)
- I like it better / best

Being indifferent
- I don't mind (him / her) V-ING…
- As you like / wish.
- It doesn't matter. / Never mind.
- Why not?
- It doesn't matter to me whether… or…
- I don't care.

Expressing wishes and intentions
- I would like to V
- I'd love to V
- I feel like GN / V-ING
- I hope to V
- I wish you'd V
- If only I / you V (prétérit modal)
- I would appreciate it if…
- I am looking forward to V-ING
- I dream of GN / V-ING
- I'm dying for GN / to V
- I want to V
- I'm thinking of V-ING
- I'm about to V
- I plan / mean / intend / aim to V
- Whether you like it or not, I'll V
- I'm determined (not) to V

Expressing regret and reproach
- I regret V-ING
- I should (not) have V-EN
- If only / I wish I had (not) V-EN
- You shouldn't have V-EN
- Why didn't you V?
- How could you V?
- What a shame!
- How awful (of you)!
- Why on earth did / didn't you V?

Giving orders
- I want you to V
- You have / have got to V
- You must V
- Will you V!
- Stop shouting! / Do be quiet.
- Dont' V
- Stop V-ING
- I'll have / make GN / V

2. Relier vos idées

Addition

- **besides / moreover / what's more**: *en outre*
I don't mind going out. **Besides**, the walk will do me good.

Purpose

- **in order (not) to / so as (not) to**: *pour (ne pas)*
He drove at 50 mph **so as to** save petrol.
- **so (that)**: *pour que, de façon que*
He lowered his voice **so (that)** Tania couldn't hear.

Cause

- **as**: *comme*
As Philip knew the road, we asked him to come with us.
- **because of**: *à cause de*
I spent three hours waiting in the rain **because of** you!
- **since**: *puisque*
Since you are unable to answer, I'll ask someone else.

Concession

- **although / though**: *bien que*
Although he's 60, he still works more than 12 hours a day.
- **despite / in spite of** (*plus courant*): *malgré, en dépit de*
Despite all our efforts to save the school, they closed it.
- **however**: *pourtant, cependant, toutefois*
This is a simple machine. **However** there are dangers.
- **still / yet**: *pourtant, cependant*
The hotel was terrible. **Still**, we were lucky with the weather.

Condition

- **as long as / so long as**: *pourvu que, à condition que*
He says he's quite willing to cooperate **as long as** he is notified in time.
- **or else / otherwise**: *sinon*
Hurry up **or else** we'll miss the train.
- **provided**: *à condition que, pourvu que*
He can come with us, **provided** he pays for his meal.
- **unless**: *à moins que*
He won't go to sleep **unless** you tell him a story.

Consequence

- **consequently / therefore / as a result**: *par conséquent*
He didn't work; **as a result** he failed.

Hypothesis

- **in case**: *au cas où*
I'll give you my number, **in case** you need to call.
- **suppose / supposing**: *en supposant que*
Supposing he can't, will you do it yourself?

Opposition

- **unlike**: *contrairement à*
Unlike most people he knew, he never came to work by car.
- **whereas / while**: *alors que, tandis que*
His first book was a flop **whereas** this one is a bestseller.

Time

- **as**: *comme, alors que, au moment où*
I saw Peter **as** I was getting off the bus.

- **as soon as**: *dès que, aussitôt que*
As soon as she entered the room, she saw him.
- **meanwhile**: *pendant ce temps*
The flight will be announced soon. **Meanwhile**, please remain seated.
- **once**: *une fois (que)*
Once they're in bed, the children usually stay there.
- **till / until**: *jusqu'à (ce que)*
He waited **until** she had finished speaking.
- **while**: *pendant que*
They arrived **while** we were having dinner.

3. Écrire un essai ou faire un exposé

Introducing the main topic

- This is a **to**pical (*d'actualité*) s**u**bject…
- This is an **e**ss**e**ntial qu**e**stion / **i**ssue (*problème*)…
- In most c**a**ses… (*Dans la plupart des cas*)
- It deals (*traite*) with…

Giving examples

- For ex**a**mple / For **i**nstance… (*Par exemple*)
- … that is to say… (*c'est-à-dire*)
- … such as… (*tel que*)

Adding an idea

- As reg**a**rds / Conc**e**rning… (*En ce qui concerne*)
- S**i**milarly… (*De la même façon*)
- As we have alr**ea**dy seen / m**e**ntioned…

Speaking about the author / the journalist

- He describes / dep**i**cts…
- She narr**a**tes / rel**a**tes…
- He wants to make us aw**a**re that…
- She stands for… / supp**o**rts (*Elle est en faveur de…*)
- He **a**rgues in f**a**vour of / ag**ai**nst…
- She den**o**unces / cond**e**mns…
- He cr**i**ticizes / blames / repr**oa**ches *GN* for sth / V-*ING*
- She approves / disappr**o**ves of…
- He sides (*prend parti*) / d**oe**sn't side with…
- She is b**ia**sed (*partiale*) ≠ unb**ia**sed

Summing up

- For all these r**ea**sons…
- In **o**ther words…
- To sum up…

Concluding

- To concl**u**de… / To sum up…
- In short / brief…
- In a n**u**tshell… (*En un mot*)
- On the whole… (*En définitive*)
- All in all… (*Tout bien pesé*)

Bac - Conseils pratiques

Vous trouverez la présentation
des épreuves pages 12-13
(BO n° 43 du 24 novembre 2011).

Bac - Conseils pratiques

1 Épreuve de compréhension orale

> Vous allez écouter trois fois un enregistrement dont le titre vous est communiqué.
>
> Chaque écoute sera séparée d'une minute. Vous aurez ensuite 10 minutes pour rendre compte en français de ce que vous avez compris.

Préparez-vous à l'écoute.

● Anticipez le sujet du document à partir du titre. Selon vous, quel va être le thème abordé ?

● Mobilisez les connaissances (lexicales, culturelles, personnelles…) que vous avez sur le sujet.

Première écoute : repérez la nature et le thème général du document.

● Repérez la nature du document : conversation privée, reportage, interview, débat, flash d'infos, documentaire, discours officiel…

● Soyez attentif à tous les indices sonores :
– nombre de voix, accent (britannique, américain, indien…) ;
– applaudissements, musique, bruits de fond…

● Quels mots et expressions reconnaissez-vous ? Notez-les.

● À la fin de la première écoute, vous aurez une minute pour réorganiser vos notes. Mettez les éléments repérés en relation afin d'identifier le thème général du document. Notez-le brièvement.
Les premières hypothèses que vous avez faites à partir du titre sont-elles confirmées ?

Deuxième écoute : relevez les informations principales.

● Relevez le plus d'informations possible en vous appuyant sur les mots porteurs de sens et les mots mis en relief que vous reconnaissez.

● Lors de la minute de pause :
– organisez vos notes : classez et mettez en relation les nouveaux éléments relevés de façon à pouvoir répondre aux questions : Qui ? Quoi ? Où ? Quand ?…
– faites aussi le point sur les informations manquantes.

Troisième écoute : revenez sur ce qui n'a pas été bien perçu.

● Concentrez-vous pour identifier les passages mal perçus. Leur sens peut être déduit du contexte.

● Soyez attentif aux formes grammaticales :
– les temps, bien sûr ;
– la présence de phrases à la voix passive, qui vous permettront de clarifier qui fait quoi et qui subit quoi ;
– les modaux qui vous donneront des renseignements sur le point de vue des locuteurs et leurs intentions.

● Efforcez-vous de repérer les liaisons, qui donnent l'impression que les mots sont collés l'un à l'autre, et les mots transparents, qui ne vous poseraient aucun problème à l'écrit, mais qui sont plus difficiles à reconnaître à l'oral.

● Faites preuve de logique. Posez-vous les questions suivantes : Pourquoi ? Comment ? Avantages / inconvénients ? Pour / contre ?

● Ne vous inquiétez pas si vous n'avez pas tout compris : il est normal que des zones d'ombre subsistent.

Rédigez le compte rendu en français.

● Utilisez au mieux les 10 minutes dont vous disposez pour rendre compte en français de ce que vous avez compris.

● Réorganisez vos notes de façon logique.

● Rédigez des phrases simples mais complètes. Rapportez non seulement le contenu informatif du document mais aussi l'attitude et les réactions éventuelles du / des locuteur(s) (ton, humour, point de vue, etc.).

● Relisez-vous ! Il est essentiel que l'on comprenne ce que vous avez voulu dire.

Épreuve d'expression orale

Première partie : prise de parole en continu

> Vous allez tirer au sort une des notions du programme étudiées dans l'année.
> Vous aurez 10 minutes pour préparer un exposé de 5 minutes sur cette notion.

Utilisez au mieux le temps de préparation.

● Vous avez étudié au cours de l'année plusieurs documents (textes, documents audio, vidéo, iconographiques) illustrant la notion tirée au sort. Pensez aux thématiques suggérées dans les pages « Bac oral » du manuel qui vous permettent d'aborder concrètement la notion que vous devez présenter. Vous pouvez bien sûr présenter toute autre thématique de votre choix.

● Sélectionnez rapidement les documents qui vous permettront de vous exprimer au mieux sur la thématique retenue (index des documents par notion culturelle, p. 222). Notez-les au brouillon.

● Notez également les mots clés liés au champ lexical de la notion.

● N'hésitez pas à utiliser vos connaissances personnelles (lectures, actualité…) pour enrichir votre présentation.

● Organisez vos idées et faites un plan rapide.

● N'oubliez pas de préparer une phrase d'introduction.

C'est à vous !

● Présentez-vous et n'oubliez pas de saluer l'examinateur.

● Posez vos notes devant vous et commencez votre présentation.

● Gérez bien votre temps : cinq minutes passent rapidement.

● Regardez votre examinateur, jetez un coup d'œil de temps à autre à vos notes, mais surtout ne les lisez pas.

● Si vous hésitez, ayez recours aux *gap fillers* (p. 163). Surtout ne restez pas muet.

● Pensez à utiliser des mots de liaison qui vont vous permettre d'enchaîner vos idées.

● Assurez-vous que l'examinateur suit bien vos propos et, si vous avez l'impression de ne pas avoir été clair, n'hésitez pas à vous reprendre et à reformuler par une périphrase ou un équivalent.

● Impliquez-vous et montrez l'intérêt de la thématique choisie : si vous semblez vous ennuyer, votre examinateur ne sera pas convaincu !

● Indiquez clairement par une phrase de conclusion que votre exposé est terminé.

Expressions utiles

● **Pour présenter la notion**

■ *The notion I'm going to deal with is The idea of progress / Myths and heroes / Places and exchanges / Seats and forms of power…*

■ *The subject of my oral presentation will be / I'm going to speak about / My topic is…*

■ *I would like to illustrate this notion through / using the theme of modernity and tradition in Britain…*

■ *I will present this notion by showing the relationship between man and machine…*

■ *I feel this notion is best illustrated by trying to see if all citizens are on an equal footing in India today…*

● **Pour introduire les documents et les exemples**

■ *In the document / text I studied about blacklisting in America…*

■ *The extract focused on / was centred on / dealt with the issue of the power of the Internet…*

■ *A good example of modernity in Britain is…*

■ *Let's take the case of girls in India…*

■ *For instance / example in the film I, Robot…*

■ *In particular / Particularly…*

■ *… such as…*

● **Pour ordonner ses idées**

■ *To begin with / First of all…*

■ *Secondly…*

■ *Then / Next…*

■ *Finally / Eventually…*

● **Pour comparer / opposer des documents ou points de vue**

■ *Similarly…*

■ *Just like…*

■ *On the one hand… on the other hand…*

■ *Contrary to / Unlike…*

■ *While / Whereas…*

● **Pour préciser ou compléter ses idées**

■ *Actually, what I mean is…*

■ *In other words, what I would like to say is…*

■ *To put it differently, what I really meant to say was…*

■ *To put it more precisely…*

■ *Moreover / What's more…*

■ *Besides…* (D'ailleurs)

■ *As regards…* (En ce qui concerne)

● **Pour résumer vos idées et conclure**

■ *To sum up the main ideas…*

■ *On the whole, it could be said that…*

■ *Last but not least, it may be said…*

■ *To conclude / In conclusion, I could say that…*

Deuxième partie : **conversation conduite par l'examinateur**

> Une conversation conduite par l'examinateur s'appuiera sur l'exposé que vous avez fait lors de la première partie de l'épreuve. Cette conversation n'excédera pas 5 minutes.

Soyez convaincant(e).

Plusieurs stratégies peuvent vous y aider :

● Donnez des exemples pour illustrer votre propos.
- *Let's take an example.*
- *For instance / example…*

● Reformulez ou répétez si vous avez l'impression de ne pas avoir été compris.
- *I must explain…*
- *In other words…*
- *Let's put it differently…*
- *I'll make myself clear…*

● Utilisez des expressions qui expriment votre forte conviction.
- *It is true to say… and yet…*
- *I'm quite sure that…*
- *I'm convinced that…*
- *I do believe that…*

● Ponctuez certains de vos énoncés par des **tags**. Dans la plupart des cas, le **tag** n'est pas une vraie question. L'intonation est alors descendante.
- *Global warming is a major issue, isn't it?* ↘
- *Most people would agree with that, wouldn't they?* ↘

● Souvenez-vous qu'en anglais les **interro-négatives** sont fréquentes dans les débats.
- *Isn't it incredibly unfair to tax them?*
- *Shouldn't the government be doing more?*

Demandez de l'aide ou des précisions.

Il se peut que vous ne soyez pas sûr(e) d'avoir compris votre interlocuteur. N'hésitez pas à le lui dire.
- *I'm sorry, what did you say?*
- *Could you repeat what you said, please?*
- *I'm sorry, I didn't hear what you said.*
- *Excuse me, I didn't understand what you said.*
- *Excuse me, what do you mean by…?*
- *I'm sorry, I don't see what you mean.*

Exprimez votre accord ou désaccord de façon authentique.

"Yes" ou *"No"* ne suffisent pas à exprimer l'accord ou le désaccord dans un échange fluide. Vous pouvez réagir aux propos de votre interlocuteur de façon nuancée et authentique à l'aide des réponses courtes.

● Utilisez les **réponses courtes avec auxiliaire**.
- *You said it was inevitable.* → *No, I didn't!*

● Pensez également aux **réponses courtes en so, not, et to**.

Rappel : *so* et *not* s'utilisent après les verbes d'opinion, tandis que l'on utilise *to* de l'infinitif après les verbes de volonté, d'intention, d'attente.
- *What you're saying is questionable.* → *I don't think so. / I suppose so. / I guess so.*
- *You don't think they're right, do you?* → *I'm afraid not. / Of course not.*
- *Would you agree to do that?* → *I'd love to, but I'm not supposed to.*

● Modulez votre réponse à l'aide de commentaires personnels, sans pour autant omettre l'auxiliaire correspondant à l'énoncé de votre interlocuteur.
- *Of course I did. / I'm sure he has. / I suppose we can. / I guess they would. / I'm surprised he did. / I don't think they should.*

Ne restez pas muet.
- *I'm afraid I don't know / remember.*
- *I'm not sure I can answer.*
- *I'm sorry, but I don't know what to say.*
- *I don't know what to think about…*
- *I have to admit I don't know much about this problem.*

3 Épreuve écrite

Première partie : **compréhension de l'écrit**

> La compréhension de l'écrit s'appuie sur un, deux ou trois textes. Certains documents peuvent comporter des éléments iconographiques.

Préparez-vous à la lecture.

Avant de lire le(s) texte(s) :

● Identifiez leur nature : article de presse, roman, pièce de théâtre…

● Identifiez les éléments périphériques : l'auteur, la source, la date de publication, le titre…

Utilisez ces éléments d'information, que vous mettrez en relation avec le document iconographique s'il y en a un, pour anticiper le thème général du ou des texte(s).

Prenez connaissance du ou des texte(s) et des questions de compréhension.

● Lisez le(s) texte(s) en entier ainsi que les notes lexicales. Cette première lecture devrait vous permettre d'identifier le narrateur ainsi que les personnages, le lieu, la période… Vos premières hypothèses sur le thème général du ou des texte(s) sont-elles confirmées ?

● Lisez ensuite les questions de compréhension. Cette étude attentive des questions vous donnera des indices sur les thèmes importants du texte. Même si les premières questions vous semblent faciles (ce qui est souvent le cas), n'y répondez pas immédiatement. Prenez connaissance de toutes les questions ainsi que des sujets d'expression.

● Assurez-vous de bien connaître le vocabulaire des consignes. Les consignes les plus courantes sont les suivantes :

■ *Pick out* the **phrases** which best **apply** to…
→ Relevez les expressions qui s'appliquent le mieux à…

■ *Explain in* **your own words**…
→ Expliquez en utilisant vos propres mots…

■ *Use* **quotes** / **quotations** from the text to **justify** your answer.
→ Utilisez des citations du texte pour justifier votre réponse.

■ *Put the* **jumbled** elements in chronological order.
→ Classez dans l'ordre chronologique les éléments donnés.

■ *Who or what do the* **underlined** elements / pronouns / adjectives **refer to**?
→ À qui ou à quoi font référence les éléments / pronoms / adjectifs soulignés ?

■ *List* the different ways Jim is **referred to** in the text.
→ Relevez dans le texte les différentes expressions utilisées pour faire référence à Jim.

■ *Discuss* / **Rephrase** the following **statement**.
→ Analysez / Reformulez l'affirmation suivante.

■ *Match* the adjectives and the **characters**.
→ Associez les adjectifs avec les personnages.

● Relisez entièrement le ou les textes. Cette deuxième lecture vous permettra d'affiner votre compréhension.

● Ne vous focalisez pas sur les mots inconnus ; ne les soulignez pas ! Vous pourrez sans doute en deviner le sens par la suite (« Les mots inconnus », p. 168). En outre, certains mots ou expressions difficiles ne feront pas nécessairement l'objet de questions.

Répondez aux questions de compréhension.

● Répondez précisément à la question posée sans anticiper sur les questions suivantes (ni revenir sur les questions précédentes) : on ne vous demande jamais deux fois la même chose.

● Prêtez attention à la consigne : le temps ou la forme verbale employés dans la question vous indiquent le temps ou la forme verbale à utiliser dans la réponse.

● On peut vous demander de citer le texte pour justifier une réponse : mettez les citations entre guillemets et accompagnez-les toujours de la mention de la ligne.

● Lorsqu'une réponse relativement longue est attendue, le nombre de mots est indiqué. Tenez-en compte (ne comptez pas les citations éventuelles dans le nombre de mots demandé). Rédigez des phrases complètes.

● Quand il n'y a pas d'indication de nombre de mots dans la question, répondez brièvement, généralement en une phrase. On vous indique parfois le passage dans lequel vous devez trouver une réponse. Ne cherchez pas celle-ci dans d'autres parties du texte.

● Si une question vous paraît difficile, passez à la suivante : les questions ne sont pas forcément liées et vous y reviendrez par la suite.

Relisez-vous !

Deuxième partie : **expression écrite**

> Vous devez rédiger un ou plusieurs textes construits en prenant appui sur des événements, faits, ou des prises de position que vous aurez identifiés dans les documents servant de support à l'épreuve de compréhension. En LV1, vous devez également construire une argumentation personnelle à partir d'un thème en relation avec ces documents.

epérez bien le type de sujet :

écit, dialogue, lettre, journal intime, essai…

• Vous adapterez le niveau de langue en conséquence : ngue informelle pour une lettre à un ami ou un dialogue, ngue plus soutenue pour un récit ou un essai. (Dans ce ernier cas, n'utilisez pas de formes verbales contractées.)

• Attention au hors-sujet. Soyez très vigilant dans votre lecure des consignes. Lorsque le sujet est lié au texte étudié n compréhension, par exemple écrire la suite d'une histoire, estez dans la logique interne du texte (époque, événement, ersonnages) et respectez le même niveau de langue.

Mobilisez le lexique et les structures que le sujet ous impose.

• Écrivez-les au brouillon ; vous vous efforcerez d'en utiliser n maximum au cours de la rédaction.

Organisez vos idées.

• Faites un plan. N'oubliez pas de rédiger une introduction et ne conclusion si vous traitez un sujet argumentatif.

aites un brouillon.

• Ceci vous permettra d'éviter les redites, de contrôler le ombre de mots et de ne pas raturer votre copie.

le rédigez pas d'abord en français pour traduire nsuite.

• Si vous êtes bloqué par un mot que vous ne connaissez as, contournez la difficulté ; ne laissez en aucun cas un blanc u un mot en français.

Reliez vos idées par des mots de liaison.

• Ayez en permanence à votre disposition une bonne quinaine de mots de liaison (→ p. 174) vous permettant de struc-turer votre discours et de rédiger un texte clairement articulé. Vous pouvez au besoin les écrire sur la feuille de brouillon fournie avant de commencer à rédiger.

Soignez la présentation et n'oubliez pas la ponctuation.

• Faites des paragraphes bien distincts. Écrivez lisiblement. Si votre copie est difficile à lire, vous serez pénalisé.

Respectez et indiquez le nombre de mots.

Gérez bien votre temps.

• Vous ne pouvez pas prendre le risque de rendre une feuille de brouillon.

Relisez-vous.

• On a souvent tendance à reproduire les mêmes erreurs… Soyez donc bien conscient des erreurs que vous avez faites au cours de l'année.

Avant de rendre votre copie, vérifiez si vous avez bien pensé à :
– conjuguer les verbes et, entre autres, à ajouter un s à la 3e personne du singulier du présent simple (sauf pour les modaux) ;
– introduire un auxiliaire aux formes négative et interrogative ;
– placer l'adjectif épithète (invariable) avant le nom qu'il qualifie ;
– former un génitif quand cela est possible ;
– ne pas mettre d'article défini devant les noms pris dans leur sens général ;
– mettre une majuscule aux adjectifs de nationalité, aux jours de la semaine, aux mois ;
– introduire des propositions relatives (en faisant la distinction entre *who* et *which*) ;
– ne pas séparer le verbe de son complément d'objet direct.

Pour s'exprimer à l'écrit ou à l'oral, il faut s'entraîner à mobiliser ses connaissances, tant pour ce qui est du lexique que de la grammaire. Apprenez à associer vos besoins d'expression à un ou des faits grammaticaux.
Sachez utiliser les points de grammaire que vous connaissez pour argumenter, prendre position sur un sujet et construire une narration.

1 Savoir argumenter

WORKBOOK → p. 68-70

Opposer « idées générales » et « situation actuelle »

FICHE 1

1 Utilisez la forme du présent qui convient.

Dans un discours argumenté, pour exposer un problème, le présent est un temps central. La difficulté en anglais est de faire la différence entre l'exposé d'idées générales et la description de la situation actuelle.

- **Pour exposer des faits stables, choisissez le présent simple.**

  Most students ***use*** *the Internet to communicate socially.*

  Do *computers* ***make*** *a difference in education?*

- **Pour une situation en évolution, utilisez le présent BE + ING.**

  Is *the world chang****ing*** *faster than we are?*
  → Le monde change-t-il plus vite que nous ?

  Things ***are not*** *gett****ing*** *any better.*
  → Les choses ne s'améliorent pas.

Attention ! **Erreurs fréquentes**

- **Avec tous les verbes d'opinion, exclure le présent BE+ING.**

  Scientists ***argue*** (prétendent) *that those lands will disappear.*

- **Le verbe *have* (« posséder / avoir ») est un verbe comme les autres. L'auxiliaire ne doit pas être omis.**

  Why ***do they have*** *so little in common?*

  They ***do not have*** *anything to say.*

- **On n'emploie pas le présent avec SINCE pour traduire « depuis » mais le *present perfect* simple ou BE+ING (voir fiche 3, p. 181).**

2 Sachez choisir les articles.

Vous n'utiliserez pas les mêmes articles selon que vous exposerez une **idée générale** (article ø) ou que vous ferez référence à une **situation particulière** (article *the*). Rappelez-vous que l'emploi de *the* est souvent source d'erreurs ! N'oubliez pas non plus que les indénombrables sont incompatibles avec l'article *a / an*.

- **Pour présenter une notion ou exposer une idée générale (« le », « la », « les »), utilisez l'article ø.**

  Racial segregation restricted access to education.
  → **La** ségregation raciale restreignait l'accès à **l'**éducation.

- **Pour faire référence à des éléments indéfinis (« du », « de la », « des »), c'est également ø que vous utiliserez.**

  He brought hope and change to his people.
  → Il a apporté **de** l'espoir et **du** changement à son peuple.

- **Réservez l'emploi de *the* à des situations particulières et bien définies ;**

  The *president they elected in* ***the*** *election of November 2008.*

- **à des faits ou des institutions connus de tous.**

  the *Internet,* ***the*** *American administration,* ***the*** *British government,* ***the*** *international Press,* ***the*** *police*

Attention ! **Erreurs fréquentes**

- **Pas d'article**

– devant le mot *society* : ~~*The*~~ *British society* ;
– devant les noms propres : ~~*The*~~ *Prime Minister Cameron* mais ***the*** *British Prime Minister* ;
– devant un génitif : ~~*The*~~ *Britain's government.* ~~*The*~~ *India's computer analysts.* ~~*The*~~ *Today's problems.*

- **Article *a* / *an* impossible**

– devant les indénombrables, qui s'accordent au singulier.

  It was ~~*an*~~ *useful information /* ~~*a*~~ *good advice. / There has been* ~~*a*~~ *progress.*

- **S'accordent au singulier malgré le *s***

– *Politics / economics / the news / the United States is...*

3 Nuancez vos propos.

Les déterminants suivants vous permettront de faire référence à une partie ou à la totalité d'un groupe et d'exprimer des quantités indéfinies.

- **« Certains », « la plupart », « tous »**

  Some *scientists.* (Certains scientifiques.) / ***Some of them.***
  Most *students.* (La plupart des étudiants.) / ***Most of them.***
  All *discoveries.* (Toutes les découvertes.) / ***All of them.***
  Every *student knows that.* Tous les étudiants savent cela. (= chaque étudiant). Verbe au singulier en anglais avec ***every***.

- **« Pas beaucoup de », « peu de »**

  They didn't have ***much*** *time. They had* ***little*** *time left.* (Nom au singulier.)
  Not ***many*** *solutions.* ***Few*** *opportunities.* (Nom au pluriel.)

Identifier un problème, envisager des solutions

1 Définissez une problématique.

• **Utilisez le gérondif (V-*ING*) pour poser un problème.**

Là où, en français, on utilise des noms, des expressions comme « le fait de » ou des verbes à l'infinitif, c'est le gérondif que l'on utilise en anglais.

Voting is an essential part of democracy.

→ **Le fait de voter** est un élément essentiel de la démocratie.

Finding a job is extremely difficult.

→ **Trouver** un emploi est extrêmement difficile.

• **Sachez utiliser les expressions suivantes pour débattre d'un problème.**

There's nothing wrong with trying to find solutions.

→ Il n'y a rien de mal à essayer de trouver des solutions.

There's no denying that it is a major issue.

→ On ne peut nier que c'est un problème majeur.

It's worth trying.

→ Cela vaut la peine d'essayer.

It is no use arguing with them.

→ Ça n'est pas la peine de discuter avec eux.

2 Formulez des propositions.

Rappelez-vous que les formes de l'infinitif (*to V*) orientent l'action vers l'avenir.

It is **necessary** / **possible** / **essential** / **vital to** develop fair trade.

I find **it important for them to** develop new projects.

→ Je pense qu'il est important qu'ils développent de nouveaux projets.

I think **it necessary for the government to** find a solution.

→ Je crois qu'il est nécessaire que le gouvernement trouve une solution.

Faire le bilan d'une situation donnée

1 Montrez le lien entre passé et présent.

Présentez les origines et les conséquences présentes d'un problème. Établissez des liens de cause à effet entre passé et présent.

• **Utilisez le *present perfect*.**

Associez dans un même énoncé ou un même paragraphe des énoncés au *present perfect* et des énoncés au présent.

The accident **has caused** *much damage and a new crisis* **is** *inevitable.*

They **are not doing** *anything about it and the situation* **has become** *critical.*

2 Présentez l'évolution du problème sur une période donnée.

• **Utilisez des expressions de temps marquant le lien passé / présent.**

Associez le *present perfect* à :

– **always** / **never** / **already** / **before** / **long** / **so far** / **over the years**

They have **always** *defended our rights.*

So far (jusqu'à présent), *there has* **never** *been a proper definition of that word.*

Crime has risen dramatically **over the past ten years**.

The number of accidents **has increased** *by 10%* **in the past few months**.

– **since** et **for** (« *depuis* »)

The country has changed a lot **since** *the 1990s.*

There has been trouble in this area **for** *a number of years.*

• **Utilisez le *present perfect* BE+ING pour exprimer la continuité ;**

This **has been** *going on for years.*

American politicians **have been debating** *this issue since the 1960s.*

• **avec des adverbes exprimant l'idée de progression.**

Demand for oil has been growing **continuously** / **regularly**.

Life expectancy has been **steadily** *increasing.*

→ L'espérance de vie ne cesse / n'a pas cessé d'augmenter / augmente régulièrement.

Attention ! Erreurs fréquentes

• **En français, on utilise le présent avec « depuis », ce qui est source d'erreur.**

They've been defending our rights since the 1960s.

→ Ils **défendent** nos droits depuis les années 1960.

• **Avec un repère de temps précis (date, *ago*) on utilise le prétérit et non pas le *present perfect*.**

It happened long ago / in 1965.

• **Le *present perfect* BE+ING est impossible avec les verbes d'état (*want, know, remember*, etc.).**

Savoir prendre position

WORKBOOK → p. 71

FICHE 4

Exprimer un jugement

Après l'exposé d'une situation donnée, on s'attend à ce que vous donniez votre avis. Exprimez-vous sur « ce qui pourrait être » ou « ce qui devrait être ».

1 **Exprimez votre opinion avec** *should, could* **et** *would.*

- **Pour une recommandation :** *should*

  The authorities **should** be doing more.
  They **should have** dealt with the problem years ago.

- **Pour des contraintes objectives :** *have to* ou *need to*

  Most of those people **have to** work very long hours.
  The problem of child poverty **needs to** be addressed urgently.

- **Pour l'expression du possible :** *could*

  They **could** find new ideas and make new proposals.
  → Ils pourraient…

They **could have** made new proposals but they didn't.
→ Ils auraient pu…

- **Pour nuancer votre avis :** *would* (conditionnel)

  It **would** be much better / far worse / totally unreasonable to change the rules.

2 **Utilisez les modaux pour exprimer certitude et incertitude.**

- *May* **et** *might* **pour l'incertitude**

  This **may** / **might** never happen.

- *Must* **et** *can't* **pour une plus grande certitude**

  They **can't have** failed.
  → Il est impossible qu'ils aient échoué.

  The proposal **must have** caused much alarm.

FICHE 5

Formuler hypothèses et souhaits

Lorsque vous utilisez les formes de l'irréel, rappelez-vous que bon nombre d'entre elles se construisent avec le prétérit modal.

1 **Faites des hypothèses en** *IF.*

- *If* **+ prétérit** → *would*

  If it were true, they would stop arguing.
  → Si c'était vrai, ils arrêteraient de débattre.

- *If* **+ pluperfect** → *would have*

  If they had done that earlier, the situation would have been totally different.
  → S'ils avaient fait cela plus tôt, la situation aurait été totalement différente.

2 **Exprimez souhaits et regrets.**

- **Sachez utiliser** *I wish.*

I wish (suivi du prétérit) se traduit souvent par « regretter » mais il faut inverser le sens de la subordonnée en français.

  I wish there was a solution.
  → Je regrette qu'il n'y ait **pas** de solution.

- **Exprimez le souhait avec** *It's (high) time.*

  It's high time they created an international organization.
  → Il est grand temps qu'ils créent une organisation internationale.

Attention ! Après *I would like*, on utilise la proposition infinitive.
  I would like the problem to be settled before it is too late.

FICHE 6

Parler de l'avenir

Vous pouvez conclure votre exposé en expliquant quelle est votre vision de l'avenir. Rappelez-vous que les formes de futur proche comme « ils vont agir » / « cela va se produire » ne se traduisent pas nécessairement par *BE GOING TO* en anglais.

1 **Utilisez** *WILL.*

Pour ce qui semble logiquement devoir se produire.

- **Avec** *if* **et** *when*

  If nothing changes, temperatures will keep increasing.
  → Si rien ne se passe, les températures vont continuer à augmenter.

Attention ! Erreur fréquente

On n'emploie ni *WILL* ni *WOULD* après *WHEN*.
  Everything will change radically when this ~~will happen~~
  → happens.
  → Tout va changer radicalement lorsque cela se produira.

- **Avec les adverbes de probabilité**

  They will probably / certainly / fail.
  No doubt they will start a new campaign.

2 **Utilisez** *BE GOING TO.*

Pour établir un lien entre la situation présente et l'avenir.
  According to the most recent studies, we **are going to** find ourselves in a very difficult situation.

3 **Utilisez des périphrases en** *TO.*

Pour énoncer des faits prévus ou imminents.
  The government **is about to** find new solutions.
  The situation **is likely to** change.
  A new project **is to** be announced soon.
  The project **is sure to** fail.

Savoir construire une narration Ⓦ ORKBOOK → p. 72

ⓌORKBOOK → p. 72

Savoir utiliser les temps du récit

Pour faire un récit, vous devez organiser l'enchaînement des événements autour d'un temps central : le prétérit simple. Évitez d'introduire par erreur des verbes au *present perfect* dans votre récit ! Faites progresser la narration à l'aide de marqueurs temporels. Lorsque vous souhaitez faire une pause dans le récit pour décrire une situation ou un personnage, utilisez le prétérit BE+ING. Utilisez le *pluperfect* pour faire des retours en arrière.

1 Sachez faire progresser un récit.

- **Privilégiez le prétérit simple et les repères passés.**

Structurez votre récit à l'aide de compléments de temps et de subordonnées de temps.

> It **happened six years ago** / **a few weeks before** Christmas / **long after** they were born.
>
> It **took** them **a while** / **years** to adapt.
>
> It **lasted a whole decade** / **for years** / **a good ten years**.
>
> **At first**… **Then**… **After a while**… **Before long**…
>
> **As** he **travelled**, he **realized** that…
>
> **While** / **All the time** she **was** there she **worked** in…
>
> **Once** it **was** over, they **left**.
>
> They **did not stop until** it was too late.

- **Exprimez l'habitude à l'aide de** WOULD.

> When / Whenever they asked him who he was, he **would** feel offended.
>
> → Lorsqu'ils lui demandaient… il se sentait…

Attention ! Dans ce cas, WOULD correspond à un simple imparfait !

- **Pensez à utiliser** USED TO.

Par exemple en début de récit, pour marquer la rupture avec la situation actuelle (« autrefois », « avant »).

> **There used to** be thousands of Aborigines in that area.
> → Avant, il y avait…

2 Apportez des précisions.

- **Ponctuez votre récit de descriptions à l'aide du prétérit BE+ING.**
> He **was talking** to the protesters when he **heard** the news.

Réservez le prétérit BE+ING aux actions en déroulement ou à l'attitude de personnages et veillez à l'opposer à un verbe au prétérit simple.

- **Insérez des retours en arrière à l'aide du *pluperfect*.**
> They sold the lands which **had belonged** to their ancestors.
> Until then they **had always lived** in small villages.
> By that time they **had built** dozens of new buildings.

Choisir un point de vue sur l'action

- Lorsque vous faites un récit, pensez à définir votre point de vue sur l'action : voix active ou voix passive ? Certaines thématiques se prêtent tout particulièrement à l'usage de la voix passive, dans la mesure où ce sont les « victimes » qui retiennent l'attention : catastrophes naturelles, accidents, conflits, etc.

- Rappelez-vous que la voix passive s'utilise plus fréquemment en anglais qu'en français lorsque l'auteur d'un acte est indéfini ou inconnu, par exemple pour traduire « on ».

1 Pensez à utiliser la voix passive.

- **Pour rendre compte des conséquences d'un événement**
> At least 4,000 people were injured.
>
> 20 thousand homes had been destroyed by the earthquake twelve months before.

Attention ! Les formes verbales à la voix passive incluent toutes l'auxiliaire BE.

> He **was** being interviewed.
> Their proposal had **been** rejected.

- **Pour traduire « on »**
> A new treatment has just been tested.

Les verbes *give, ask, tell* se prêtent tout particulièrement à la voix passive.

> He was given a fine and six months' probation.
> → On lui a donné une amende et six mois de sursis.

2 Inspirez-vous du style journalistique.

- **Utilisez** *are expected to, are said to, are reported to*.
> All residents are expected to respect the rules.
> → Tous les habitants sont censés respecter le règlement.
>
> Thousands of victims are said to have run away.
> → On dit que des milliers de victimes se sont enfuies.
>
> 280 people are reported to have died in the accident.
> → On rapporte que 280 personnes sont mortes dans l'accident. / 280 personnes seraient mortes…

FICHE 7

FICHE 8

Précis grammatical

1 — Le présent simple

A Formes

● À la **forme affirmative**, on utilise la **base verbale** et on ajoute *s* à la 3e personne du singulier. Pour les **questions** et les **négations**, on emploie l'auxiliaire *DO / DON'T* (*DOES / DOESN'T* à la 3e personne du singulier) suivi de la base verbale.

I know him and he knows me.
➤ Je le connais et il me connaît.

Does he know me? ➤ Est-ce qu'il me connaît ?

● Formes

■ **affirmative** : *I / You like him. – He / She likes you. – We / You / They like him.*

■ **interrogative** : *Do I like him? – Does he / she like me? – Do we / you / they like them?*

■ **négative** : *I don't like you. – He / She doesn't like you. – We / You / They don't like him.*

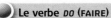

> **Le verbe *DO* (FAIRE)**
> Il se conjugue aussi avec l'auxiliaire *DO*, aux formes interrogative et négative du présent simple.
> *Does he often do that?*
> ➤ Est-ce qu'il fait cela souvent ?

B Emplois

● On emploie le présent simple pour :

■ **définir** une personne ou un objet (métier, goûts, opinion, etc.).

He works on a farm. ➤ Il travaille dans une ferme.

He likes animals. ➤ Il aime les animaux.

■ mentionner une **action habituelle** ou **fréquente**.

They always come back. ➤ Ils reviennent toujours.

■ exprimer une **vérité générale**.

The earth revolves around the sun.
➤ La terre tourne autour du soleil.

● **On utilise aussi le présent simple pour donner des informations lorsque :**

■ on **raconte une histoire** (**présent de narration**).

Then he stops and looks at them.
➤ Puis il s'arrête et les regarde.

■ on **s'informe sur ce qui va se passer**.

What happens after that? ➤ Qu'est-ce qui se passe après ?

Who speaks next? ➤ Qui parle ensuite ?

> ***HAVE* et *HAVE GOT* (POSSÉDER)**
> Le verbe *HAVE* se conjugue obligatoirement avec l'auxiliaire *DO* (aux formes interrogative et négative).
> *Do you have a car?* ➤ Est-ce que tu as une voiture ?
> *Yes I do. / No, I don't.*
> *I have a motorbike.* ➤ J'ai une moto.
>
> ***HAVE GOT* :** *HAVE* est un auxiliaire.
> *Have you got a computer?* ➤ As-tu un ordinateur ?
> *Yes, I have. / No, I haven't.*
> *I have got (I've got) two computers.*
> ➤ J'ai deux ordinateurs.

2 — Le présent *BE+ING*

A Formes

● On utilise l'auxiliaire *BE* à toutes les formes. On accole *-ING* au verbe.

● Formes

■ **affirmative** : *I am sleeping. – You are sleeping. – He / She is sleeping. – We / You / They are sleeping.*

■ **interrogative** : *Am I sleeping? – Are you sleeping? – Is he / she sleeping? – Are we / you / they sleeping?*

■ **négative** : *I am not sleeping. – You are not sleeping. – He / She is not sleeping. – We / You / They are not sleeping.*

B Emplois

● **On emploie le présent *BE+ING* pour décrire :**

■ une action **en cours de déroulement** dont on est **témoin**.

Listen! The phone is ringing!
➤ Écoute ! Il y a le téléphone qui sonne !

■ la **position** de quelqu'un.

She is sitting on her bed. ➤ Elle est assise sur son lit.

● **On emploie également le présent *BE+ING* pour :**

■ faire un **commentaire** (positif ou négatif) **sur le sujet** de l'énoncé.

She's always nagging at me!
➤ Elle n'arrête pas de m'embêter !

■ exprimer la **volonté du sujet** (intention ou refus).

I'm not talking to her. ➤ Je refuse de lui parler.

☰ Verbes d'état / verbes d'action et la forme *BE+ING*

● Les verbes suivants (verbes d'état) **ne peuvent normalement pas s'utiliser à la forme** *BE+ING* : *be, have, agree, believe, belong, hate, know, like, look, mean, prefer, remember, see, seem, sound, think, understand, want.*

What do you want? ▶ Qu'est-ce que tu veux ?

● Parmi ces verbes, certains peuvent changer de sens et être utilisés au **présent** *BE+ING* lorsque l'on parle d'une **situation particulière**.

S'emploient toujours au présent simple	Peuvent s'employer au présent *BE+ING*
THINK : lorsqu'il signifie CROIRE (opinion). *I think you're wrong.* ▶ Je pense / crois que tu as tort. *SEE* : pour la **perception** ou une **faculté intellectuelle**. *I don't see what you're talking about.* ▶ Je ne vois pas / comprends pas de quoi tu parles. *HAVE* : lorsqu'il signifie POSSÉDER et dans les expressions : **have an idea, no idea, a problem, time, a headache.** *Do you have any idea where he's been?* ▶ Sais-tu où il est allé ?	*THINK* : lorsqu'il signifie PENSER À, RÉFLÉCHIR, ENVISAGER DE. *Who are you thinking of?* ▶ À qui penses-tu ? *We're thinking of leaving London.* ▶ Nous envisageons de quitter Londres. *SEE* : lorsqu'il signifie RENCONTRER. *Who are you seeing today?* ▶ Qui vois-tu / Avec qui as-tu rendez-vous aujourd'hui ? *HAVE* : dans les expressions **have dinner, lunch, an appointment, a bath, a rest, a good time.** *Are you having a good time?* ▶ Est-ce que tu t'amuses ?

☲ Le prétérit

A Prétérit simple

● À la **forme affirmative**, il se forme avec *-ED* (sauf dans le cas des verbes irréguliers ; voir pages 206-207).

● Aux **formes interrogative** et **négative**, il se forme avec l'auxiliaire *DID* / *DIDN'T*. Les formes sont identiques à toutes les personnes.

- **affirmative** : *He laughed.*
- **interrogative** : *Did you laugh?*
- **négative** : *They didn't laugh.*

● Le prétérit est le **temps du récit** (de la narration). Les mots exprimant la **succession dans le temps** (*FIRST, AND THEN*, etc.) entraînent obligatoirement le prétérit.

He looked up and then smiled.
▶ Il leva les yeux, puis il sourit.

B *USED TO* et *WOULD*

● *USED TO* est une forme de prétérit qui exprime la rupture avec la situation présente : ce qui était vrai dans le passé ne l'est plus.

He used to wake up at night.
▶ Avant, il se réveillait la nuit. → Ce n'est plus le cas.

● *WOULD* (auxiliaire modal, suivi de la base verbale) peut exprimer l'habitude au passé.

As a child, he would wake up at night.
▶ Quand il était enfant, il se réveillait la nuit. → C'était une habitude.

C Prétérit *BE+ING*

● Il sert à la **description dans le passé**. On l'utilise souvent pour parler d'une **action en cours de déroulement dans le passé** et qui s'oppose à un événement ponctuel (au prétérit simple).

When I came in, they were watching TV.
▶ Lorsque je suis entré, ils regardaient la télévision.

☴ Le *present perfect*

A *Present perfect* simple

● L'auxiliaire est *HAVE*. Le verbe est au **participe passé**. (La formule *HAVE -EN* symbolise le *present perfect*.)

● On utilise *HAVE* à toutes les personnes, sauf à la 3e personne du singulier → *HAS*.

● Formes
- **affirmative** : *I have finished. He has finished.*
- **interrogative** : *Have you finished?*
- **négative** : *He has not finished.*

● Le *present perfect* permet de présenter le **résultat présent** d'une action.

He's opened the door. ⟫ Il a ouvert la porte.
→ La porte est ouverte.

● Il permet de faire le **bilan** d'une situation dans le présent. On le trouve donc souvent associé à des verbes au présent ou à des adverbes établissant un lien avec le présent. (Voir **Gr. 6 B.**)

I've often talked to him lately. He doesn't agree with us.
⟫ Je lui ai souvent parlé ces derniers temps. Il n'est pas d'accord avec nous.

B *Present perfect* BE+ ING

● On associe la forme BE+ING au *present perfect*.

● Il exprime le **résultat d'une activité** qui a eu lieu, activité dont on voit souvent des traces dans le présent.

You've been crying. ⟫ Tu as pleuré.
→ J'en vois des traces (larmes, etc.).

C *Present perfect* simple ou *present perfect* BE+ ING ?

● Le *present perfect* simple met l'accent sur le **résultat** obtenu et le *present perfect* BE+ING sur l'**activité** qui a eu lieu.

You've painted the door. ⟫ Tu as peint la porte.
(On s'intéresse à la porte.)

You've been painting. ⟫ Tu as fait de la peinture.
(On s'intéresse à ce qu'a fait le sujet.)

● Avec une **mesure précise** (*three times, by 10%*, etc.), on utilise le *present perfect* simple et non pas BE+ING.

Prices have risen by 10%. ⟫ Les prix ont augmenté de 10 %.

● **Attention !** Le *present perfect* BE+ING à lui seul ne signifie **pas** que l'action dure encore ! Pour exprimer cette idée, il faut l'associer à *for* ou *since*.

Prices have been rising regularly since last year / for a few months. ⟫ Les prix augmentent régulièrement depuis l'an dernier / depuis quelques mois.

6 *Present perfect* ou prétérit ?

A Choix de « l'éclairage »

● On peut répondre à une question au *present perfect* par un **prétérit**, lorsqu'on donne une information sur **le moment** ou **le lieu**. Comparez les deux réponses possibles à la question suivante :

Have you seen them lately? ⟫ Tu les a vus récemment ?

Réponse 1 :

Yes, I have. ⟫ Oui.

C'est le résultat présent qui compte. (Je sais qu'ils sont là.)
→ *Present perfect*.

Réponse 2 :

Yes, I saw them in the park yesterday.
⟫ Oui, je les ai vus hier dans le parc.

Information sur le lieu et le moment où s'est produit l'événement passé. → **Prétérit**.

B Adverbes et expressions de temps

● La présence d'**adverbes de temps** ou d'**expressions renvoyant au passé** (*AGO, LAST YEAR, WHEN*…) entraîne obligatoirement le **prétérit**.

He found a new job two months ago.
⟫ Il a trouvé un nouvel emploi il y a deux mois.

● Certains adverbes et expressions de temps sont fréquemment associés au **present perfect**. C'est parce qu'ils peuvent exprimer un **lien avec le présent** : *ALREADY, ALWAYS, BEFORE, EVER / NEVER, NOT YET* (NE PAS… ENCORE), *OVER THE PAST FEW MONTHS* (CES DERNIERS MOIS), *JUST, RECENTLY, SO FAR* (JUSQU'À PRÉSENT), *SINCE* (DEPUIS).

We've just started. ⟫ Nous venons de commencer.

Have you ever been there? ⟫ Tu y es déjà allé ?

C Traduction du passé composé

● Si le passé composé renvoie à un **événement passé**, on le traduit par un **prétérit. C'est le cas le plus fréquent.**

Je les ai vus hier. ⟫ *I saw them yesterday.*

● On ne traduit le passé composé par un **present perfect** que s'il exprime un **résultat présent**.

Oui, je sais. Je les ai vus. ⟫ *Yes, I know. I've seen them.*

7 FOR - SINCE - AGO / PENDANT - DEPUIS - IL Y A

A FOR

● FOR et le prétérit

Le **prétérit** indique que l'action n'a **aucun lien avec le présent**. On traduit FOR par PENDANT.

He stayed with them for two months last year.
➤ Il a vécu chez eux pendant deux mois l'année dernière.

● FOR avec le *present perfect* simple et le *present perfect* BE+ING

Le *present perfect* met en évidence le **lien avec le présent**. On traduit FOR par DEPUIS et le verbe par un **présent**.

I've had this CD for years.
➤ J'ai ce CD depuis des années. / Cela fait des années que j'ai ce CD.

He's been sleeping for more than three hours now.
➤ Il dort depuis plus de trois heures. / Cela fait plus de trois heures qu'il dort.

B SINCE

● SINCE est suivi d'une **date ou** d'une **expression indiquant le point de départ de l'action** : since yesterday, since last year, since that time, etc.

● SINCE exprime un **lien entre le point de départ d'une action (dans le passé) et le présent**. C'est pourquoi le verbe principal est au *present perfect* : il peut s'agir du *present perfect* simple ou du *present perfect* BE+ING.

● On traduit SINCE par DEPUIS et le verbe par un **présent**.

I've known him since Xmas.
➤ Je le connais depuis Noël.

She's been living in London since June.
➤ Elle vit à Londres depuis juin.

● FOR ou SINCE ?

■ **FOR** : on additionne des moments : for two weeks, for days, etc. (Voir **Gr. 7 A.**)

■ **SINCE** est suivi d'un élément qui a la valeur d'une **date**. Parfois, cet élément est un **verbe au prétérit**.

She's been working here since January / since she came back.
➤ Elle travaille ici depuis janvier / depuis qu'elle est revenue.

> ● Le *present perfect* BE+ING avec FOR ou SINCE → DEPUIS
> ■ La forme BE+ING du *present perfect* n'est possible qu'avec les **verbes d'action** qui sont compatibles avec l'idée de déroulement.
> *I've been running for twenty minutes.*
> ➤ Je cours depuis vingt minutes.
> ■ La forme BE+ING, qui souligne l'activité du sujet, est impossible avec les verbes d'état. (Voir **Gr. 3.**)

■ Avec FOR ou SINCE, **on traduit** de la même manière le *present perfect* simple et le *present perfect* BE+ING → **présent en français**.

C AGO

● AGO se place **après le complément de temps** et ne s'emploie qu'avec le **prétérit** car l'expression en AGO joue le rôle d'une date.

He sent me a message two days ago (on Sunday).
➤ Il m'a envoyé un message il y a deux jours (dimanche).

D « PENDANT » : FOR ou DURING ?

● FOR, qui exprime la **durée**, répond à la question HOW LONG? (COMBIEN DE TEMPS ?). Il s'utilise :

■ chaque fois que l'on **additionne** des jours, des semaines, etc. → for **two** days, for **three** weeks, for **days**, for **weeks**, for **ages**, for **centuries**, etc.

■ avec **time**, **long** et **ever** → for **a long time**, for **some time**, for **so long**, for **ever**, etc.

● DURING est suivi d'un groupe nominal et répond à la question WHEN? (QUAND ?). Il renvoie à **un moment précis**, situé à l'intérieur d'une période de temps. DURING signifie À UN MOMENT DONNÉ DE : during the holidays, during that time, during the weekend, etc.

● Comparez les deux traductions de PENDANT.

Il l'a appelée **pendant la pause** et lui a parlé **pendant plus de vingt minutes**.
➤ *He called her **during the break** and talked to her **for more than twenty minutes**.*

E « DEPUIS »

● Attention au temps ! À la différence du français, on n'emploie pas le présent en anglais lorsqu'on traduit un énoncé avec DEPUIS. On emploie le *present perfect*.

J'ai cette voiture **depuis** un mois / **depuis** Janvier.
➤ *I've had this car **for** a month / **since** January.*

● IL Y A ou DEPUIS ?

■ **IL Y A** s'utilise pour un événement **passé**. On traduit par le **prétérit + AGO**.

Ils sont partis il y a une semaine. (partir : *leave*)
➤ *They left one week ago.*

■ On peut parfois exprimer à peu près la même idée avec DEPUIS. Mais dans ce cas, on parle d'un état qui dure jusqu'au moment présent (et non plus d'un événement passé). On doit **changer de temps et de verbe**. On traduit par le *present perfect* + FOR ou SINCE.

Ils sont partis depuis une semaine / depuis lundi.
(être parti : *be away*)
➤ *They've been away for a week / since Monday.*

8   Le *pluperfect*

A *Pluperfect* simple

● Il se forme comme le *present perfect* avec l'auxiliaire *HAVE* et le **participe passé** du verbe. Cependant, à la différence du *present perfect*, **l'auxiliaire est au passé** : *HAD*. (Pour parler du *pluperfect*, on utilise parfois la formule *HAD -EN*, dans laquelle *-EN* symbolise le participe passé.)

He had finished. – Had he finished? – He had not finished.

● Il correspond souvent au *present perfect* dans un **contexte passé**. Ainsi il est souvent associé à des adverbes comme *ALREADY, ALWAYS, BEFORE, EVER / NEVER*, etc.

I knew that he had already told her.
➤ Je savais qu'il le lui avait déjà dit.

● On l'utilise pour bouleverser l'ordre des événements (ordre chronologique) et faire des retours en arrière (flash-back).

She realized that he had left a few minutes before.
➤ Elle se rendit compte qu'il était parti quelques minutes auparavant.

Contractions de *HAD*

■ À l'oral, on contracte souvent *HAD* en *'D* et *HAD NOT* en *'D NOT* ou *HADN'T*.
She'd not / hadn't eaten what I'd prepared.
➤ Elle n'avait pas mangé ce que j'avais préparé.
■ Ne pas confondre *HAD* et *WOULD* (auxiliaire du conditionnel) dans leur forme contractée *'D* :
– *HAD* est suivi du **participe passé** :
He'd told me. ➤ Il me l'avait dit.
– *WOULD* est suivi de la **base verbale** :
I'd tell you if I knew. ➤ Je te le dirais si je le savais.

B *Pluperfect* BE+ING

● Comme le **present perfect** BE+ING, il est formé avec *HAVE -EN* et *BE+ING*. Mais à la différence du *present perfect*, l'auxiliaire *HAVE* est au passé : *HAD*. Il correspond au *present perfect* BE+ING dans un **contexte passé**.

I could see that she had been crying.
➤ Je voyais bien qu'elle avait pleuré.

9   L'irréel

A Les deux valeurs du passé

● Un temps du passé (prétérit ou *pluperfect*) ne renvoie pas toujours à un événement qui s'est produit dans le passé. Il peut être utilisé pour des **faits irréels**, souhaités ou imaginés.

● **Comparez** :

■ **événement passé : valeur temporelle du prétérit**
He asked me long ago.
➤ Il me l'a demandé il y a longtemps.

■ **fait irréel : valeur modale (= prétérit modal)**
If he asked me, I would help him.
➤ S'il me le demandait, je l'aiderais.

B Hypothèse

● **Hypothèse simple :** *IF* + présent / *WILL* BV
If she calls me, I will talk to her.
➤ Si elle m'appelle, je lui parlerai.

● **Hypothèse incertaine :** *IF* + prétérit modal / *WOULD* BV
If she called me, I would talk to her.
➤ Si elle m'appelait, je lui parlerais.

● **Hypothèse non réalisée :** *IF* + *pluperfect* modal / *WOULD HAVE -EN*
If she had called me, I would have talked to her.
➤ Si elle m'avait appelé, je lui aurais parlé.

C Souhait – regret

On emploie le prétérit modal après :

● *IF ONLY*   *If only she was / were with us!*
➤ Si seulement elle était avec nous !

    WERE s'emploie à **toutes les personnes** dans une langue plus formelle.

● *I'D RATHER* *I'd rather you left / you didn't stay.*
➤ Je préfèrerais que tu partes / que tu ne restes pas.

Lorsque la phrase ne comporte qu'**un sujet**, on emploie l'**infinitif sans** *TO*.

I'd rather do it myself.
➤ Je préfèrerais le faire moi-même.

● *IT'S TIME* *It's time you bought a new computer.*
➤ Il est temps que tu achètes un nouvel ordinateur.

● *I WISH* *I wish he was (were) younger.*
➤ J'aimerais qu'il soit plus jeune. / Je regrette qu'il ne soit pas plus jeune.

D Regret d'un fait passé

● Lorsqu'on veut exprimer le **regret à propos d'un fait passé**, on emploie le *pluperfect* **modal** après WISH et I'D RATHER.

I wish you had talked to him. ➤ J'aurais aimé que tu lui parles. / Je regrette que tu ne lui aies pas parlé.
I'd rather you had told me.
➤ J'aurais préféré que tu me le dises.

Traduction de REGRETTER

WISH signifie SOUHAITER (qui est l'inverse de REGRETTER). On doit donc inverser le sens de la subordonnée lorsqu'on traduit en français : le négatif devient positif et inversement.

Je regrette qu'il soit si tard.
➤ *I wish it were **not** so late.*

Je regrette que tu ne sois pas mon frère.
➤ *I wish you were my brother.*

Je regrette que tu aies vu cela.
➤ *I wish you had **not** seen that.*

---

10   Expressions du futur

A WILL et BE GOING TO

● **WILL : on prévoit que l'action se réalisera dans l'avenir** (exemple : prévision météo).

It will snow tomorrow. ➤ Il neigera demain.

● **BE GOING TO :** l'action future est étroitement **liée à la situation présente** → « Étant donné ce que je sais du présent / ce que je vois, j'en conclus que… »

Careful! It's going to fall! ➤ Attention ! Ça va tomber !

● **On emploie WILL :**

▪ avec un **repère de temps futur**, et donc avec une **subordonnée de temps**.

I'll ask her later / on Monday / when she comes back.
➤ Je le lui demanderai plus tard / lundi / quand elle reviendra.

Attention : WILL ne peut **pas** s'utiliser **dans la subordonnée**. (Voir **Gr. 10 C.**)

▪ avec une **subordonnée en IF**.

If you ask me, I'll help you.
➤ Si tu me le demandes, je t'aiderai.

● **On emploie BE GOING TO :**

▪ lorsqu'il y a **observation de la situation présente**.

Look! It's going to rain. ➤ Regarde ! Il va pleuvoir.

▪ généralement, lorsqu'il n'y a **pas de repère temporel**.

There's going to be a great change.
➤ Il va y avoir un grand changement.

B Autres expressions du futur

Comme BE GOING TO, elles sont construites avec BE et TO. *To* indique qu'il y a **projection dans l'avenir**.

● **BE TO**

Indique que quelque chose est **prévu** ou **a été arrangé à l'avance**. On traduit souvent par DEVOIR.

The meeting is to take place next week.
➤ La réunion doit avoir lieu la semaine prochaine.

● **BE ABOUT TO**

Indique que quelque chose est **sur le point de se produire**.

He is just about to leave. ➤ Il est sur le point de partir.

● **BE LIKELY TO**

Indique qu'il y a de **fortes chances pour que quelque chose se produise**.

It is likely to happen again.
➤ Il y a beaucoup de chances pour que cela se reproduise.

● **BE SURE TO / BE BOUND TO**

Expriment la **certitude d'un événement futur**.

She is sure to win. ➤ Il est certain qu'elle va gagner.

They are bound to come back.
➤ Il est certain qu'ils vont revenir.

C Subordonnées en WHEN et le futur

● **On n'emploie pas WILL dans une subordonnée de temps :** après WHEN, AS SOON AS (DÈS QUE), WHILE (PENDANT QUE), AS LONG AS (TANT QUE), UNTIL (JUSQU'À CE QUE / AVANT QUE). Pour exprimer l'idée d'avenir, on emploie le présent ou le *present perfect*.

I'll get a new one when I have a little money.
➤ J'en prendrai un autre lorsque j'aurai un peu d'argent.

I won't go until I have finished.
➤ Je ne partirai pas avant d'avoir fini.

Remarque : Si la subordonnée est remplaçable par LATER, c'est bien une subordonnée de temps.

Je lui écrirai quand j'aurai le temps / plus tard.
➤ *I'll write to him when I have time / later.*

● **On maintient WILL après WHEN** lorsqu'il s'agit d'une **interrogative** au style direct ou indirect.

Quand reviendra-t-elle ?
➤ *When will she come back?*

Je ne sais pas quand elle reviendra.
➤ *I don't know when she will come back.*

11 Les modaux : introduction

Les modaux *CAN, COULD, MAY, MIGHT, WILL, WOULD, MUST, SHALL, SHOULD* sont des **auxiliaires** qui ont un sens bien particulier : ils expriment **le possible, le certain, l'impossible, l'obligation, la permission**, etc.

She may call later. ➤ Il se peut qu'elle appelle plus tard.
I must leave. ➤ Il faut que je parte. / Je dois partir.

A Formes

● Ils ne prennent pas de **s** à la 3e personne et ne sont jamais suivis de *TO*, ni de *V-ING*.

● On utilise **un seul modal** par forme verbale. Par exemple, *WILL* n'est jamais suivi de *CAN* ou *MUST*.

● Les modaux peuvent être suivis de :

■ *BE+ING* pour une action vue sous l'angle du **déroulement**.
He may be sleeping. ➤ Peut-être est-il en train de dormir.

■ l'auxiliaire *HAVE* suivi du **participe passé** (*HAVE -EN*) pour **un fait accompli ou passé**.

She may have finished by now.
➤ Peut-être a-t-elle fini maintenant.

B Les deux sens des modaux

La modalité renvoie au domaine du **jugement**. Il y a deux types de jugement possibles. Selon le contexte, chaque modal peut avoir l'un ou l'autre sens :

■ celui qui parle estime que **le sujet de la phrase a la capacité / l'obligation / la permission / la volonté** de faire quelque chose : on parle de **sens 1** du modal.

She must accept it! ➤ Elle doit l'accepter !
→ Moi qui parle, j'affirme qu'il faut qu'elle l'accepte.

■ celui qui parle dit qu'il est **plus ou moins certain** de quelque chose : on parle de **sens 2** du modal.

She must be very happy. ➤ Elle doit être très heureuse.
→ Je suis certain qu'elle est très heureuse.

12 Les modaux : sens 1

A Capacité / incapacité : *CAN* / *CAN'T*

Can you help him? ➤ Peux-tu l'aider ? → En es-tu capable ?
I can't stay much longer.
➤ Je ne peux pas rester beaucoup plus longtemps.
I can drive a lorry. ➤ Je sais conduire un camion.

B Permission / absence de permission : *MAY* / *MAY NOT*

You may stay if you like. ➤ Tu peux rester si tu veux.
Visitors may not feed the animals. ➤ Les visiteurs ne sont pas autorisés à donner de la nourriture aux animaux.

Remarque : Dans la langue courante, la permission et l'interdiction sont souvent exprimées par *CAN* et *CAN'T*.

You can stay, but you can't smoke.
➤ Tu peux rester, mais tu ne peux pas fumer.

C Obligation / interdiction : *MUST* / *MUSTN'T*

You must tell me everything. ➤ Tu dois tout me dire.
You must not tell anyone. ➤ Tu ne dois le dire à personne.

D Conseil : *SHOULD* / *SHOULD NOT*

You should ask him first. ➤ Tu devrais lui demander d'abord.
You shouldn't say that. ➤ Tu ne devrais pas dire ça.

E Volonté / refus : *WILL* / *WON'T*

Will you marry me? ➤ Veux-tu m'épouser ?
He won't do it! ➤ Il refuse de le faire !

Remarque : Dans la plupart des cas, le verbe VOULOIR se traduit par *WANT*.

She wants to leave. He doesn't want to go.

F Nécessité / absence de nécessité : *NEED* / *NEEDN'T*

Need I tell you what I feel?
➤ Ai-je besoin de te dire ce que je ressens ?
You needn't tell me why you did it.
➤ Tu n'as pas besoin de me dire pourquoi tu l'as fait.

13 « Équivalents » des modaux (sens 1)

● *HAVE TO* (DEVOIR), *BE ABLE TO* (ÊTRE CAPABLE DE), *BE ALLOWED TO* (ÊTRE AUTORISÉ À), *BE FORBIDDEN TO* (ÊTRE INTERDIT / AVOIR L'INTERDICTION DE) expriment des notions proches de celles exprimées par les modaux de sens 1.

● Au passé et au futur, ils s'utilisent à la place des modaux.

● À la différence des modaux, ces verbes n'expriment **aucun jugement** de la part de celui qui parle. Ils présentent l'obligation, la permission, etc., sous l'angle de la **simple constatation**.

Notion	Forme non modale : simple constatation	Modal : jugement ou pression de celui qui parle
Obligation	**Présent :** *Sorry, I have to go now.* ➤ Désolé, il faut que je parte maintenant. **Futur :** *He will have to…* **Passé : *Did he have to…?***	*You **must** go now!* ➤ Tu dois partir maintenant ! → C'est moi qui le veux.
Interdiction	**Présent :** *They're **forbidden to** go out.* ➤ Il leur est interdit de sortir. **Futur :** *They **will be forbidden to…*** **Passé :** *They **were forbidden to…***	*They **mustn't** go out!* ➤ Ils ne doivent pas sortir ! → Je le leur interdis.
Absence d'obligation	**Présent :** *You **don't have to** answer.* ➤ Tu n'es pas obligé de répondre. **Futur :** *You **won't have to…*** **Passé :** *You **didn't have to…***	*You **needn't** shout!* ➤ Tu n'es pas obligé de crier ! → Cette forme peut indiquer le reproche fait à l'autre.
Permission	**Présent :** *They're **allowed to** leave now.* ➤ Ils ont le droit de partir maintenant. **Futur :** *They'll **be allowed to…*** **Passé :** *They **were allowed to…***	*You **may** leave now.* ➤ Vous pouvez partir maintenant. → Celui qui parle accorde la permission.
Ce qui n'est pas permis	**Présent :** *You're **not allowed to** turn left.* ➤ Tu n'as pas le droit de tourner à gauche. **Futur :** *You **won't be allowed to…*** **Passé :** *We **weren't allowed to…***	*Visitors **may not** take photos.* ➤ Il est interdit aux visiteurs de prendre des photos. → Ce sont les autorités qui le disent.
Volonté (refus)	**Présent :** *He **doesn't want to** answer.* ➤ Il ne veut pas répondre. **Passé :** *He **didn't want to…***	**Présent :** *He **won't** answer me!* ➤ Il refuse de me répondre ! **Passé :** *I insisted but he **wouldn't** answer me.* ➤ J'ai insisté, mais il a refusé de me répondre.
Conseil	*Why don't you help them?* ➤ Pourquoi ne les aides-tu pas ?	*You **should** help them.* ➤ Tu devrais les aider. *You really **ought to** help them.* ➤ Tu devrais vraiment les aider. → OUGHT TO exprime une **obligation morale** plus fortement que SHOULD.
Reproche	*Why didn't you ask them?* ➤ Pourquoi ne le leur as-tu pas demandé ?	*You **should have** asked them.* ➤ Tu aurais dû le leur demander.
(In)capacité	**Présent :** *Is he **able to** handle the situation?* ➤ Est-il capable de faire face à la situation ? **Futur :** *He'll **be able to…*** **Passé :** *He **was able to…***	**Présent :** *I **can** stay with you.* ➤ Je peux rester avec toi. **Passé :** *I **couldn't** stay with you.* ➤ Je ne pouvais pas rester avec toi.

14   Les modaux (sens 2) : la probabilité

A Degrés de probabilité

On peut classer les modaux selon le **degré de probabilité** qu'ils expriment, **du moins certain au plus certain** :

It might rain tonight. » Il se pourrait qu'il pleuve ce soir.

It may rain tonight. » Il est possible qu'il pleuve ce soir.

It will rain tonight. » Il pleuvra ce soir.
→ J'affirme qu'il pleuvra ce soir.

He must be older than her. » Il doit être plus âgé qu'elle.
→ J'en suis à peu près sûr.

She can't be his daughter!
» Il est impossible que ce soit sa fille !
→ J'en suis certain.

B MAY NOT et CAN'T

● **MAY NOT :** « Il est possible que cela **ne soit pas**… »

She may not know that we're back.
» Peut-être ne sait-elle pas que nous sommes revenus.

● **CAN'T :** « Il est **impossible** que cela soit… »

He can't be that young!
» Il n'est pas possible qu'il soit si jeune !

B Probabilité d'un fait présent, passé, futur

● On peut exprimer un jugement de probabilité sur un fait présent, passé ou futur : « Il est possible que cela se passe en ce moment / cela se soit passé / cela se produise dans l'avenir. » Le jugement est fait dans le présent par celui qui parle. **Ce n'est pas le modal qui exprime le passé, présent ou futur de l'action ; c'est la forme du verbe qui le suit et le contexte.**

● Fait présent

■ La **forme** BE+ING est possible avec les **verbes de processus** (actions) et impossible avec les verbes d'état (BE, HAVE, KNOW, WANT, etc.).

I must be dreaming! » Je dois rêver !

She may be sleeping.
» Il se peut qu'elle soit en train de dormir.

■ Avec les **verbes d'état**, on emploie la **base verbale** pour indiquer que le fait est possible / probable dans le présent.

You must know her. » Tu dois la connaître.

He may not want to stay.
» Il se peut qu'il ne veuille pas rester.

● Fait passé

On utilise le **modal suivi de l'auxiliaire** HAVE et du participe passé du verbe (modal + HAVE -EN).

You may have left it in the car.
» Il se peut que tu l'aies laissé dans la voiture.

He must have changed his mind.
» Il a dû changer d'avis.

● Fait futur

La **base verbale** (infinitif sans TO) peut renvoyer à un **fait futur**.

You may get a promotion if you work hard enough.
» Il se peut que tu sois promu si tu travailles suffisamment.

D Forme passée du modal

COULD est le passé de CAN ; MIGHT est le passé de MAY ; WOULD le passé de WILL. La forme passée du modal exprime souvent l'**irréel**, c'est-à-dire ce qui est **moins certain**. Par exemple, MIGHT exprime une possibilité plus incertaine que MAY.

He may know the answer.
» Il se peut qu'il connaisse la réponse.

He might know the answer.
» Il se pourrait qu'il connaisse la réponse.

15   Les modaux : CAN, COULD, MAY, MIGHT

A CAN / COULD : le possible

SENS 1	SENS 2
CAN : capacité *Can you see it?* » Tu le vois ? → Tu peux le voir ? *I can read Spanish.* » Je lis l'espagnol. → Je sais lire l'espagnol.	**CAN : possibilité** (seulement à la forme interrogative) *Can he be that stupid?* » Est-il possible qu'il soit aussi bête ?
CAN'T : incapacité *He can't explain it. He knows nothing about it.* » Il ne peut pas l'expliquer. Il n'en sait rien.	**CAN'T : l'impossible** *She can't be right!* Elle ne peut pas avoir raison. → C'est impossible.
CAN / CAN'T : permission / interdiction *Can I open the window? – No you can't.* » Puis-je ouvrir la fenêtre ? – Non.	

SENS 1	SENS 2
COULD / *COULDN'T* : **capacité / incapacité – possibilité au passé ou au conditionnel** ■ **Passé :** *He couldn't sleep for weeks.* ❯ Il n'a pas pu dormir pendant des semaines. ■ **Possibilité irréelle :** *We could try and phone him.* ❯ On pourrait essayer de lui téléphoner. ■ **Possibilité non réalisée :** *He could have sold it.* ❯ Il aurait pu le vendre. → Mais il ne l'a pas vendu.	*COULD* : **possibilité plus incertaine que** *can* *It could well be the last time.* ❯ Il se pourrait bien que ce soit la dernière fois.

B *MAY* : le possible à 50 %

SENS 1	SENS 2
MAY : **permission** *May I have a look at your notebook?* ❯ Puis-je jeter un coup d'œil à votre carnet ?	*MAY* : **possibilité** *She may call you any minute.* ❯ Il est possible qu'elle appelle d'une minute à l'autre. → Il y a autant de chances que cela arrive, que l'inverse.
MAY NOT : **ce qui n'est pas permis** *You may not use your mobile phone.* ❯ Vous n'avez pas le droit d'utiliser votre portable.	*MAY NOT* : **il est possible que cela ne se passe pas / ne soit pas le cas** *Even if I invite him he may not come.* ❯ Même si je l'invite, il est possible qu'il ne vienne pas.

C *MIGHT* : le possible très atténué

SENS 1	SENS 2
MIGHT : **permission au style indirect** *She asked if she might leave.* ❯ Elle a demandé si elle pouvait partir.	*MIGHT* : **possibilité très incertaine** *The rumour might be true.* ❯ Il se pourrait que la rumeur soit fondée.

16　Les modaux : *MUST, SHALL, SHOULD*

A *MUST* : la nécessité, ce qui doit être

SENS 1	SENS 2
MUST : **obligation** *You must believe me!* ❯ Tu dois / Il faut me croire !	*MUST* : **certitude** *She must be his wife.* ❯ Ce doit être sa femme. → C'est certainement vrai.
MUSTN'T : **interdiction** *You mustn't bother her.* ❯ Tu ne dois pas l'embêter.	*CAN'T* : **on est certain que cela n'est pas vrai** *She can't be his sister!* ❯ Cela ne peut être sa sœur ! → Ce n'est pas possible.

B SHALL / SHOULD : la contrainte, ce qui doit être

SENS 1	SENS 2
SHALL : s'utilise pour faire une **suggestion** (presque toujours à la forme interrogative). *Shall I let them in?* » Je les fais entrer ?	SHALL : **sens futur** (à la première personne du singulier et du pluriel, mais beaucoup plus rarement que *WILL*) *When shall I see you again?* » Quand vous reverrai-je ?
SHOULD : **conseil** (forme atténuée de contrainte) *You should leave her alone.* » Tu devrais la laisser tranquille.	SHOULD : **probabilité forte** *It shouldn't be difficult to convince them.* » Cela ne devrait pas être difficile de les convaincre.
SHOULD HAVE -EN : **reproche** / **regret** (fait passé) *You should have told me before.* » Tu aurais dû me le dire plus tôt. *I should have told her.* » J'aurais dû le lui dire.	SHOULD HAVE -EN : **probabilité forte** (fait passé) *She should have found it by now.* » Elle a dû le trouver à l'heure qu'il est. → Elle doit l'avoir trouvé.

C Traduction de DEVOIR

● DEVOIR / NE PAS DEVOIR peut exprimer **l'obligation**, **l'interdiction** ou **l'absence d'obligation**. Une erreur fréquente consiste à confondre ces notions lorsque l'on traduit « il ne doit pas », « il ne devait pas », « il n'a pas besoin de », « il n'a pas été obligé de ».

● DEVOIR peut également exprimer une **quasi-certitude**. On utilise *MUST* ou *CAN'T* lorsque l'on est certain que quelque chose est vrai ou n'est pas vrai.

● Avant de choisir la forme verbale en anglais, il faut **identifier la notion** exprimée.

Français	Notion	Anglais
Tu dois le leur dire.	Obligation au présent	*You must tell them. / You have to tell them. / You've got to tell them.*
Il ne doit pas le leur dire.	Interdiction au présent	*He mustn't tell them.*
Il ne devait pas sortir. (= Il n'en avait pas le droit.)	Interdiction au passé	*He wasn't allowed to go out.* → On n'utilise pas *MUST* au passé.
Tu n'as pas besoin de le leur dire.	Absence d'obligation au présent	*You needn't tell them. / You don't have to tell them.*
Il n'a pas eu besoin de le leur dire.	Absence d'obligation au passé	*He didn't have to tell them.*
Il doit être très jeune. Elle doit être en train de travailler. Ils ont dû être très contents.	Forte probabilité affirmative	*He must be very young.* *She must be working.* *They must have been very glad.*
Il ne doit pas faire très froid. Elle ne devait pas être très âgée.	Forte probabilité négative	*It can't be very cold.* *She can't have been very old.*

17 Les modaux : WILL, WOULD

WILL / WOULD : projection vers la réalisation d'un acte

SENS 1	SENS 2
WILL : **volonté** *Stand up, will you?* » Lève-toi, veux-tu ? / Lève-toi, s'il te plaît.	WILL : **sens futur (prédiction)** *I will let you know.* » Je te tiendrai au courant.
WON'T : **refus** *I won't speak to him!* » Je refuse de lui parler !	WON'T : **sens futur** *The results won't be announced until Tuesday.* » Les résultats ne seront pas annoncés avant mardi.

SENS 1	SENS 2
WILL : **ce qui est prévisible et caractéristique du sujet** *He will talk all the time.* » Il ne peut pas s'empêcher de parler.	
WOULD : **volonté atténuée** *Do you know anyone who would do it?* » Connais-tu quelqu'un qui voudrait bien le faire ?	*WOULD* : **conditionnel** *It would be wonderful if they came.* » Ce serait merveilleux s'ils venaient. → Fait irréel, soumis à condition : conditionnel présent
WOULD : **habitude au passé** (ce qui caractérisait le sujet dans le passé) *The children would be up at dawn.* » Les enfants étaient toujours debout à l'aube.	*If we had left later we would have missed the train.* » Si nous étions partis plus tard, nous aurions manqué le train. → Fait non réalisé : conditionnel passé

18 Prépositions et particules adverbiales

Ce sont souvent les mêmes mots qui servent de préposition et de particule adverbiale (ou postposition).

He goes in. » Il entre. / *He goes out.* » Il sort.
→ *In* et *out* sont des particules adverbiales. **Chacune donne** au verbe *GO* un **sens particulier.**

The money is in my bag. » L'argent est dans mon sac.
→ *In* est ici une préposition. Elle a pour fonction **d'introduire un complément** (*in my bag* → complément de lieu).

A Verbes à particule

● Dans certains cas, la particule donne au verbe un sens immédiatement compréhensible.

ACROSS :	à travers	→ *get across* :	traverser
BACK :	idée de retour	→ *get back* :	revenir
DOWN :	vers le bas	→ *look down* :	regarder vers le bas
IN :	à l'intérieur	→ *get in* :	entrer
UP :	vers le haut	→ *look up* :	regarder vers le haut
OUT :	à l'extérieur	→ *get out* :	sortir

● Mais la particule ne permet pas toujours de comprendre le sens du verbe.

get by : se débrouiller   *give in* : céder
give up : renoncer, abandonner   *look after* : s'occuper de

● **Si le complément est un pronom**, il se place **entre le verbe et la particule.**

He gave it up. » Il l'abandonna.

B Verbes prépositionnels

● Certains verbes comme *bring* (apporter), *give* (donner), *send* (envoyer), *write* (écrire) ont **deux constructions** :

■ **avec préposition :**

I sent the book to her. » Je lui ai envoyé le livre.
→ C'est à elle que j'ai envoyé le livre.

■ **sans préposition :**

I sent her the book. » Je lui ai envoyé le livre.

● **Attention : À la différence du français**, on maintient la **préposition à droite du verbe** dans les cas suivants :

■ **Questions**

Who are you thinking of?
» À qui penses-tu ?

■ **Relatives**

The lady we talked to is our new tenant.
» La dame à qui nous avons parlé est notre nouvelle locataire.

■ **Passives**

That problem has never been dealt with.
» On ne s'est jamais occupé de ce problème.

AS **ou** *LIKE* **?**
■ Les deux mots expriment la comparaison, mais *LIKE* indique que **les deux éléments sont différents**, alors que *AS* signifie que **les deux éléments sont identiques.**

As a father, Charles will disagree.
» En tant que père, Charles ne sera pas d'accord.
→ Charles est le père.

Bill behaves like my father.
» Bill se comporte comme mon père.
→ Ce n'est pas mon père, je le compare à mon père.

■ On utilise *LIKE* après les verbes exprimant les cinq sens : *SOUND* (OUÏE), *SMELL* (ODORAT), *TASTE* (GOÛT), *FEEL* (TOUCHER), *LOOK* (VUE).

She sounds like my mother.
» Quand elle parle, on dirait ma mère.

It tastes like honey.
» Ça a un goût de miel.

Look at the sand. It looks like salt!
» Regarde le sable. On dirait du sel !

19 Les noms

A Dénombrables et indénombrables

● Le choix des déterminants, articles et quantifieurs par exemple, dépend de la nature des noms, qui peuvent être **dénombrables** ou **indénombrables**.

● Un **dénombrable** est un nom qui désigne un ou des éléments que l'on **peut compter**. On peut donc l'employer au **singulier** ou au **pluriel**, par exemple le nom *film*: *a film, one film, two films, several films*, etc.

● Un **indénombrable** est un mot qui désigne **un objet ou une activité vu(e) dans son ensemble, comme un tout qu'on ne peut pas compter, et qui est toujours au singulier en anglais**: *luggage* (des bagages), *information* (des informations / renseignements), *advice* (des conseils), etc.

B Indénombrables

● **Noms de matériaux et d'aliments**: *silk* (la soie), *iron* (le fer), *steel* (l'acier), *wood* (le bois), *bread*, *tea*, *milk*, etc.

● **Noms renvoyant à un ensemble**:

■ concret: *furniture* (des meubles), *hair* (des cheveux), *luggage* (des bagages), *rubbish* / *refuse* (des détritus), *trash* (déchets), etc.

■ abstrait: *accommodation* (le logement), *advice* (des conseils), *business* (les affaires), *damage* (les dégâts), *evidence* (des preuves), *growth* (la croissance), *information* (des renseignements), *knowledge* (le savoir), *luck* (la chance), *progress* (des progrès), *news* (des nouvelles), *nonsense* (des absurdités), *research* (la [des] recherche[s]), *trouble* (des ennuis), *work* (l'emploi), etc.

● **Noms formés à partir de verbes**: *swimming* (la natation), *housing* (le logement), *laughter* (le rire), etc.

● **Noms formés à partir d'adjectifs**: *homelessness* (le fait d'être sans abri), *joblessness* (le chômage), *optimism*, *whiteness* (la blancheur), *youth* (la jeunesse), etc.

● **Autres noms**: *weather*, *smoke*, *thunder* (le tonnerre), etc.

● Les indénombrables sont **incompatibles** avec:

■ l'article indéfini A / *AN* et *ONE*.

■ le pluriel, donc avec A FEW, FEW, MANY, SEVERAL, TWO, THREE, etc.

● Le **verbe** est toujours au **singulier**.

This news is good. ≫ Les nouvelles sont bonnes.

C Dénombrables ou indénombrables?

Certains mots peuvent être dénombrables dans un certain contexte et indénombrables dans un autre. Lorsqu'ils renvoient à une **notion**, ils sont **indénombrables**.

■ Indénombrable:

Time is money. ≫ Le temps, c'est de l'argent.

■ Dénombrable:

*We had **a** wonderful **time** together.*
≫ On a passé un très bon moment ensemble.

Certaines réalités peuvent être exprimées en anglais par deux mots, l'un dénombrable (article *a*), l'autre indénombrable (*ø*).

■ **Dénombrable ≫ Indénombrable**

a house: une maison. ≫ *housing*: le logement (en géneral).

a job: un emploi. ≫ *work / employment*: le travail / l'emploi.

■ *Pity* et *shame* sont indénombrables. Mais dans les exclamations en *WHAT* et *SUCH*, ces mots s'emploient avec l'article *A*.

What a pity! ≫ Quel dommage !

It's such a shame! ≫ C'est une honte !

> **A PIECE OF**
> En anglais, on peut, pour certains indénombrables, employer l'expression A PIECE OF qui signifie littéralement « un morceau de »: *a piece of furniture / information / luggage / news*.
> Mais ce n'est pas d'un emploi très courant.
> **L'article UN, UNE devant un mot qui est indénombrable en anglais, se traduit le plus souvent par l'absence d'article.**
> C'était **un** bon conseil. ≫ *It was good advice.*

D Singuliers et pluriels particuliers

● **Toujours** suivis d'un verbe au **singulier**, malgré le *s* en fin de mot:

■ les noms de sciences en *-ics*: *Economics / Mathematics is*…

■ autres: *The news is at eight… The United States is*…

● **Toujours** suivis d'un verbe au **pluriel**: *police*, *clothes* (des vêtements), *cattle* (le bétail).

● **Souvent** suivis d'un verbe au **pluriel**: *government*, *audience* (le public), *family*, *crowd* (la foule), *sheep* (les moutons).

> **S et le pluriel**
> ■ *S* n'est pas toujours la marque du pluriel, par exemple *news*, *mathematics*, etc.
> ■ Certains mots ont la même forme au singulier et au pluriel: *a series*, *series* (une série, des séries); *a means*, *means* (un moyen, des moyens).

20 Le génitif ou cas possessif ('s)

● Le **génitif** est un **déterminant du nom**. (Il se substitue par exemple à un article.) Il se forme avec **'s**. Le premier élément permet d'identifier le deuxième.

It's my sister's computer. ≫ C'est l'ordinateur de ma sœur.
→ Le génitif (*my sister's*) permet d'identifier l'ordinateur.

● Le **génitif** ou **cas possessif** peut exprimer la **possession**.

Lisa's father was out.
≫ Le père de Lisa était sorti.

James's /'dʒeɪmsɪz/ *room is untidy.*
≫ La chambre de James est en désordre.

● Les **pluriels en s** forment leur cas possessif par le simple **ajout d'une apostrophe**.

Where are the students' books?
≫ Où sont les livres des élèves ?

● Le **génitif n'exprime pas toujours la possession**. On peut former le génitif avec un grand nombre de mots. Le premier élément doit être clairement reconnaissable ou avoir déjà été mentionné.

Le génitif peut exprimer :

■ une **durée** :
It's a few minutes' walk from the station.
≫ C'est à quelques minutes à pied de la gare.

After a hard day's work, he was exhausted.
≫ Après une dure journée de travail, il était épuisé.

■ un **repère dans le temps** : *today's TV programme* (le programme télé d'aujourd'hui), *last year's events* (les événements de l'année dernière), *yesterday's newspaper* (le journal d'hier).

■ un **repère dans l'espace** (noms de villes ou de lieux connus ou déjà mentionnés) : *London's museums* (les musées de Londres), *New York's national parks* (les parcs nationaux de New York).

■ des **éléments du monde connus de tous** ou des **groupes humains** : *the government's decisions* (les décisions du gouvernement), *the world's biggest cities* (les plus grandes villes du monde).

■ **magasins** ou **résidences** : *at the baker's, at Janet's* (chez le boulanger, chez Janet).

● Le **génitif générique** : certains génitifs ne désignent pas un objet particulier mais un type (ou genre) d'objet : *a woman's magazine* (un magazine féminin), *an officer's cap* (une casquette d'officier).

🔵 Attention !

■ Pour former un génitif, **l'ordre des mots doit être inversé** par rapport au français ; c'est le possesseur qui vient en premier en anglais.
le téléphone portable de Mike ≫ *Mike's mobile*

■ Lorsque le **possesseur** est **sans article**, le **génitif** est également **sans article**. Par exemple, lorsque le possesseur est un **nom propre** :
le bateau de Ben ≫ *Ben's boat (the Ben's boat* est impossible.)

■ L'anglais est plus logique que le français : lorsqu'il y a **plusieurs possesseurs** et **plusieurs objets possédés**, les objets possédés sont au pluriel.
la vie de nos enfants ≫ *our children's lives*

21 Les articles

A Un ou des éléments indéfinis

● Pour désigner **un** élément parmi d'autres, on emploie l'article *A* / *AN*.

She's bought a new flat.
≫ Elle a acheté un nouvel appartement.

● On emploie *A* devant les consonnes (sauf « h » non-aspiré comme dans *hour, honest, honour, heir* [héritier]) ou devant les voyelles « fortes », comme par exemple celles qu'on prononce /j/ ou /juː/ : *year* /jɪə/, *yellow* /'jeləʊ/, *European* /jʊərə'piːən/, *uniform* /'juːnɪfɔːm/, *useful* /'juːsfʊl/.

an honest man, a quarter of an hour, a year ago, a European country

● On emploie *AN* devant les autres voyelles.
It is an interesting discovery.
≫ C'est une découverte intéressante.

● Pour désigner **des** éléments parmi d'autres, on emploie **l'article zéro (ø)**, ce qui signifie qu'aucun article n'apparaît. Le nom est un **dénombrable au pluriel**.

I've often seen birds on that tree.
≫ J'ai souvent vu des oiseaux sur cet arbre.

B Le particulier

● Lorsqu'un ou des éléments sont **particuliers** et **bien définis**, on emploie l'article *THE*, au singulier et au pluriel.

● Le nom peut être défini par :

■ ce qui le suit : les **relatives** ou **compléments en** *OF* permettent souvent de particulariser un nom.
The baby who's crying is my nephew.
≫ Le bébé qui pleure est mon neveu.

It was the beginning of a new story.
≫ C'était le début d'une nouvelle histoire.

■ **la situation** dans laquelle on se trouve : le nom peut ainsi désigner un objet ou une personne **immédiatement reconnaissables ou connus de tous.**

Open the door. ❯ Ouvre la porte.
→ On sait de quelle porte il s'agit, elle est devant nous.

Sont censés être connus de tous :

■ les éléments naturels : *the earth, the sky, the sea,* etc.

■ les personnalités ou structures d'un pays : *the press, the president, the government,* etc.

C La généralité

La **généralité** s'exprime en anglais par **l'absence d'article** pour les **noms dénombrables au pluriel** et les **indénombrables.**

■ **Dénombrables au pluriel**

I don't like cats. ❯ Je n'aime pas les chats.
→ Les chats en général.

■ **Indénombrables :** ces mots ne se mettent pas au pluriel.

Time does fly! ❯ Comme **le** temps passe !

D Emplois particuliers de A / AN

À la différence du français, on emploie A / AN :

■ lorsqu'on définit une personne (ou un objet) à l'aide d'un nom et donc devant les noms de métiers.

She is a doctor. ❯ Elle est médecin.

■ après les prépositions (sauf si le mot est indénombrable).

He went out without a coat. ❯ Il est sorti sans manteau.
He talked without enthusiasm. ❯ Il parlait sans enthousiame.

■ devant les expressions de mesure ou de temps pour traduire PAR.

It's 1.99 euro a litre. ❯ Cela vaut 1,99 euro le litre.
We see them once a week.
❯ On les voit une fois par semaine.

Attention !

■ **Traduction de LE, LA, LES**

L'erreur la plus fréquente consiste à utiliser *THE* dans un contexte de généralité puisqu'en français on dit LE, LA, LES dans ce cas. En anglais, on utilise l'article ø (absence d'article).

Les jeunes enfants aiment **les** dessins animés.
❯ *Young children like cartoons.*

■ A / AN

En français, on utilise l'article ø pour définir des personnes, ce qui est source d'erreur lorsqu'on traduit en anglais.

Lorsque j'étais **enfant**... ❯ *When I was a child*...

E Emplois particuliers de THE

● **On emploie THE :**

■ devant les superlatifs (*last, first, best*) et les adjectifs restrictifs (*only*), car ils désignent l'élément comme unique.

She was the best writer and the only French girl in the contest. ❯ C'était le meilleur écrivain et la seule Française en compétition.

■ devant les instruments de musique après le verbe PLAY. Mais devant les noms de sports, on emploie **ø**.

He plays the piano and she plays football.
❯ Il joue du piano et elle joue au foot.

● **Noms de pays**

■ **au singulier,** ils s'emploient généralement **sans article :** *England, France, Spain,* etc.

■ **au pluriel,** ils sont précédés de *THE* :

the United States (les États-Unis)
the Netherlands (les Pays-Bas)
the Canaries (les Canaries), etc.

F Noms propres et fonctions officielles

● Le **nom propre** s'emploie toujours avec l'**article ø**, même s'il est précédé d'un titre ou d'un grade, ce qui n'est pas le cas en français.

President Obama (**le** Président Obama)
Prime Minister Gordon Brown (**le** Premier ministre Gordon Brown)
Queen Elizabeth (**la** reine Elizabeth)
General Patton (**le** général Patton)
Admiral Nelson (**l'**amiral Nelson), etc.

● En revanche, lorsqu'aucun nom propre ne suit la fonction, on emploie l'article *THE.*

the *French Prime Minister*
the *President of the US,* etc.

G Groupes et individus

Certains adjectifs peuvent être utilisés avec des noms et des articles différents, selon qu'ils renvoient à **la totalité du groupe,** à **un ensemble** d'individus ou bien à **un individu.**

● **Le groupe dans sa totalité** ❯ *THE* + adjectif au singulier.

the English (les Anglais)
the poor (les pauvres)
the homeless (les sans-abri)
the jobless (les personnes aux chômage)

● **Un ensemble d'individus** ❯ Ø + adjectif + *people.*

homeless people: les / des sans-abri
jobless people: les / des gens au chômage

● **Un individu** ❯ A + adjectif + *man / woman / person.*

a homeless man: un sans-abri
a jobless person: une personne au chômage

22 Les quantifieurs

La nature du nom (dénombrable ou indénombrable) permet de choisir le quantifieur qui convient.

A « Une certaine quantité de » : *SOME, ANY*

	Indénombrable	Dénombrable pluriel
Dans les affirmations : *SOME* ■ *SOME* désigne « **une certaine quantité de...** », non précisée. ■ L'article *ø* peut être employé à la place de *SOME* ou *ANY* lorsqu'il s'agit **d'opposer un élément à un autre.**	*Let's have some tea!* » Prenons du thé ! *Do you want milk or cream?* » Tu veux du lait ou de la crème ?	*There are some messages for you.* » Il y a des messages pour toi.
Dans les questions : *SOME* ou *ANY* ■ On emploie *SOME* lorsqu'on attend une **réponse positive**, par exemple pour une offre. ■ *ANY* dans la question implique qu'**on ne sait pas quelle réponse va être faite.**	*Would you like some water?* » Désirez-vous de l'eau ? *Is there any coffee?* » Est-ce qu'il y a du café ?	*Can you give me some biscuits?* » Pouvez-vous me donner des biscuits ? *Are there any people around?* » Est-ce qu'il y a des gens dans le coin ?
ANY peut également signifier N'IMPORTE LEQUEL. On le trouve alors aux trois formes (affirmative, interrogative et négative).	*Any student can do it.* » N'importe quel élève peut le faire. *Give me just any pencil.* » Donne-moi n'importe quel crayon.	

B Petite / grande quantité : *MUCH, MANY, LITTLE, FEW, A LOT OF, PLENTY OF*

	Indénombrable	Dénombrable pluriel
Grande quantité : BEAUCOUP DE	*a lot of* money, **plenty of** time	*a lot of* books, **plenty of** friends
(Pas) grande quantité : PAS BEAUCOUP DE	There is **not much** time.	There are **not many** people.
Petite quantité : (TRÈS / TROP / SI) PEU DE, UN PEU DE, QUELQUES	(**very / too / so**) **little** time, **a little** money	(**very / too / so**) **few** people, **a few** people
Plus grande quantité : PLUS DE	**more** money	**more** people
Plus petite quantité : MOINS DE	**less** money	**fewer** people

---

● Traduction des quantifieurs

Pour **traduire** les quantifieurs, il faut se poser la question de la nature du nom : **dénombrable pluriel** (ex. *friends*) ou **indénombrable singulier** (ex. *money*).

● PAS BEAUCOUP DE

■ Dénombrable pluriel : Il n'a **pas beaucoup d'**amis.
» *He hasn't got **many** friends.*

■ Indénombrable : Il n'a **pas beaucoup d'**argent.
» *He hasn't got **much** money.*

Remarque : *HOW MUCH* et *HOW MANY* signifient COMBIEN ?.

● PEU DE

■ Dénombrable pluriel : Il a **peu d'**amis.
» *He's got **few** friends.*

■ Indénombrable : Il a **peu d'**argent.
» *He's got **little** money.*

Remarque : *LITTLE* et *FEW* peuvent être précédés de *VERY* ou *TOO* : very / too little time (très / trop peu de temps), very / too few friends (très / trop peu d'amis).

● PEU DE / UN PEU DE

■ *LITTLE* et *FEW* (**sans article**) expriment une **quantité insuffisante**. Ils ont les mêmes règles d'emploi que *much* et *many*.
J'ai eu peu (= pas suffisamment) de temps.
» *I had **little** time.*

Il y avait peu (= pas assez) d'enfants.
» *There were **few** children.*

■ *A LITTLE* et *A FEW* (**avec article**) expriment seulement l'idée d'une **quantité faible** (UN PEU DE, QUELQUES).
Nous avons encore un peu de temps.
» *We still have **a little** time.*

Il y avait quelques enfants. » *There were **a few** children.*

C Quantité nulle : *NO, NOT ANY, NONE*

	Indénombrable	**Dénombrable pluriel**
Avec un nom : *NOT ANY* OU *NO*	*There isn't any time / There's no time left.* » Il ne reste plus de temps.	*There weren't any / There were no passengers on the platform.* » Il n'y avait pas de voyageurs sur le quai.
À la place d'un nom : pronom *NONE*	*– How many cars have they got?* » Combien ont-ils de voitures ? *– None.* » Aucune. **Ne pas confondre** *NONE* (en un mot → *AUCUN*) avec *NO ONE* (en deux mots → *PERSONNE*). *No one likes him.* » Personne ne l'aime.	

NOT ANY OU NOT A ?

Attention ! Avec un nom dénombrable singulier *NOT ANY* est impossible. On emploie *NOT A.*

*I haven't got **a** car* » Je n'ai pas de voiture.

D De l'unité à la totalité

Les quantifieurs suivants se construisent avec un **nom** (*all books, the whole bottle*, etc.) ou avec *OF* (*most of the kids, most of her friends, most of them*, etc.).

ONE : UN **(et un seul)** *BOTH* : LES DEUX	*one child, one of the children* *both children, both of the children*
EACH (toujours suivi du singulier ; le pluriel n'est possible qu'après *OF*) : CHAQUE *EVERY* (toujours suivi du singulier) : CHAQUE, TOUS	*each child, each of the children* *every child* (pas de construction en *OF*)
ALL : TOUT, TOUS *THE WHOLE* : TOUT ENTIER / ENTIÈRE	*all day, all that time, all his children, all those people, all of them* *the whole town, the whole of it*
EITHER (toujours suivi du singulier ; le pluriel n'est possible qu'après *OF*) : L'UN OU L'AUTRE *NEITHER* (toujours suivi du singulier ; le pluriel n'est possible qu'après *OF*) : NI L'UN NI L'AUTRE	*in either case, either of them* *neither dress fitted, neither of them*
MOST : LA PLUPART DE	*most people, most of the children I know* **Ne pas confondre** *most* avec *the most* (superlatif). *It's the most beautiful painting in the museum.* C'est le plus beau tableau du musée.

Traduction de TOUT, TOUS
- ***ALL*** exprime l'idée d'ensemble (TOUT, TOUS) : *all day* (toute la journée), *all the children* (tous les enfants).
- ***WHOLE*** exprime l'idée de totalité (TOUT ENTIER) : *the whole country* (tout le pays).
- À la différence de *ALL, WHOLE* se place après *THE, MY, YOUR*, etc.
  toute ma vie → *all my life / my whole life*
- ***EVERY*** (CHAQUE) peut s'utiliser pour traduire TOUS LES. On insiste alors sur CHAQUE élément. Le mot qui suit *EVERY* est au singulier.
  tous les enfants (= chaque enfant) » *every child*

E Le nombre

● **Nombre précis**

DOZEN, HUNDRED, THOUSAND, MILLION ne se mettent pas au pluriel lorsqu'ils sont précédés d'un nombre précis : *two dozen eggs* (deux douzaines d'œufs), *three hundred kilos* (trois cents kilos), *four thousand people* (quatre mille personnes), *five million dollars* (cinq millions de dollars).

● **DES CENTAINES / MILLIERS / MILLIONS DE**

On emploie le pluriel lorsque le nombre est précédé de l'article ø.

There were hundreds of boats and thousands of people.
» Il y avait des centaines de bateaux et des milliers de gens.

23 Les pronoms

A Pronoms personnels

● **Pronoms personnels sujets et compléments**

■ **Sujet** : *I, YOU, HE / SHE / IT, WE, YOU, THEY*

■ **Complément** : *ME, YOU, HIM / HER / IT, US, YOU, THEM*

<u>He</u> never talks to <u>me</u>.
sujet   complément

● *HE* (masculin) et *SHE* (féminin) s'emploient pour les êtres humains et les animaux familiers. *IT* s'emploie pour les objets et animaux.

B Possessifs

> **Déterminants possessifs**
> *MY, YOUR, HIS / HER / ITS, OUR, YOUR, THEIR*

● Ce sont des génitifs (Voir **Gr. 20.**) appliqués aux pronoms personnels. Ils sont **suivis de l'élément possédé**.

Where's your sister? ▶ Où est ta sœur ?

● À la différence du français, les possessifs en anglais **s'accordent** en nombre (et en genre à la 3ᵉ personne du singulier) **avec le possesseur**.

La voiture de Paul ▶ *sa voiture* ▶ *his car*.

→ *HIS* est masculin comme le possesseur, Paul.

● Pour les parties du corps et les vêtements, on emploie le possessif en anglais (alors qu'en français, on emploie LE, LA, LES).

*He had **his** hands in **his** pockets.*
▶ Il avait les mains dans les poches.

● On peut renforcer le possessif par *OWN*.

We have our own swimming pool.
▶ Nous avons notre propre piscine.

> **Pronoms possessifs**
> *MINE, YOURS, HIS / HERS, OURS, YOURS, THEIRS*

● On peut éviter la répétition de l'objet possédé grâce aux pronoms possessifs.

Is this bag yours (= your bag)? ▶ Ce sac est-il à toi ?

● Pour dire « **un(e) de mes / tes / ses / nos / vos / leurs + groupe nominal** », on emploie : **groupe nominal + *OF* + pronom possessif**.

She is a cousin of mine. ▶ C'est une de mes cousines.

I met a good friend of theirs.
▶ J'ai rencontré un de leurs bons amis.

● *THEY, THEIR, THEIRS, THERE'S*

■ *THEY, THEIR, THEIRS* renvoient à des **personnes** ou **objets**.

***Tom and Lisa** are gone. **They**'re in Spain now.*
→ *They = Tom et Lisa* → **pronom sujet**

*Sue is looking after **their** dog.*
→ *their* = appartenant à Tom et Lisa
→ **déterminant possessif**

*She is a friend of **theirs**.*
→ *of theirs* = parmi les amis de Tom et Lisa
→ **pronom possessif**

■ *THERE* est un adverbe qui signifie LÀ. (*HERE* signifie ICI.) L'expression *there's* (= *there is*) signifie donc littéralement « là est ». Par extension, *THERE* permet de dire « quelque chose existe (là) ». Au pluriel, on utilise *THERE ARE*.

There's a new shop in Dawson Street.
▶ Il y a une nouvelle boutique rue Dawson.

There are huge difficulties.
▶ Il y a d'énormes difficultés.

C Pronoms réfléchis

> **Pronoms réfléchis**
> *MYSELF, YOURSELF, HIMSELF / HERSELF / ITSELF, OURSELVES, YOURSELVES, THEMSELVES*

● On emploie le pronom réfléchi lorsque **le sujet et l'objet sont la même personne**.

*He looked at **himself** in the mirror.*
▶ Il se regarda dans la glace.

● Le pronom réfléchi peut également permettre d'**insister sur une personne ou un objet**.

*Why don't **you** do it **yourself**?*
▶ Pourquoi ne le fais-tu pas toi-même ?

● **Certains verbes français** se construisent avec un pronom réfléchi mais pas leur équivalent anglais. → se laver (*wash*), se sentir (*feel*), se raser (*shave*), se rencontrer (*meet*), s'excuser (*apologize*), se lever (*stand up*), se baigner (*have a bath*), etc.

*Elle **s'**habille très bien.* ▶ *She dresses very well.*
*Comment **vous** sentez-vous ?* ▶ *How do you feel?*

D Pronoms réciproques

On utilise *EACH OTHER* (deux éléments) et *ONE ANOTHER* (deux ou plusieurs éléments) pour exprimer l'idée d'un **échange entre deux ou plusieurs personnes**.

The two girls looked at each other / one another.
▶ Les deux filles échangèrent un regard.

E Pronoms indéfinis

● **Composés de** *SOME, ANY, NO* **et** *EVERY*

	–BODY	*–ONE*	*–THING*	*–WHERE*
SOME	*somebody*	*someone*	*something*	*somewhere*
ANY	*anybody*	*anyone*	*anything*	*anywhere*
NO	*nobody*	*no one*	*nothing*	*nowhere*
EVERY	*everybody*	*everyone*	*everything*	*everywhere*

Remarque : *No one* (PERSONNE) s'écrit en deux mots. Ne pas confondre avec *NONE* (AUCUN). (Voir **Gr. 22.**)

● Les composés de *SOME, ANY, NO* et *EVERY* suivent les mêmes règles d'emploi que *SOME, ANY, NO* et *EVERY*. (Voir **Gr. 22.**)

Someone has slept in my bed.
➢ Quelqu'un a dormi dans mon lit.

He has nowhere to go. ➢ Il n'a nulle part où aller.

Everything is fine. ➢ Tout va bien.

● Les composés de *ANY* peuvent avoir la valeur de N'IMPORTE LEQUEL. *Any* est alors accentué à l'oral.

*Any*body could have done it.
➢ N'importe qui aurait pu le faire.

24 THIS / THAT

● *THIS* (pluriel : *THESE*) désigne un objet qui est seulement **connu de celui qui parle** (d'où l'idée de « proximité »). *THIS* sert souvent par conséquent à présenter une personne ou un objet nouveau.

This is my brother. ➢ Voici mon frère.
→ Je vous présente mon frère.

There are more and more homeless people these days.
➢ De nos jours, il y a de plus en plus de sans-abri.
→ De nos jours = dans le présent.

● *THAT* (pluriel : *THOSE*) est utilisé pour tout objet ou fait qui est **éloigné de celui qui parle**, dans le temps ou l'espace.

People worked longer hours in those days.
➢ Les gens avaient des journées de travail plus longues en ce temps-là. → en ce temps-là = dans le passé.

● On emploie aussi *THAT* et non pas *THIS* lorsque celui qui parle et celui auquel il s'adresse savent tous deux de quel objet il s'agit.

Give me that, please. ➢ Donne-moi ça, s'il te plaît.
→ Les interlocuteurs savent tous deux de quoi il s'agit car ils l'ont sous les yeux.

25 Les adjectifs

A Place et ordre des adjectifs

● Les adjectifs **épithètes** se placent toujours **devant le nom**, même s'il y en a plusieurs.

I just love your little black dress.
➢ J'adore ta petite robe noire.

● Certains adjectifs sont **toujours attributs**. Ils se placent après un verbe d'état comme *BE*. Ce sont les adjectifs : *alive* (en vie), *asleep* (endormi), *afraid* (effrayé), *awake* (éveillé), *cross* (fâché), *ill* (malade), *glad* (joyeux).

● Lorsqu'il y a plusieurs adjectifs devant le nom, l'adjectif exprimant un jugement **subjectif** (*nice, good, bad, stupid, rich*, etc.) se place **en tête**. Les autre adjectifs se placent en général dans cet ordre : **taille** (forme, dimension), **âge**, **couleur**, **origine** (nationalité, religion, origine géographique ou politique), **matière**. (Formule : **S.T.A.C.O.M.**)

a huge old dark Italian wooden door
a small new red American car
a lovely tall young dark-haired Indian girl

B Comparatif des adjectifs (PLUS, MOINS)

● **Adjectifs courts :** adjectifs d'**une syllabe** ou de deux syllabes terminés par *-ER*, *-Y*, *-OW* et *-LE* : *big, old, small, tall, short, long, clever, happy, narrow, gentle*, etc.

● **Adjectifs longs :** adjectifs de **deux syllabes ou plus** (sauf ceux terminés par *-ER*, *-Y*, *-OW* et *-LE*) : *stupid, expensive, interesting, intelligent, difficult*, etc.

	Adjectifs courts	Adjectifs longs
Supériorité (PLUS)	*-ER … THAN* *She's younger than you.* ➢ Elle est plus jeune que toi.	*MORE … THAN* *It's more interesting than it used to be.* ➢ C'est plus intéressant qu'avant.
Égalité ou inégalité (AUSSI / PAS AUSSI)	*AS … AS / NOT SO (AS) … AS* *He's as smart / intelligent as his mother.* ➢ Il est aussi intelligent que sa mère. *It's not (so) as hard / difficult as I thought.* ➢ Ce n'est pas aussi difficile que je le pensais.	

	Adjectifs courts	Adjectifs longs
Infériorité (MOINS)	*LESS ... THAN* *He is less dumb / stupid than I thought.* » Il est moins bête que je ne le pensais.	
DE PLUS EN PLUS	*-ER AND -ER* *It's getting smaller and smaller.* » Ça devient de plus en plus petit.	*MORE AND MORE ...* *It's more and more interesting.* » C'est de plus en plus intéressant.
DE MOINS EN MOINS	*LESS AND LESS ...* *His work is less and less satisfactory.* » Son travail est de moins en moins satisfaisant.	

C Superlatif des adjectifs (LE PLUS, LE MOINS)

	Adjectifs courts	Adjectifs longs
Supériorité (LE PLUS)	*THE -EST* *It's the biggest mistake you've ever made.* » C'est la plus grosse erreur que tu aies jamais faite.	*THE MOST ...* *It's the most difficult task we've ever had to do.* » C'est la tâche la plus difficile que nous ayons jamais eu à faire.
Infériorité (LE MOINS)	*THE LEAST* *She's the least clever of the three children.* » C'est la moins intelligente des trois enfants.	*THE LEAST ...* *We bought the least expensive of all.* » Nous avons acheté le moins cher de tous.

D Comparatifs et superlatifs irréguliers

	Comparatif	Superlatif
GOOD / WELL	*BETTER*	*THE BEST*
BAD	*WORSE*	*THE WORST*
FAR	*FURTHER*	*FARTHER*
	THE FURTHEST	*THE FARTHEST*

E Adjectifs en -ED et -ING

Ces adjectifs sont dérivés de verbes.

- Les adjectifs en **-ING** ont un sens **actif**.

  I'm sure it's a fascinating / exciting job.
  » Je suis sûr que c'est un travail passionnant.

- Les adjectifs en **-ED** ont un sens **passif**.

  I'm not really interested.
  » Ça ne m'intéresse pas vraiment.

  I was shocked to hear these words.
  » J'ai été abasourdi d'entendre ces mots.

F Adjectifs composés

● À partir d'un verbe

- Comme les adjectifs simples en **-ING** (voir **Gr. 25 E**), les adjectifs composés en **-ING** ont un sens **actif**.

  a student who works hard → *a hard-working student*
  a job that breaks your back → *a back-breaking job*

- De même, les adjectifs composés en **-ED** ont un sens **passif** (sauf dans *well-behaved* : « qui se comporte bien »).

  an institution controlled by the state
  → *a state-controlled institution*

  a machine operated by a battery
  → *a battery-operated machine*

● À partir d'un adjectif et d'un nom + -ED

L'adjectif composé indique une **caractéristique** de la personne ou de l'objet.

She has dark hair. → *She's dark-haired.*

He's a man with a cold heart.
→ *He's a cold-hearted man.*

It's a jacket with red stripes (rayures).
→ *It's a red-striped jacket.*

He's wearing a shirt with long sleeves (manches).
→ *He's wearing a long-sleeved shirt.*

● Expression de l'âge

- Après **BE**, on utilise la forme ... *YEARS OLD* :

  *She is twenty **years old**.* » Elle a vingt ans.
  → *year* est au pluriel.

- Lorsque l'adjectif est placé **avant le nom** :

  They have a twenty-year-old son.
  » Ils ont un fils de vingt ans.
  → *year* est au singulier + trait d'union entre les trois mots.

26 Les noms composés

A Élément principal

● Dans un nom composé, **le premier élément sert à préciser le sens du deuxième. C'est le deuxième élément qui est le mot principal**. Le premier élément ne se met jamais au pluriel (sauf exception).

paper **bag**, hand**bag**, air **bag**, tea **bag**, sand**bag**, doggy **bag**

● Les mots composés ne sont pas systématiquement soit séparés, soit attachés, soit reliés par un tiret. Il n'y a en fait pas de règle précise, sinon l'usage, donné par le dictionnaire : dining room, schoolfriend, coffee-maker, etc.

B Nom + nom

Le nom 1 indique...	Nom composé
... à quoi sert le nom 2	teaspoon, breadknife, meat hook, fish fork
... comment fonctionne le nom 2	gas cooker, steamboat, petrol engine, atom bomb
... la matière du nom 2	silver chain, glass building, gold tooth, steel guitar
... de quoi fait partie le nom 2	doorknob, lampshade, chair back, table leg
... le sexe du nom 2	manservant, boy soprano, boyfriend, girl guide
... le lieu du nom 2	seabird, streetlamp, roadblock, village idiot
... le moment du nom 2	night train, morning paper, day nurse, afternoon tea
... le métier, l'occupation du nom 2 (**man, woman, girl, boy**)	newspaperman, businesswoman, schoolgirl, message-boy
... la fonction du nom 2 et ce qu'il contient	wine glass, teapot, butter dish, bookshelf

C Nom + forme verbale

	La forme verbale désigne...	Mot composé
Nom + BV-*ER*	... la personne ou l'instrument qui fait l'action	taxi driver, opera singer, coat hanger, bottle-opener
Nom + BV-*ING*	... une profession ou une activité	window cleaning, bungee jumping, sightseeing, bird-watching
BV-*ING* + nom	... l'usage d'un objet ou d'un lieu	driving licence, dining room, riding boots, looking-glass

27 Énoncés affirmatifs

A Ordre des mots

● À la différence du français, on ne sépare pas le **complément d'objet direct** (COD) du **verbe** en anglais.

Il y avait, dans la voiture, **un chien noir** (COD).
» ~~There was in the car a black dog.~~
» There was **a black dog** in the car.

● Le **complément de manière** ou d'intensité (**well, very much**, etc.) se place **après le complément d'objet**. (Il se place avant en français.)

J'aime **beaucoup** ce livre.
» ~~I like very much this book.~~
» I like this book **very much**.

● On place les **adverbes de fréquence** (**always, often, sometimes, usually**, etc.) :

■ **avant le verbe** (sauf pour *BE*), alors qu'en français, on les place après.

Je le vois **souvent**. » I **often** see him.

■ **après le verbe** lorsque celui-ci est *BE*.

He **is often** angry. » Il est souvent en colère.

■ **après le premier auxiliaire**, s'il y en a un ou plusieurs.

I have **never** liked them. » Je ne les ai jamais aimés.

● Les **autres compléments de temps** (**last year, yesterday, in those days**, etc.) se placent **en fin d'énoncé**.

We never visited them **in those days**.
» On ne leur rendait jamais visite **à cette époque**.

B *Do* / *DID* de reprise

● La présence de l'auxiliaire *DO* / *DID* dans les énoncés affirmatifs a un sens bien particulier car le présent simple et le prétérit simple ne font normalement pas apparaître d'auxiliaire à la forme affirmative.

● *Do* permet de **reprendre ce qui vient d'être dit pour confirmer ou contredire**. Le verbe peut rester sous-entendu.

*I thought that she would phone me and she **did** phone / and she **did**.*
  ➤ Je pensais qu'elle me téléphonerait et, effectivement, elle m'a téléphoné.

■ *You don't like her very much.*
  ➤ Tu ne l'aimes pas beaucoup.

■ *That's not true. I **do** like her, but she hates me.*
  (L'auxiliaire est accentué à l'oral.)
  ➤ Ce n'est pas vrai. Moi, je l'aime bien, mais c'est elle qui me déteste.

28 Énoncés négatifs

● La forme négative fait toujours apparaître un auxiliaire.
  *She **doesn't** know you. He **didn't** want to talk.*

● Avec un terme **négatif ou restrictif** comme *NEVER, HARDLY EVER* (PRESQUE JAMAIS), *NOBODY, NOTHING*, l'emploi de *NOT* est **inutile** et le verbe reste à la forme affirmative.

*He **never** wrote to me.* ➤ Il ne m'a jamais écrit.

*We **hardly ever** agree.*
  ➤ Nous ne sommes presque jamais d'accord.

● On peut mettre en relief un terme **négatif ou restrictif** (*NEVER, NO SOONER … THAN*) en le plaçant en **tête de phrase**. Ceci entraîne une **inversion sujet / auxiliaire**. (Attention : **l'auxiliaire** est toujours nécessaire dans un cas d'inversion, y compris au présent simple et au prétérit simple.) Cette inversion se trouve dans un **anglais très soutenu**.

She never saw him again.
  → ***Never did she** see him again.*
  ➤ Elle ne l'a jamais revu.

He got in the car and fell asleep at once.
  → ***No sooner had he** got in the car **than** he fell asleep.*
  ➤ À peine était-il entré dans la voiture qu'il s'endormit.

Autres termes négatifs ou restrictifs pouvant être placés en tête de phrase : *HARDLY / SCARCELY … WHEN* (À PEINE), *LITTLE, NOR, NOT ONLY, NOWHERE, SELDOM* (RAREMENT).

Scarcely had the car stopped when the police surrounded it.
  ➤ À peine la voiture s'était-elle arrêtée que les policiers l'encerclèrent.

Little did she think that her novel would sell so well.
  ➤ Elle était loin de se douter que son roman se vendrait si bien.

29 Énoncés interrogatifs

A Questions

● En français, pour poser une question à l'oral, on utilise souvent la forme affirmative, avec une intonation montante : « Tu la connais ? » / « Elle est venue ? ».

En anglais, l'inversion sujet / auxiliaire est toujours nécessaire (sauf lorsque *WHO* ou *WHAT* est sujet de l'énoncé : voir ci-après).

Do you know her? / Did she come?

● Lorsqu'il y a une **préposition**, elle est maintenue **à droite du verbe**.

À qui penses-tu ? ➤ *Who are you thinking **of**?*

De quoi parliez-vous ? ➤ *What were you talking **about**?*

B Mots interrogatifs

● *WHO* s'emploie pour une **personne**, en fonction **sujet ou complément**.

Who saw the murderer? ➤ Qui a vu le meurtrier ?
  (*WHO* est **sujet**.)

Who did you see? ➤ Qui as-tu vu ?
  (*WHO* est **complément**.)

Remarque : Les auxiliaires *DO* (au présent) et *DID* (au passé) n'apparaissent pas lorsque *WHO* et *WHAT* sont sujet.

● *WHOM* s'emploie (rarement) en fonction **complément**, dans une langue plus formelle.

Whom do you like best? ➤ Qui préfères-tu ?

● *WHAT* s'emploie pour un **non-animé**, en fonction **sujet ou complément**.

What happened? ➤ Que s'est-il passé ?
  (*WHAT* est **sujet**.)

What did you find? ➤ Qu'as-tu trouvé ?
  (*WHAT* est **complément**.)

WHAT peut être suivi d'un **nom**.

What colour is it? ➤ C'est de quelle couleur ?

What subjects did you choose?
  ➤ Quelles matières as-tu choisies ?

● ***Which*** : **choix entre plusieurs possibilités** (réduites).

Which of the two brothers did he call?
› Lequel des deux frères a-t-il appelé ?

Which peut être suivi d'un **nom** ou de ***one***.

Which book is it? › C'est quel livre ?

Which one is it? › Lequel est-ce ?

● ***What ... like*** s'emploie pour une demande de **description**. ***Like*** se place en fin de phrase.

– *What is her brother like?* › Comment est son frère ?
– *He's tall and thin.* › Il est grand et maigre.

● ***Whose*** : question sur la **possession**. ***Whose* est suivi de l'élément possédé sans article**.

– *Whose bike is it?* › À qui est ce vélo ?
– *It's Paul's.* › À Paul.

● ***Where*** : question sur le **lieu**.

Where is it? › Où est-ce ?

● ***When*** : question sur le **moment**.

When did he call? › Quand a-t-il appelé ?

● ***Since when*** : question sur le **point de départ** d'une action ou d'un fait.

Since when have you been here?
› Depuis quand es-tu là ?

● ***Why*** porte sur la **cause**. On trouve ***because*** dans la réponse.

– *Why did she laugh at him?* › Pourquoi s'est-elle moquée de lui ?
– *Because she found him stupid.* › Parce qu'elle a trouvé qu'il était idiot.

● ***What ... for*** porte sur le **but**. On répond souvent par **l'infinitif**. ***For*** se place en fin de phrase.

– *What did you call him* ***for****?* › Pourquoi l'as-tu appelé ?
– ***To*** *tell him how sorry I was.* › Pour lui dire combien j'étais désolé.

● ***How long*** : question sur la **durée**.

– *How long has she known them?* › Cela fait combien de temps qu'elle les connaît ?
– *(For) two years.* › Deux ans.

● ***How long ago*** : question sur la **date**.

– *How long ago did she leave?* › Il y a combien de temps qu'elle est partie ?
– *Two hours ago.* › Il y a deux heures.

● ***How often*** : question sur la **fréquence**.

How often do you feed the cat?
› Tous les combien donnes-tu à manger au chat ?

● ***How* + adjectif** permet d'évaluer le **degré d'un adjectif**.

How big is his house?
› Quelle est la taille de sa maison ?
→ Quel est son « degré de grandeur » ?

How old is she? › Quel âge a-t-elle ?

● ***How far*** : question sur la **distance**.

How far is it? › C'est à combien / à quelle distance d'ici ?

● ***How much / how many*** : questions sur la **quantité**. ***How much*** s'emploie également pour **demander un prix**.

How much money do you have?
› Combien d'argent as-tu ?

How many children are there?
› Combien d'enfants y-a-t-il ?

How much is it? › C'est combien ?

Remarque : Lorsque ***how much*** est suivi d'un nom, celui-ci est nécessairement **indénombrable** et donc au **singulier**. ***How many*** est suivi d'un nom au **pluriel**.

● ***How*** : question sur le **moyen**, la **manière**.

How did you get out of the car?
› Comment es-tu sorti de la voiture ?

How s'emploie aussi pour questionner sur l'**état de santé**.

How is he? › Comment va-t-il ?

30 Les réponses courtes et les *tags*

A « Oui / non »

● **Oui** ou **non** suffisent en français pour faire une réponse courte. En anglais, **on utilise très souvent l'auxiliaire** (précédé du sujet) dans la réponse courte. On fait apparaître l'auxiliaire correspondant au premier énoncé.

– Tu as fini ? › *Have you finished?*
– Non. › *No,* ***I haven't****.*

● Au **présent simple** et au **prétérit simple**, l'auxiliaire ne figure pas dans l'énoncé affirmatif ; il faut le faire apparaître dans la réponse.

– *You agree with me, I suppose.*
› Je suppose que vous êtes d'accord avec moi.
– *Yes, I do. / No, I don't.* › Oui. / Non.

B « Moi aussi / moi non plus »

On utilise ***so*** lorsque le premier énoncé est **affirmatif** et ***neither*** lorsque le premier énoncé est **négatif**. ***So*** et ***neither*** sont directement **suivis de l'auxiliaire**.

– *I often watch that TV show.* › Je regarde souvent ce show télévisé.
– *So do I.* › Moi aussi.

– *I didn't tell him about it.* › Je ne lui en ai pas parlé.
– *Neither did I.* › Moi non plus.

C « Moi si / pas moi »

La reprise courte permet de **s'opposer** à ce qui vient d'être dit. On utilise le même auxiliaire que dans la phrase de départ, à la forme affirmative ou négative selon le cas. Si l'auxiliaire ne figure pas dans la première phrase, il faut le faire apparaître dans la deuxième : *DO* / *DID* au **présent simple** et au **prétérit simple**. Le sujet est accentué.

– *She won't come.* ≫ Elle ne viendra pas.
– *I will.* ≫ Moi si.
– *They tried hard.* ≫ Ils ont fait beaucoup d'efforts.
– *Well, you didn't.* ≫ Pas toi.

D Réponses courtes en *SO* et *NOT*

On utilise *so* après **I think, I don't think, I hope, I suppose** et *NOT* après **I'm afraid, I hope, I suppose** et *of course*. *So* et *NOT* ont pour fonction de reprendre ce qui précède. On n'utilise pas d'auxiliaire dans ce cas.

– *Did he understand what she said?*
≫ A-t-il compris ce qu'elle a dit ?
– *Yes, I think so. / No, I don't think so. / I suppose so.*
≫ Oui, je crois. / Non, je ne crois pas. / Je crois que oui.
– *Well, I hope not. / I'm afraid not. / Of course not.*
≫ Eh bien, j'espère que non. / Je crains que non. / Bien sûr que non.

E *TAGS* interrogatifs

Ce sont de brèves formes interrogatives (sujet + auxiliaire) que l'on trouve à la fin d'énoncés affirmatifs ou négatifs. Souvent traduit par N'EST-CE PAS ?, le *tag* permet de **demander confirmation de ce qui a été déclaré.**

They have finished, haven't they?
≫ Ils ont fini, non / n'est-ce pas ?

● Il faut parfois faire apparaître dans le *tag* un auxiliaire qui ne figure pas dans la première partie de la phrase.

■ **Au présent simple** et au **prétérit simple** : *DO* / *DID*

She talks too much, doesn't she?
≫ Elle parle trop, n'est-ce pas ?

He gave up at once, didn't he?
≫ Il a tout de suite abandonné, n'est-ce pas ?

■ **À l'impératif** : *SHALL* ou *WILL*

Let's go out, shall we? ≫ Sortons, voulez-vous ?

Stay there, will you? ≫ Reste-là, s'il te plaît.

● Après un terme négatif ou restrictif comme *NEVER, HARDLY EVER, NOTHING,* le *tag* est **positif.**

She never complains, does she?
≫ Elle ne se plaint jamais, n'est-ce pas ?

● Les indéfinis *EVERYBODY, NOBODY* sont repris par *THEY* bien que le verbe soit au singulier.

Everybody was there, weren't they?
≫ Tout le monde était là, n'est-ce pas ?

Nobody knows him, do they?
≫ Personne ne le connaît, n'est-ce pas ?

Première forme verbale affirmative → *tag* interro-négatif	Première forme verbale négative → *tag* interrogatif
He **is** swimming, **isn't** he?	He **isn't** swimming, **is** he?
He **was** swimming, **wasn't** he?	He **wasn't** swimming, **was** he?
They'**ve** changed, **haven't** they?	They **haven't** changed, **have** they?
They **had** changed, **hadn't** they?	They **hadn't** changed, **had** they?
He **will** change, **won't** he?	He **won't** change, **will** he?

31 Énoncés exclamatifs

A L'exclamation sur un groupe nominal

● On emploie *WHAT* avec l'article *A, AN* ou le pluriel sans article si le nom est dénombrable.

What a nice trip! ≫ Quel voyage agréable !
What fools we are! ≫ Que nous sommes bêtes !

● On utilise *WHAT* avec ø si le nom est indénombrable.
What awful weather! ≫ Quel temps affreux !

● On peut formuler les exclamations en *WHAT* avec *SUCH.*
What a nice boy he is! → *He's such a nice boy!*
≫ C'est un garçon si gentil !

B L'exclamation sur un adjectif

● On emploie *HOW* immédiatement suivi de l'adjectif.
How terrible! ≫ Comme c'est affreux !

● On peut formuler les exclamations en *HOW* avec *SO.*
How disappointed I was!
→ *I was ever so disappointed!* ≫ J'étais tellement déçu !
(*EVER* renforce un adjectif précédé de *SO.*)

32 Énoncés à l'impératif

- **Ordre adressé à** *YOU*
- **Forme affirmative :** *Try this one!* » Essaie celui-ci !
- **Forme négative :** *Don't get out!* » Ne sors pas !

- **Ordre adressé à** *WE*
- **Forme affirmative :**
  Let's go to bed! » Allons nous coucher !

- **Forme négative :**
  Let's not forget to sign the book!
  » N'oublions pas de signer le livre !

ou (plus formel) : *Don't let's forget to sign the book!*

- L'auxiliaire *DO* **a une valeur de persuasion à l'impératif.**
  Do try! » Mais essaie donc !

33 L'infinitif

A Infinitif complet

- C'est **l'infinitif précédé de** *TO*. Il désigne généralement un **acte à venir** ou un **acte qu'on envisage de faire.**
  He intends to go. » Il a l'intention de partir.

- **On trouve l'infinitif complet :**
- **après les verbes projetant l'action dans l'avenir.**
  → Verbes de **volonté** (refus) ou **désir** : *decide, plan, refuse, want,* etc.
  We've decided to stay. » Nous avons décidé de rester.

  → *allow, can't afford, ask, expect, force, try*
  You're not allowed to go out on your own.
  » Tu n'as pas le droit de sortir tout seul.

- pour exprimer la **visée** (action projetée dans l'avenir) après *BE*.
  The show is to start at 10 p.m.
  » Le spectacle doit commencer à 10 heures.

- **en complément d'adjectif.**
  This language is pleasant to hear but difficult to understand.
  » Cette langue est agréable à entendre mais difficile à comprendre.

- **en complément de certains pronoms indéfinis** (*NOTHING, NOBODY, NOWHERE*).
  We have nothing to do and nowhere to go.
  » Nous n'avons rien à faire et nulle part où aller.

- La **négation** se place **avant** *TO*.
  We tried not to argue with him.
  » On a essayé de ne pas se disputer avec lui.

- L'infinitif complet peut exprimer le **but.**
  I went to your room to get a clean T-shirt.
  » Je suis allé dans ta chambre pour y prendre un T-shirt propre.

- **Formes de l'infinitif complet**
- **Forme simple**
  Le verbe renvoie au **présent** ou à l'**avenir.** Cela dépend du verbe et du contexte.
  He seems to know you. » On dirait qu'il te connaît.

- **Forme** *BE+ING*
  Le verbe renvoie souvent à une **action en cours.**
  He seems to be waiting for someone.
  » Il semble qu'il soit en train d'attendre quelqu'un.

- **Forme** *HAVE -EN*
  Le verbe renvoie à un **fait accompli ou passé.**
  He seems to have given up. » Il semble qu'il ait abandonné.

B Proposition infinitive

- Lorsque **l'infinitif est précédé d'un sujet**, on parle de **proposition infinitive.** Si le **sujet** est un pronom, on utilise le **pronom complément**, car la proposition infinitive est complément du premier verbe.
  *Would you like **Sarah / her** to help you?*
  » Voudrais-tu que Sarah / qu'elle t'aide ?
  → La proposition infinitive (*Sarah / her to help you*) est complément du premier verbe (*Would you like*).

- **Verbes acceptant la proposition infinitive :** *allow, advise, ask, expect, force, order, prefer, tell, wait for, want.*
  *What do you expect **me to say**?*
  » Qu'attends-tu que je dise ?

  *They advised **us not to buy** anything in that shop.*
  » Ils nous ont conseillé de ne rien acheter dans cette boutique.

- La proposition infinitive peut exprimer le **but.** Le sujet est alors introduit par *FOR*.
  *She turned round **for him to see** her new hairdo.*
  » Elle se tourna pour qu'il voie sa nouvelle coiffure.

- La proposition infinitive peut **suivre un adjectif.** Le sujet est alors introduit par *FOR*.
  *It was **difficult / impossible for me to admit** the truth.*
  » Il m'a été difficile / impossible d'admettre la vérité.

  *It is **necessary / important for him to do** this.*
  » Il est nécessaire / important qu'il le fasse.

- *IT* **est nécessaire pour annoncer une proposition infinitive après** *find, know, consider.*
  *I find **it** hard **to get an answer**.*
  » Je trouve qu'il est difficile d'obtenir une réponse.

∃Ч Le gérondif

On forme le gérondif en accolant la marque *-ING* au verbe (**V-*ING***). Le gérondif désigne une **activité**, c'est-à-dire un ensemble d'actes ou un acte vu dans son déroulement.

I hate staying indoors.
➤ J'ai horreur de rester à l'intérieur.

A Gérondif utilisé comme un nom

On le trouve :

■ **en fonction de sujet ou complément.**

Reading is his favourite activity.
➤ Lire (la lecture) est son activité préférée.

He loves dancing. ➤ Il adore danser (la danse).

■ **après les prépositions** (*OF, WITH, ABOUT, FOR, IN*, etc.). Les prépositions sont normalement suivies de noms ; le gérondif étant proche d'un nom, on le trouve donc aussi après les prépositions.

I'm no longer interested in doing this.
➤ Je ne m'intéresse plus à cela.

B Prépositions *TO* et *FOR*

● *To* est parfois préposition, donc suivi du gérondif.

I don't object to inviting them.
➤ Je ne suis pas contre le fait de les inviter.

● *To* est préposition avec les verbes suivants : **be used to** (être habitué à), **be reduced to**, **devote time to** (consacrer du temps à), **get used to** (s'habituer à), **look forward to** (avoir hâte de / attendre avec impatience), **limit oneself to** (se limiter à), **object to** (avoir une objection contre), **take to** (se mettre à).

I look forward to meeting them. ➤ J'ai hâte de les rencontrer.

 BE / GET USED TO et USED TO

■ Dans **BE USED TO** (ÊTRE HABITUÉ À) et **GET USED TO** (S'HABITUER À), *TO* est préposition et donc suivi du gérondif (V-*ING*).

I'm not used to driving on the left.
➤ Je ne suis pas habitué à conduire à gauche.
I never got used to driving on the left.
➤ Je ne me suis jamais habitué à la conduite à gauche.

■ *USED TO* est une forme de prétérit qui exprime la **rupture totale avec le présent** (voir **Gr. 4 B**). Le verbe qui suit *USED* est à **l'infinitif avec** *TO*.

I used to drive a smaller car.
➤ Avant, je conduisais une voiture plus petite.

● *FOR* suivi du gérondif exprime la cause

He blamed me for letting the cat out.
➤ Il m'a reproché d'avoir laissé sortir le chat.

● En revanche, pour exprimer le **but**, on emploie *FOR* + **GN** + infinitif complet, avec *TO*. (Voir **Gr. 33 B**.)

I brought it for you to see.
➤ Je l'ai apporté pour que vous le voyiez.

C Gérondif désignant une activité

On le trouve :

■ **après les verbes exprimant le goût** : *like, love, enjoy, fancy* (avoir envie de), *feel like* (avoir envie de), *resent* (ne pas apprécier), *hate, can't stand / bear* (ne pas supporter de), etc.

I love going to the cinema but I can't stand queuing.
➤ J'adore aller au cinéma mais je ne supporte pas de faire la queue.

Remarque : Certains de ces mêmes verbes peuvent exprimer le **désir** et sont alors suivis de **l'infinitif complet**. (Voir **Gr. 33 A**.)

■ **après certains adjectifs ou verbes qui décrivent une action déjà en cours** : *be busy* (être occupé à), *go on / keep on* (continuer à), *keep* (ne pas cesser de), *spend time* (passer du temps à), *can't help* (ne pas pouvoir s'empêcher de), *stop*.

Why do they keep asking questions?
➤ Pourquoi n'arrêtent-ils pas de poser des questions ?

■ **après les verbes impliquant que l'action a été réalisée** : *remember, regret*.

I regret speaking to her. ➤ Je regrette de lui avoir parlé.

D Autres verbes et expressions suivis du gérondif

● *acknowledge* (reconnaître), *avoid* (éviter), *consider* (envisager de), *delay* (retarder), *have difficulty* (avoir du mal à), *give up* (cesser de, abandonner), *I don't mind* (ça ne me gêne pas / ça ne m'ennuie pas de), *postpone* (remettre à plus tard), *resist, risk*.

You should avoid driving and consider taking the train.
➤ Tu devrais éviter de conduire et envisager de prendre le train.

● *It's no use / It's worth / There's no*

It's no use trying.
➤ Cela ne vaut pas la peine d'essayer.

It's worth going.
➤ Cela vaut la peine d'y aller.

There's no denying that she's a liar.
➤ On ne peut pas nier que c'est une menteuse.

35 — Infinitif ou gérondif ?

A — Verbes à deux constructions

Certains verbes peuvent être suivis soit de l'infinitif, soit du gérondif : *like*, *love*, *hate*, *begin*, *start*, *remember*, *try*.

- **Action déjà réalisée ou en cours → gérondif**

  *I remember **talking** to him.*
  ≫ Je me rappelle lui avoir parlé.

  *Stop **asking** silly questions!*
  ≫ Arrête de poser des questions idiotes !

  *I tried **rock climbing** once.*
  ≫ Une fois, j'ai essayé de faire de l'escalade.

- **Action non encore réalisée → infinitif**

  *Remember **to talk** to him.*
  ≫ N'oublie pas de lui parler.

*He stopped **to ask** a question.*
≫ Il s'est arrêté pour poser une question.

*I tried **to stop** but I couldn't.*
≫ J'ai essayé de m'arrêter mais je n'ai pas pu.

B — Propositions en -*ING*

● Le gérondif peut être **précédé d'un sujet** qui peut avoir la forme d'un possessif, d'un génitif, d'un pronom ou d'un nom.

*He objected to **their** going out (to **the children's** going out).*
*He objected to **them** going out (to **the children** going out).*
≫ Ça l'ennuyait qu'ils sortent (que les enfants sortent).
→ *TO* est ici préposition.

36 — La base verbale

A — Emplois de la base verbale

La base verbale est « l'infinitif sans *TO* ». On la trouve :

- **après les modaux.**

  She should stay. ≫ Elle devrait rester.

- **après les expressions modales** *YOU'D BETTER* **et** *I'D RATHER*.

  You'd better ask them first.
  ≫ Tu ferais mieux de leur demander avant.

  I'd rather stay on my own. ≫ Je préférerais rester seul.

- **à l'impératif :**

  Stay back! ≫ N'avancez pas !

- **après** *WHY* / *WHY NOT* **dans les questions sans sujet.**

  Why see her? Why not write to her?
  ≫ Pourquoi la voir ? Pourquoi ne pas lui écrire ?

- **après les verbes de perception.**

  I heard him come in. ≫ Je l'ai entendu entrer.

  I saw someone fall off the roof.
  ≫ J'ai vu quelqu'un tomber du toit.

Remarque : Les verbes de perception peuvent être aussi suivis de la **forme en -*ING*.** Dans ce cas, l'action est vue dans son **déroulement**.

  I heard him singing. ≫ Je l'ai entendu chanter.
  → Il était en train de chanter.

B — « Faire faire »

● *MAKE* **ou** *HAVE* **+ base verbale**

The police made the terrorist talk.
≫ La police a fait parler le terroriste.

Juliet had us talk all night.
≫ Juliet nous a fait parler toute la nuit.

  → *MAKE* exprime plus la contrainte que *HAVE*.

● *HAVE* **+ participe passé**

We've had the lock changed.
≫ Nous avons fait changer la serrure.
→ On ne nous dit pas qui a changé la serrure mais seulement que la serrure a été changée. Le participe passé a un sens passif. *MAKE* est impossible dans ce cas.

Remarque : *GET* **+ participe passé** a le même sens.

I got my car serviced. ≫ J'ai fait réviser ma voiture.

> **Traduction de FAIRE FAIRE**
> Il faut se demander si l'énoncé a un **sens passif** ou **actif**.
> - **Sens passif :** *HAVE* **+ participe passé**
>   Elle s'est fait livrer de la nourriture.
>   ≫ De la nourriture a été livrée.
>   ≫ *She's had some food delivered.*
> - **Sens actif (quelqu'un accomplit une action à la demande de quelqu'un d'autre) :** *MAKE* **ou** *HAVE* **+ base verbale**
>   Elle les a fait sortir de la pièce.
>   ≫ Ils sont sortis de la pièce.
>   ≫ *She made / had them go out of the room.*

C — « Laisser faire »

On utilise *LET*, qui signifie DONNER LA POSSIBILITÉ DE. On utilise alors la base verbale pour le deuxième verbe.

He let us stay a little longer.
≫ Il nous a laissé rester un peu plus longtemps.
Remarque : Ne pas confondre *LET*, *LET'S* et *LEAVE*.

- *LET'S* sert à former **l'impératif** à la 1ʳᵉ personne du pluriel.

  Let's go! ≫ Allons-y !

- *LEAVE* signifie généralement PARTIR OU LAISSER.

  He left Paris in 2002. ≫ Il a quitté Paris en 2002.

  They left me alone. ≫ Ils m'ont laissé tout seul.

37 Les subordonnées en *THAT* et *WHAT*

A Subordonnées en *THAT* (QUE)

On les trouve :

■ après les verbes exprimant un savoir ou une opinion : *believe, know, suppose, think*.

I think (that) it is too late. ≫ Je pense qu'il est trop tard.

THAT est souvent effacé à l'oral dans ce cas.

■ après les verbes servant à rapporter des paroles : *answer, say, tell*. (Voir **Gr. 42 D**.)

He said (that) he didn't need any help.
≫ Il a dit qu'il n'avait pas besoin d'aide.

■ après *suggest, demand, insist, recommend*. Dans ce cas, *THAT* est souvent suivi de *SHOULD* ou de la **base verbale** (anglais soutenu, pas de *s* à la 3ᵉ personne du singulier).

*Your brother has suggested that **she should stay** here / that **she stay** here.*
≫ Ton frère a suggéré qu'elle reste ici.

 TELL et SAY

■ *TELL* a deux constructions :

– Lorsque *TELL*, suivi d'une proposition, signifie DIRE QUE, il se construit avec une proposition en *THAT*.

He told me that I was in danger.
≫ Il m'a dit que j'étais en danger.

– Lorsque *TELL* signifie DIRE DE (= ORDONNER), il se construit avec une **proposition infinitive**.

*They told **me to** stop there.*
≫ Ils m'ont dit (ordonné) de m'arrêter là.

Remarque : Le verbe est à l'infinitif précédé de *TO*. Lorsque le sujet est un pronom, il se met au cas complément.

■ *SAY*, qui signifie aussi DIRE, se construit généralement avec *THAT*.

*He **said (to me) that** I was in danger.*
≫ Il (m') a dit que j'étais en danger.

 Traduction de QUE

■ **On ne traduit pas toujours QUE par *THAT*.** Beaucoup de verbes se construisent en anglais avec la **proposition infinitive** (voir **Gr. 33 B**) et tout particulièrement les verbes exprimant le **désir** ou une **attente**.

Je veux qu'ils m'écoutent.
≫ *I want them to listen to me.*

Je ne m'attends pas à ce qu'elle me comprenne.
≫ *I don't expect her to understand me.*

■ Certains QUE sont des **relatifs**. (Voir **Gr. 38**.)

C'est le seul bateau que j'aie vu.
≫ *It's the only boat (that) I have seen.*

B Subordonnées en *WHAT* (CE QUE)

On les trouve en position de **sujet** ou de **complément** de la phrase. *WHAT* se traduit alors par CE QUE.

***What happened** was unpredictable.* (sujet)
≫ Ce qui s'est passé n'était pas prévisible.

*I'll do **what I can**.* (complément)
≫ Je ferai ce que je pourrai.

 Traduction de TOUT CE QUE

TOUT CE QUE se traduit par *ALL THAT* et non par ~~ALL WHAT~~. *THAT* peut être effacé.

C'est tout ce que j'ai. ≫ *This is all (that) I have.*

38 Les subordonnées relatives

A Qu'est-ce qu'une relative ?

● C'est une proposition subordonnée qui apporte une information sur un nom.

Voici le livre **que tu voulais**. → La relative (en gras) apporte une précision concernant le nom « livre » que l'on vient de mentionner. On appelle ce nom l'**antécédent**.

● Les subordonnées relatives sont introduites par des **pronoms relatifs**. En anglais, les **pronoms relatifs** expriment la **distinction entre « humain » et « non-humain »** :

■ Pronoms relatifs pour un **humain** : *WHO, THAT, WHOM*.

■ Pronoms relatifs pour un **non-humain** : *THAT, WHICH*.

B Fonction du pronom relatif

Outre la différence entre « humain » et « non-humain », il faut déterminer si le pronom relatif est **sujet** de la relative ou bien **complément**.

■ **Pronom sujet :** il est placé juste **avant le verbe de la subordonnée**. On emploie *WHO* pour un **humain**, et *THAT* ou *WHICH* pour un **non-humain**.

*The man **who's** painting the front door is the caretaker.*
≫ L'homme qui est en train de peindre la porte d'entrée est le gardien.

*You'll have to clean the couch **that** / **which** is in your study.*
≫ Il va falloir que tu nettoies le canapé qui est dans ton bureau.

■ **Pronom complément** : on emploie *THAT* ou *WHO*(*M*) pour un **humain** et *THAT* ou *WHICH* pour un **non-humain**.

Remarque : *WHOM* est de moins en moins fréquemment utilisé. *THAT* **est souvent effacé**.

Here is the lady that / whom / ø I've told you about.
❯ Voici la dame dont je t'ai parlé.

The CD that / which / ø you've lent me is in the drawer.
❯ Le CD que tu m'as prêté est dans le tiroir.

C Absence du pronom relatif

● Dans un grand nombre de cas, la relative suit directement le nom, **sans aucun pronom relatif**.

You can use the new computer I've bought.
❯ Tu peux te servir du nouvel ordinateur **que j'ai acheté**.

● On pourrait introduire *THAT* devant la relative.

You can use the new computer that I've bought.

● **Dans quel cas peut-on « effacer »** *THAT* ? **Uniquement lorsque** *THAT* **est complément**. Dans l'exemple ci-dessus, *THAT* peut être effacé car il est complément du verbe *I've bought*.

En revanche lorsque *THAT* est **sujet, on ne peut pas l'effacer**.

It's the tallest skyscraper that was ever built.
❯ C'est le plus grand gratte-ciel qui ait jamais été construit.

● **On efface le plus souvent** *THAT* **après** :

■ *ALL, THE ONLY, THE FIRST, THE LAST* et les **superlatifs** (*THE MOST*…, *THE BEST*…, etc.).

All I need is a little rest.
❯ Tout ce dont j'ai besoin, c'est d'un peu de repos.

He's the funniest man I know.
❯ C'est l'homme le plus drôle que je connaisse.

■ **les prépositions** : si le verbe est construit avec une préposition (*look at, laugh at, look for*, etc.), la **préposition** est maintenue **à droite du verbe** et *THAT* **peut être effacé**.

This is the baby she's been looking after.
❯ C'est le bébé dont elle s'est occupée.

D Les deux types de relatives

● Si la relative est **essentielle au sens**, c'est-à-dire qu'elle **permet d'identifier l'élément dont on parle**, on dit qu'elle est « **déterminative** » ou « **restrictive** ». Ces relatives sont **les plus fréquentes**. On emploie le plus souvent les pronoms *THAT* et *WHO*.

This is the car that I'd like to buy.
❯ C'est la voiture que j'aimerais acheter.
→ Cette voiture-là et pas une autre.

Here is the journalist who wrote the article you liked so much.
❯ C'est le journaliste qui a écrit l'article que tu as tant apprécié. (*THAT* est possible.)

● Si la relative apporte une **précision accessoire**, un **détail supplémentaire** qui n'est pas essentiel au sens, on dit que la relative est « **non-déterminative** ». Ces relatives se placent généralement **entre virgules**. On emploie les pronoms *WHICH* et *WHO* (ou, plus rarement, *WHOM* en fonction complément).

*Her house, **which was built by a famous architect**, overlooks the bay.*
❯ Sa maison, qui a été construite par un architecte célèbre, domine la baie.
→ On comprend de quelle maison il s'agit, même si l'on supprime la relative.

*His father, **who used to work in publishing**, is now retired.*
❯ Son père, qui travaillait dans l'édition, est maintenant à la retraite.

E « CE QUE / CE QUI »

● On utilise *WHAT* pour **annoncer quelque chose qui va être précisé**.

What you did was sheer madness.
❯ Ce que tu as fait était de la folie pure.

● On utilise *WHICH* lorsqu'on **reprend la proposition qui précède**.

I didn't ask him why he'd done that, which was a mistake.
❯ Je ne lui ai pas demandé pourquoi il avait fait cela, ce qui était une erreur.

Rappel : **TOUT CE QUE** se traduit par *ALL THAT*. On n'utilise pas *WHAT* dans ce cas. (*THAT* est souvent effacé.)

Donne-moi tout ce que tu as.
❯ *Give me all (that) you have.*

Elle m'a dit tout ce qu'elle savait.
❯ *She told me all (that) she knew.*

F « DONT »

● Lorsque *DONT* exprime la **possession**, on utilise le pronom *WHOSE*.

*C'est la fille **dont** les parents travaillent dans un hôpital.*
❯ *This is the girl **whose** parents work in a hospital.*

*C'est un pays **dont** j'aime le climat.*
❯ *It's a country **whose** climate I like.*

● Lorsque *DONT* n'exprime pas la possession, il correspond souvent en français à un verbe suivi de la préposition **DE**. Il faut donc trouver le verbe correspondant en anglais. La préposition, en anglais, est placée **à droite du verbe**. (Le pronom complément *THAT* peut être effacé.)

*Les enfants **dont** elle s'occupe ne parlent qu'allemand.*
❯ *The children (that) she's looking after only speak German.*

G « OÙ »

En anglais, on utilise *WHERE* pour le lieu et *WHEN* pour le temps.

*C'est l'endroit **où** cela s'est passé.*
❯ *This is the place **where** it happened.*

*Il fut un temps **où** tu avais besoin de lui.*
❯ *There was a time **when** you needed him.*

39 Les subordonnées de condition et de temps

A Condition

● IF

■ **Condition simple**

If you help me, I will succeed. ➤ Si tu m'aides, je réussirai.

■ **Condition incertaine**

If you helped me, I would succeed.
➤ Si tu m'aidais, je réussirais.

■ **Condition non-réalisée**

If you had helped me, I would have succeeded.
➤ Si tu m'avais aidé, j'aurais réussi.

● PROVIDED : À CONDITION QUE / POURVU QUE

I will do the job provided I get a reward.
➤ Je ferai le travail à condition que j'obtienne une récompense.

● UNLESS : À MOINS QUE

I won't do it unless they offer to help me.
➤ Je ne le ferai pas, à moins qu'ils ne proposent de m'aider.

● WHETHER correspond à une **interrogation** et présente toujours **deux possibilités**.

I still wonder whether it's true (or not).
➤ Je me demande encore si c'est vrai.
→ « Est-ce vrai ? Oui ou non ? »

Ne pas confondre WHETHER avec IF, qui exprime la **condition**.

B Temps

● WHEN : QUAND

When you're older, you'll understand.
➤ Quand tu seras plus grand, tu comprendras.

● Les subordonnées de temps et le futur

En anglais, les subordonnées de temps, **comme les subordonnées en** IF, ne sont pas compatibles avec WILL. Pour exprimer le futur, on emploie le présent ou le *present perfect* dans la subordonnée. (Voir **Gr. 10 C.**)
Je lui parlerai **si** je le vois / **quand** je le **verrai**.
➤ *I'll talk to him if I see him / when I see him.*

● WHENEVER : CHAQUE FOIS QUE

He calls me whenever he feels low.
➤ Il m'appelle **chaque fois qu'**il se sent déprimé.

● AS SOON AS : DÈS QUE / AUSSITÔT QUE

Let me know as soon as you've finished.
➤ Prévenez-moi **dès que** / **aussitôt que** vous aurez fini.

● BEFORE : AVANT QUE

Try to find him before it's too late.
➤ Essaie de le retrouver **avant qu'**il ne soit trop tard.

● UNTIL : JUSQU'À CE QUE / AVANT QUE

I'll stay until you tell me he's safe.
➤ Je resterai **jusqu'à ce que** tu me dises qu'il est en sécurité.

Avec une forme négative, on traduit UNTIL par AVANT QUE.

I won't move until you tell me we're safe.
➤ Je ne m'en irai pas **avant que** tu ne me dises que nous sommes en sécurité.

● WHILE : PENDANT QUE

He slept while I was working.
➤ Il a dormi **pendant que (tout le temps que)** je travaillais.

● AS : ALORS QUE / TANDIS QUE / COMME

As she got on the bus, she saw him cross the street.
➤ **Alors / Tandis qu'**elle montait dans le bus, elle le vit traverser la rue.

40 Les subordonnées de cause et de but

A Cause

● BECAUSE (PARCE QUE) répond à la question WHY ?

– **Why** *did you turn down his offer?* ➤ Pourquoi as-tu refusé sa proposition ?
– **Because** *it wasn't very sensible.* ➤ Parce qu'elle n'était pas très raisonnable.

● AS / SINCE : COMME / PUISQUE

As it was getting late, we decided to pack up.
➤ **Comme** il se faisait tard, nous avons décidé de faire nos bagages.

Since it's over, we can leave.
➤ **Puisque** c'est fini, nous pouvons partir.

● FOR + -ING ou **GN**

He was blamed for smoking too much.
➤ On lui a reproché **de trop fumer**.

B But

● TO / IN ORDER TO / SO AS TO (POUR / AFIN DE) répondent à la question WHAT ... FOR ?

– **What** *did you do that for?* ➤ **Dans quel but** as-tu fait cela ?
– *I did it to help you / in order to help you / so as to help you.* ➤ Je l'ai fait **pour** t'aider.

● FOR + GN + TO (POUR QUE / AFIN QUE)

We bought a piano for him to practise at home.
➤ Nous avons acheté un piano **pour qu'**il puisse faire ses exercices à la maison.

41 Subordonnées d'opposition, de concession, de manière

A Opposition

● WHEREAS / WHILE : ALORS QUE

*She's never been to New York, **whereas / while** most of her friends have been there several times.*
❯ Elle n'est jamais allée à New York **alors que** la plupart de ses amis y sont allés plusieurs fois.

B Concession

● ALTHOUGH / THOUGH : BIEN QUE / QUOIQUE

Ils sont proches par le sens de AND YET (ET POURTANT).

*I'll stay **although** I don't feel like it.*
❯ Je vais rester, **bien que / quoique** je n'en aie pas envie.

*I'll stay **and yet** I don't feel like it.*
❯ Je vais rester, **et pourtant** je n'en ai pas envie.

Ne pas confondre ALTHOUGH (conjonction, suivie d'une phrase) et DESPITE / IN SPITE OF (MALGRÉ), qui sont des prépositions (suivies d'un GN).

***Despite / In spite of** his despondency, he went on working.*
❯ **Malgré** son abattement, il continua à travailler.

***Although** he felt despondent, he went on working.*
❯ **Bien qu'**il se sentît abattu, il continua à travailler.

● HOWEVER : BIEN QUE / QUOIQUE

Dans ce sens, HOWEVER est suivi d'un adjectif ou d'un adverbe.

*However **sweet** she may be now, I can't forgive her.*
❯ **Bien qu'elle soit gentille** maintenant (pour aussi gentille qu'elle puisse être maintenant), je ne peux lui pardonner.

HOWEVER signifie aussi CEPENDANT.

*We've been asked to wait. **However**, we've decided to leave as soon as possible.*
❯ On nous a demandé d'attendre ; **cependant**, nous allons partir dès que possible.

C Manière

● *How* introduisant une subordonnée signifie LA MANIÈRE DE / COMMENT.

I wonder how she managed to do it.
❯ Je me demande comment (de quelle manière) elle a réussi à le faire.

● *How* peut aussi exprimer le degré :

■ **d'un adjectif.**

Ask them how big / deep / wide it is.
❯ Demande-leur quelle est sa taille / quelle est sa profondeur / quelle est sa largeur.

■ **d'un adverbe** (HOW MUCH, HOW OFTEN).

Do you have any idea how much they need you?
❯ Sais-tu combien / à quel point ils ont besoin de toi ?

42 Le style indirect

On peut transformer un énoncé au style direct (phrase d'un dialogue, par exemple) en un énoncé introduit par un verbe comme SAY ou TELL au passé (DIRE QUE), ou bien ASK (DEMANDER SI), etc. On a alors un énoncé au style indirect. Cette transformation entraîne des modifications **dans les formes verbales, les pronoms, les possessifs, l'ordre des mots et les repères de lieu et de temps.**

A Formes verbales

Style direct	Style indirect passé
*"**I'm watching TV**," said Paul.*	*Paul said (that) **he was watching TV**.*
*"**I don't believe you**," he said to them.*	*He said (that) **he didn't believe them**.*
*"**I have never talked to her**," she said.*	*She said (that) **she had never talked to her**.*
*"**He's been crying**," she said.*	*She said that **he had been crying**.*
*"**I saw them yesterday**," he said.*	*He said (that) **he had seen them the day before**.*
Modaux	
*"**I will help you**," he said.*	*He said (that) **he would help her**.*
*"**I can't drive**," she said.*	*She said that **she couldn't** drive.*
*"**May I** sit next to **you**?" asked Paul.*	*Paul asked whether **he might** sit next to **her**.*
*"You **must** wait for him," I said.*	*I said that they **were to** wait for him (that they **must** wait for him).*
	On peut conserver MUST, mais on emploie souvent WAS / WERE TO (forme non-modale) qui exprime la contrainte.

● **Could, could have, might, should** et **should have** restent inchangés au style indirect.

*"You **should** see this film,"* he said.

» «Tu devrais voir ce film,» dit-il.

→ *He said that I **should** see this film.*

» Il a dit que je devrais voir ce film.

● Le prétérit devient *pluperfect* lorsque le verbe désigne un **événement unique** qui est **antérieur** au moment où on en parle.

*"I **didn't eat** much last night,"* he said.

» «Je n'ai pas beaucoup mangé hier soir,» dit-il.

→ *He said that he **had not eaten** much the night before.*

» Il a dit qu'il n'avait pas beaucoup mangé la veille au soir.

● **On maintient le prétérit** lorsque l'énoncé décrit une **habitude** et lorsque le verbe est un **verbe d'état**, comme par exemple *BE, HAVE, HATE, KNOW, LIKE, WANT*.

*"When Helen **was** in Chester, we sometimes **went out** for a drink."*

» «Lorsqu'Helen était à Chester, nous sortions parfois boire un verre ensemble.»

→ *He said that when Helen **was** in Chester, they sometimes **went out** for a drink.*

» Il a dit que lorsqu'Helen était à Chester, ils sortaient parfois boire un verre ensemble.

B Questions : ordre des mots

Au style indirect, on n'inverse jamais le sujet et le verbe.

"Where's your car?" » «Où est ta voiture?»

→ *She asked me where **my car was**.*

» Elle m'a demandé où **était ma voiture**.

C Expressions de temps et de lieu

Au style indirect passé, certains repères de temps et de lieu sont modifiés :

– yesterday	→ the day before
– two days ago	→ two days before
– last year	→ the year before
– tomorrow	→ the following day / the day after
– next week	→ the following week / the week after
– here	→ there

"I'll buy my ticket tomorrow," he said.

» «J'achèterai mon billet demain,» dit-il.

→ *He said (that) he would buy his ticket **the following day**.*

» Il a dit qu'il achèterait son billet le lendemain.

D Verbes introducteurs du style indirect

● **DIRE QUE : SAY ou TELL ?**

■ Pour rapporter des paroles, on peut utiliser **SAY** ou **TELL** suivis de **THAT**. La différence est que **SAY** peut se construire sans complément, alors que ce n'est pas le cas de **TELL**.

*She said that he was silly. / She told **him** that he was silly.*

» Elle (lui) a dit qu'il était idiot.

■ **SAY** peut aussi se construire avec un complément, bien que ce ne soit pas obligatoire. Dans ce cas, on utilise la **préposition** *TO* (alors qu'on place le complément directement après **TELL**, sans préposition).

*She said **to John** that he was silly.*

» Elle a dit à John qu'il était idiot.

Remarque : *TELL* peut signifier ORDONNER (= dire à quelqu'un de faire quelque chose). Dans ce cas la **proposition infinitive** est obligatoire.

*She told **me to** do it.* » Elle m'a dit (ordonné) de le faire.

● **ASK : DEMANDER / WONDER : SE DEMANDER**

"When are they coming?" she asked him.

» «Quand arrivent-ils?»

→ *She asked him when they were coming.*

» Elle lui a demandé quand ils arrivaient.

On utilise *WHETHER* (SI) pour transformer une **question attendant une réponse** en *YES / NO*.

"Will they like it?" » «Est-ce que ça leur plaira?»

→ *She wondered whether (if) they would like it.*

» Elle se demanda si ça leur plairait.

● **ORDER / TELL : expression de l'ordre**

"Close your eyes! Don't laugh!" he said to her.

» «Ferme les yeux! Ne ris pas!»

→ *He ordered her / told her **to close her eyes** and **not to laugh**.*

» Il lui a ordonné / dit de fermer les yeux et de ne pas rire.

● **ADVISE : CONSEILLER**

"Why don't you buy a new one?"

» «Pourquoi n'en achètes-tu pas un neuf?»

→ *She advised him to buy a new one.*

» Elle lui a conseillé d'en acheter un neuf.

● **BLAME FOR / REPROACH FOR : expression du reproche**

"You shouldn't have laughed at her."

» «Tu n'aurais pas dû te moquer d'elle.»

→ *He reproached him **for** / blamed him **for laughing** at her.*

» Il lui reprocha de s'être moqué d'elle.

● **APOLOGIZE FOR : S'EXCUSER**

"I'm sorry I'm late," he said.

» «Je suis désolé d'être en retard», dit-il.

→ *He apologized **for being** late.*

» Il s'excusa d'être en retard.

● **SUGGEST : SUGGÉRER QUE**

On utilise la **base verbale simple** après *SUGGEST*, quelle que soit la personne (anglais soutenu).

"Why don't you try another one?"

» «Pourquoi n'en essaies-tu pas un autre?»

→ *He suggested that she **try** the other one.*

» Il proposa / suggéra qu'elle en essaie un autre.

43 La voix passive

A Formes

La voix passive met l'**objet** sur lequel porte l'action en **tête de l'énoncé**. L'auxiliaire de la voix passive est *BE*. Le verbe est au **participe passé**.

- **Voix active :**

  They built the new museum in 2009.
  - Ils ont construit le nouveau musée en 2009.

- **Voix passive :**

  The new museum was built in 2009.
  - Le nouveau musée a été construit en 2009.

Formes verbales	Voix active	Voix passive
Présent simple	*They never **discuss** our plans.*	*Our plans **are** never **discussed**.*
Prétérit	*They **discussed** it.*	*It **was discussed**.*
Présent *BE+ING*	*They **are discussing** it.*	*It **is being discussed**.*
Prétérit *BE+ING*	*They **were discussing** it.*	*It **was being discussed**.*
Present perfect	*They **have discussed** it.*	*It **has been discussed**.*
Pluperfect	*They **had discussed** it.*	*It **had been discussed**.*
Modal	*They **will discuss** it. / They **can't discuss** it.*	*It **will be discussed**. / It **can't be discussed**.*

B Sens

● **Pourquoi la forme passive ?**

- Si l'on parle de l'**événement lui-même**, on utilise la **voix active**.

  *The authorities **cancelled** the performance.*
  - Les autorités ont annulé la représentation.

- Si l'on parle de l'**objet sur lequel porte l'action** (la «victime», la personne ou l'objet qui subissent l'action), on utilise la **voix passive**.

  *The performance **was cancelled** by the authorities.*
  - La représentation a été annulée par les autorités.

● **Traduction de** *ON*

On utilise très fréquemment la voix passive en anglais lorsque l'agent (celui qui fait l'action) n'est pas identifié. En français, on utilise souvent *ON* dans ce cas-là.

On a créé **deux mille nouveaux sites Internet** la semaine dernière.
- ***Two thousand new websites** were created last week.*

On **m**'a donné le code d'accès. ● *I was given the passcode.*

On ne **les** a jamais revus. ● ***They** were never seen again.*

● **Complément d'agent (celui qui fait l'action)**

On ne le mentionne que si celui-ci a une importance particulière. Il est introduit par *BY*.

*The dress was offered to her **by a British designer**.*
- La robe lui a été offerte par un grand couturier britannique.

C Verbes à deux compléments

● **Il y a deux façons en anglais de former la voix passive** à partir de la phrase suivante :

Someone gave me the key. ● Quelqu'un m'a donné la clé.

- **Le complément d'attribution** (ME) devient **sujet**.

  I was given the key. ● On m'a donné la clé.

C'est la forme du passif **la plus fréquente en anglais avec ce type de verbe**, car c'est un être humain qui est placé en tête d'énoncé. Cette forme est impossible en français : on traduit par *ON*.

- **Le complément d'objet direct** (*the key*) devient **sujet**.

  ***The key** was given to me.* ● La clé m'a été donnée.

● Les verbes *ASK, SHOW, TELL, TEACH, OFFER, SEND, LEND* peuvent se construire à la voix passive de la même manière que *GIVE*.

I was asked / told to keep silent.
- On m'a demandé de me taire.

She was lent / offered / shown a new car.
- On lui a prêté / offert / montré une nouvelle voiture.

D Les verbes prépositionnels

● On maintient la **préposition à droite du verbe** à la voix passive.

- **Voix active :**

  *Somebody **will look after** him.*
  - Quelqu'un s'occupera de lui.

- **Voix passive :**

  *He **will be looked after**.*
  - On s'occupera de lui.

● Cette forme passive est impossible en français : on traduit par *ON*.

E -ING après *NEED* et *WANT*

WANT peut signifier AVOIR BESOIN DE, comme *NEED*.

*The flowers need / want **watering**.*
➧ Les fleurs ont besoin d'être arrosées.

-ING a ici un sens **passif**.

F Construction passive de certaines phrases complexes

Les trois phrases complexes suivantes se passivent de la même façon. On fait apparaître *TO* à la voix passive.

● **Rapporter des paroles ou une opinion**

■ On utilise *BELIEVE, CONSIDER, DECLARE, HEAR, KNOW, REPORT, SAY, THINK* au passif, suivis de *TO*.

They are said to… ➧ On dit qu'ils…

She is believed to… ➧ On pense qu'elle…

He is thought to… ➧ On pense qu'il…

■ S'il n'y a pas de décalage temporel entre les deux propositions, on utilise l'infinitif simple.

They say that she is a secret agent.
→ *She is said **to be** a secret agent.*
➧ On dit qu'elle est agent secret.

They believe he has a chance of succeeding.
→ *He is believed **to have** a chance of succeeding.*
➧ On pense qu'il a des chances de succès.

■ Si le fait dont on parle est antérieur à *SAY, THINK*, etc., on utilise l'infinitif à la forme *HAVE -EN*.

They think that he died in Africa.
→ *He is thought **to have died** in Africa.*
➧ On pense qu'il est mort en Afrique.

It is reported that a prisoner has escaped.
→ *A prisoner is reported **to have escaped**.*
➧ Un détenu se serait évadé.

● **Propositions infinitives exprimant la pression** (*ASK, EXPECT, TELL, ORDER*)

They told him to hang up the phone.
→ *He was told to hang up the phone.*
➧ On lui a dit de raccrocher le téléphone.

● **Structures causatives en *MAKE*** (voir **Gr. 36 B**)

She made us unpack at once.
→ *We were made to unpack at once.*
➧ On nous a immédiatement fait défaire nos affaires.

Les points de grammaire sont référencés par rapport aux fiches.

Verbes irréguliers

	Base verbale	Prétérit	Participe passé	Traduction
	Trois formes identiques			
C	cut /ʌ/	cut /ʌ/	cut /ʌ/	couper
H	hurt /ɜː/	hurt /ɜː/	hurt /ɜː/	blesser
L	let /e/	let /e/	let /e/	permettre, louer
P	put /ʊ/	put /ʊ/	put /ʊ/	mettre, poser
R	read /iː/	read /e/	read /e/	lire
S	set /e/	set /e/	set /e/	fixer
	shut /ʌ/	shut /ʌ/	shut /ʌ/	fermer
	Prétérit et participe passé identiques			
B	bend /e/	bent /e/	bent /e/	(se) courber
	bring /ɪ/	brought /ɔː/	brought /ɔː/	apporter
	build /ɪ/	built /ɪ/	built /ɪ/	construire
	burn /ɜː/	burnt /ɜː/	burnt /ɜː/	brûler
	buy /aɪ/	bought /ɔː/	bought /ɔː/	acheter
C	catch /æ/	caught /ɔː/	caught /ɔː/	attraper
D	dream /iː/	dreamt /e/	dreamt /e/	rêver
F	feel /iː/	felt /e/	felt /e/	(se) sentir, éprouver
	fight /aɪ/	fought /ɔː/	fought /ɔː/	se battre, combattre
	find /aɪ/	found /aʊ/	found /aʊ/	trouver
G	get /e/	got /ɒ/	got /ɒ/	obtenir
H	have /æ/	had /æ/	had /æ/	avoir
	hear /ɪə/	heard /ɜː/	heard /ɜː/	entendre
	hold /əʊ/	held /e/	held /e/	tenir
K	keep /iː/	kept /e/	kept /e/	garder
L	lead /iː/	led /e/	led /e/	mener, guider
	learn /ɜː/	learnt /ɜː/	learnt /ɜː/	apprendre
	leave /iː/	left /e/	left /e/	laisser, quitter
	lend /e/	lent /e/	lent /e/	prêter
	light /aɪ/	lit /ɪ/	lit /ɪ/	allumer
	lose /uː/	lost /ɒ/	lost /ɒ/	perdre
M	make /eɪ/	made /eɪ/	made /eɪ/	faire, fabriquer
	mean /iː/	meant /e/	meant /e/	signifier, vouloir dire
	meet /iː/	met /e/	met /e/	(se) rencontrer
P	pay /eɪ/	paid /eɪ/	paid /eɪ/	payer
S	say /eɪ/	said /e/	said /e/	dire
	sell /e/	sold /əʊ/	sold /əʊ/	vendre
	send /e/	sent /e/	sent /e/	envoyer
	shoot /uː/	shot /ɒ/	shot /ɒ/	tirer
	sit /ɪ/	sat /æ/	sat /æ/	être assis
	sleep /iː/	slept /e/	slept /e/	dormir
	smell /e/	smelt /e/	smelt /e/	sentir (odorat)
	spend /e/	spent /e/	spent /e/	dépenser, passer (le temps)
	stand /æ/	stood /ʊ/	stood /ʊ/	être debout
	stick /ɪ/	stuck /ʌ/	stuck /ʌ/	coller
	strike /aɪ/	struck /ʌ/	struck /ʌ/	frapper
T	teach /iː/	taught /ɔː/	taught /ɔː/	enseigner
	tell /e/	told /əʊ/	told /əʊ/	dire, raconter
	think /ɪ/	thought /ɔː/	thought /ɔː/	penser
U	understand /ʌ/ə/æ/	understood /ʌ/ə/ʊ/	understood /ʌ/ə/ʊ/	comprendre
W	win /ɪ/	won /ʌ/	won /ʌ/	gagner

Base verbale	Prétérit	Participe passé	Traduction
Deux formes identiques			
B beat /iː/	beat /iː/	beaten /iː/ə/	*battre*
become /ɪ/ʌ/	became /ɪ/eɪ/	become /ɪ/ʌ/	*devenir*
C come /ʌ/	came /eɪ/	come /ʌ/	*venir*
R run /ʌ/	ran /æ/	run /ʌ/	*courir*
Trois formes différentes			
A awake /ə/eɪ/	awoke /ə/əʊ/	awoken /ə/əʊ/ə/	*(se) réveiller*
B be /iː/	was /ɒ/ / were /ɜː/	been /iː/	*être*
bear /ɛə/	bore /ɔː/	borne /ɔː/	*supporter*
begin /ɪ/ɪ/	began /ɪ/æ/	begun /ɪ/ʌ/	*commencer*
bite /aɪ/	bit /ɪ/	bitten /ɪ/ə/	*mordre*
blow /əʊ/	blew /uː/	blown /əʊ/	*souffler*
break /eɪ/	broke /əʊ/	broken /əʊ/ə/	*casser*
C choose /uː/	chose /əʊ/	chosen /əʊ/ə/	*choisir*
D do /uː/	did /ɪ/	done /ʌ/	*faire*
draw /ɔː/	drew /uː/	drawn /ɔː/	*dessiner*
drink /ɪ/	drank /æ/	drunk /ʌ/	*boire*
drive /aɪ/	drove /əʊ/	driven /ɪ/ə/	*conduire*
E eat /iː/	ate /e/	eaten /iː/ə/	*manger*
F fall /ɔː/	fell /e/	fallen /ɔː/ə/	*tomber*
fly /aɪ/	flew /uː/	flown /əʊ/	*voler*
forbid /ə/ɪ/	forbade /ə/eɪ/	forbidden /ə/ɪ/ə/	*interdire*
foresee /ɔː/iː/	foresaw /ɔː/ɔː/	foreseen /ɔː/iː/	*prévoir*
forget /ə/e/	forgot /ə/ɒ/	forgotten /ə/ɒ/ə/	*oublier*
forgive /ə/ɪ/	forgave /ə/eɪ/	forgiven /ə/ɪ/ə/	*pardonner*
freeze /iː/	froze /əʊ/	frozen /əʊ/ə/	*geler*
G give /ɪ/	gave /eɪ/	given /ɪ/ə/	*donner*
go /əʊ/	went /e/	gone /ɒ/	*aller*
grow /əʊ/	grew /uː/	grown /əʊ/	*grandir, faire pousser*
H hide /aɪ/	hid /ɪ/	hidden /ɪ/ə/	*(se) cacher*
K know /nəʊ/	knew /njuː/	known /nəʊn/	*savoir, connaître*
L lie /aɪ/	lay /eɪ/	lain /eɪ/	*être étendu*
R ride /aɪ/	rode /əʊ/	ridden /ɪ/ə/	*aller (à cheval / vélo)*
ring /ɪ/	rang /æ/	rung /ʌ/	*sonner*
rise /aɪ/	rose /əʊ/	risen /ɪ/ə/	*s'élever, se lever*
S see /iː/	saw /ɔː/	seen /iː/	*voir*
shake /eɪ/	shook /ʊ/	shaken /eɪ/ə/	*secouer*
show /əʊ/	showed /əʊ/	shown /əʊ/	*montrer*
sing /ɪ/	sang /æ/	sung /ʌ/	*chanter*
speak /iː/	spoke /əʊ/	spoken /əʊ/ə/	*parler*
steal /iː/	stole /əʊ/	stolen /əʊ/ə/	*voler, dérober*
swear /ɛə/	swore /ɔː/	sworn /ɔː/	*jurer*
swim /ɪ/	swam /æ/	swum /ʌ/	*nager*
T take /eɪ/	took /ʊ/	taken /eɪ/ə/	*prendre*
tear /ɛə/	tore /ɔː/	torn /ɔː/	*déchirer*
throw /əʊ/	threw /uː/	thrown /əʊ/	*jeter*
U undergo /ʌ/ə/əʊ/	underwent /ʌ/ə/e/	undergone /ʌ/ə/ɒ/	*subir*
W wake (up) /eɪ/ʌ/	woke (up) /əʊ/ʌ/	woken (up) /əʊ/ə/ʌ/	*(se) réveiller*
wear /ɛə/	wore /ɔː/	worn /ɔː/	*porter (des vêtements)*
write /aɪ/	wrote /əʊ/	written /ɪ/ə/	*écrire*

Index par notion culturelle

Dans cet index, les documents proposés dans chacune des unités du manuel sont classés par notion culturelle du programme. Cet index vous aidera à préparer l'épreuve d'expression orale.

Lieux et formes du pouvoir
Seats and forms of power

Mythes et héros
Myths and heroes

Crédits photographiques

Crédits textes

Crédits sonores

N° éditeur 10206622 - Dépôt légal Juin 2014 - Imprimé en Italie par BONA